Mastering QlikView

Unleash the power of QlikView and Qlik Sense to make optimum use of data for Business Intelligence

Stephen Redmond

BIRMINGHAM - MUMBAI

Mastering QlikView

First published: November 2014

Production reference: 1191114

Published by Packt Publishing Ltd.
Livery Place
35 Livery Street
Birmingham B3 2PB, UK.

ISBN 978-1-78217-329-8

www.packtpub.com

Credits

Author
Stephen Redmond

Reviewers
Ralf Becher
Gert Jan Feick
Miguel Ángel García
Barry Harmsen

Commissioning Editor
Akram Hussain

Acquisition Editor
Kevin Colaco

Content Development Editors
Samantha Gonsalves
Azharuddin Sheikh

Technical Editors
Mrunal M. Chavan
Dennis John

Copy Editors
Maria Gould
Paul Hindle
Deepa Nambiar

Project Coordinator
Kinjal Bari

Proofreaders
Simran Bhogal
Ameesha Green
Paul Hindle

Indexers
Priya Sane
Tejal Soni

Graphics
Abhinash Sahu

Production Coordinator
Manu Joseph

Cover Work
Manu Joseph

About the Author

Stephen Redmond is the CTO and Qlik Luminary at CapricornVentis (http://www.capventis.com)—a QlikView Elite Partner. He is the author of several books, including *QlikView for Developers Cookbook* and *QlikView Server and Publisher*, both published by Packt Publishing. He is also the author of the popular *DevLogix* series for SalesLogix developers.

In 2006, after many years of working with CRM systems, reporting and analysis solutions, and data integration, Stephen started working with QlikView. Since then, CapricornVentis has become QlikView's top partner in the UK and Ireland territories, and with Stephen as the head of the team, they have implemented QlikView in a wide variety of enterprise and large-business customers across a wide range of sectors, from public sector to financial services to large retailers.

In 2014, Stephen was awarded the Luminary status by Qlik in recognition of his product advocacy. He regularly contributes to online forums, including the Qlik Community. His QlikView blog is at http://www.qliktips.com, and you can follow him on Twitter at @stephencredmond where he tweets about QlikView, BI, data visualization, technology in general, and occasionally, on marathon running.

As always, thanks to my family for their constant support—I couldn't do this without them.

Thanks to the technical reviewers—they helped me remain honest and make this a better publication.

Special thanks to Colman Walsh of UXTraining.ie for his permission to reuse his photograph that so well represents a Donald Door—I have been using it for several years in presentations and I am delighted to be able to use it here.

About the Reviewers

Ralf Becher has worked as an IT system architect and as an IT consultant since 1989 in banking, insurance, logistics, automotive, and retail sectors. He founded TIQ Solutions GmbH in 2004 with his partners. The company specializes in modern, quality-assured data management.

Since 2004, they have been helping their customers process, evaluate, and maintain the quality of company data, helping them introduce, implement, and improve complex solutions in the fields of data architecture, data integration, data migration, master data management, metadata management, data warehousing, and Business Intelligence.

Ralf is an internationally recognized QlikView expert with a strong position in the Qlik Community. He started working with QlikView in 2006 and has contributed QlikView add-on solutions for data quality and data integration, especially for connectivity in the Java and Big Data realms. He runs his QlikView data integration blog at `http://tiqview.tumblr.com/`.

Gert Jan Feick studied Informatics (language, knowledge, and interaction) at Technical University of Enschede (NL). He started his career as a project manager at a medium-sized software development company, specializing in requirements analysis and project management. From 2005 onward, he was responsible for the buildup of a company in the areas of software development, reporting and visualizations, and analysis. In 2011, he moved to Germany and became a management consultant at Infomotion GmbH, where he is responsible for the team that works on self-service and Agile BI as well as reporting and analysis.

He regularly contributes to online forums (including the Qlik Community), speaks at conventions, and writes articles. You can follow him on Twitter at `@gdollen` where he tweets about QlikView, Agile and self-service BI, data visualization, and other topics in general.

Miguel Ángel García is a Business Intelligence consultant and QlikView Solutions Architect, based in Monterrey, Mexico. Having worked throughout many successful QlikView implementations, from inception through implementation, and performed across a wide variety of roles on each project; his experience and skills range from presales to applications development and design, technical architecture, system administration, as well as functional analysis and overall project execution.

He is the co-author of *QlikView 11 for Developers*, *Packt Publishing*, which was published in November 2012, and its corresponding translation into Spanish, *QlikView 11 para Desarrolladores*, *Packt Publishing*, published in December 2013. He has also worked as a technical reviewer for several other QlikView books.

He is the cofounder of Q-On Training Center (`www.q-on.bi`), a place where users, developers, and enthusiasts can get access to online QlikView training, with options that cover all the skill levels.

He currently holds the QlikView Designer, QlikView Developer, and QlikView System Administrator certifications issued by Qlik, for Versions 9, 10, and 11.

In 2014, he was awarded the Qlik Luminary distinction in recognition for his active participation and collaboration in the QlikView ecosystem.

Barry Harmsen is the owner of Bitmetric, a boutique consulting firm that specializes in QlikView and is based in the Netherlands. Originally from a background of traditional Business Intelligence, data warehousing, and performance management; in 2008 he made the shift to QlikView and a more user-centric form of Business Intelligence.

Since switching over to QlikView, Barry and his team have completed many successful implementations in many different industries, from financial services to telecom and from manufacturing to healthcare. His QlikView experience covers a wide variety of roles and subjects including requirements analysis, design, development, architecture, infrastructure, system administration, integration, project management, and training.

In 2012, he co-authored *QlikView 11 for Developers*, *Packt Publishing*. This book has quickly established itself as one of the best ways to teach yourself QlikView. He is also one of the core speakers at the Masters Summit for QlikView. This 3-day conference for QlikView developers covers advanced topics and is designed to take your QlikView skills to the next level. More information about the Masters Summit can be found at www.masterssummit.com.

Barry maintains a QlikView blog at www.qlikfix.com and can be followed on Twitter at @meneerharmsen.

www.PacktPub.com

Support files, eBooks, discount offers, and more

For support files and downloads related to your book, please visit www.PacktPub.com.

Did you know that Packt offers eBook versions of every book published, with PDF and ePub files available? You can upgrade to the eBook version at www.PacktPub.com and as a print book customer, you are entitled to a discount on the eBook copy. Get in touch with us at service@packtpub.com for more details.

At www.PacktPub.com, you can also read a collection of free technical articles, sign up for a range of free newsletters and receive exclusive discounts and offers on Packt books and eBooks.

https://www2.packtpub.com/books/subscription/packtlib

Do you need instant solutions to your IT questions? PacktLib is Packt's online digital book library. Here, you can search, access, and read Packt's entire library of books.

Why subscribe?

- Fully searchable across every book published by Packt
- Copy and paste, print, and bookmark content
- On demand and accessible via a web browser

Free access for Packt account holders

If you have an account with Packt at www.PacktPub.com, you can use this to access PacktLib today and view 9 entirely free books. Simply use your login credentials for immediate access.

Instant updates on new Packt books

Get notified! Find out when new books are published by following @PacktEnterprise on Twitter or the *Packt Enterprise* Facebook page.

Table of Contents

Preface

This is a book about mastery. But what does this mean? What does being a QlikView master mean?

When I wrote *QlikView for Developers Cookbook*, *Packt Publishing*, I started the preface with the sentence:

> *"There is no substitute for experience."*

When it comes to QlikView, experience is the thing that makes a difference. Experience is the difference between the developers who can create good applications and the consultants who can create real business solutions that solve real business problems.

I have been working with QlikView since 2006, and in this time, I have created some fantastic solutions. I also created applications that I cringe to look at today. I like to think that I have mastered the subject, even though I am still learning.

At CapricornVentis, I work with one of the brightest bunch of consultants; it has ever been my pleasure to work with them. I get to teach a lot but I also get to learn a tremendous amount from these guys. We are constantly pushing the boundaries of the product to get to the right solution. As a beginner in this area, I would have wanted to work for an organization like CapricornVentis, where I could really learn and grow as a consultant.

Let's be clear; I do not know every little detail about QlikView, but I do know most of them. What I think I know, and know really well, are the important things to know about when creating QlikView solutions. This knowledge is what I have tried to distil down into this book.

You won't be a master by just reading this book. As Alfred Korzybski famously stated:

> *"The map is not the territory."*

This book is not an ultimate mastering guide, rather is a like a map that guides us towards our common destination—to become a QlikView master. Study the map well and you will get there.

Qlik Sense

During the development of this book, Qlik released their next generation product, Qlik Sense. Qlik Sense is not, currently, a replacement product for QlikView, and Qlik has announced that they will have a two-product strategy and sell QlikView for guided BI applications and Qlik Sense for self-service BI applications. A new version, QlikView 12.0, is slated for release in the second half of 2015.

While Qlik Sense is a new product, it is built on the same heritage as QlikView. There is a new data engine, QIX, that stores the data in a format more columnar than that of QlikView. However, the inference engine is still the same (green, white, and gray). The script syntax is still the same; in fact, we can use QlikView scripts in Qlik Sense. The frontend is very different because it is based on a new web design, but the expression syntax is still the same.

Therefore, much of what is written in this book about QlikView will still apply to Qlik Sense. Anyone who masters QlikView will be well on their way to mastering Qlik Sense.

What this book covers

Chapter 1, Performance Tuning and Scalability, is where we look at understanding how QlikView stores its data so that we can optimize that storage in our applications. We will also look at topics such as Direct Discovery and testing implementations using JMeter.

Chapter 2, QlikView Data Modeling, looks in detail at dimensional data modeling and learning about fact and dimension tables and using best practices from Ralph Kimball in QlikView. We also learn about how to handle slowly changing dimensions (SCDs), multiple fact tables, and drilling across with document chaining.

Chapter 3, Best Practices for Loading Data, is where we look at implementing ETL strategies with QVD files. We also introduce QlikView Expressor.

Chapter 4, Data Governance, looks at areas such as implementing metadata in QlikView and managing our implementation with QlikView Governance Dashboard.

Chapter 5, Advanced Expressions, is where we look at areas such as the Dollar-sign Expansion, set analysis, and vertical calculations using Total and Aggr.

Chapter 6, Advanced Scripting, looks at optimizing loads, Dollar-sign Expansion in the script, and control structures. We also introduce the concept of code reuse.

Chapter 7, Visualizing Data, is where we look at the historical background to data visualization; we gain an understanding of the human relationship with numbers and learn some good design principles to bring to our applications.

What you need for this book

You need a copy of QlikView Desktop, which you can download for free from `http://www.qlikview.com/download`. After this, you shouldn't need anything else. You can also test the examples in Qlik Sense.

To demonstrate the different techniques and functions, I will usually get you to load a table of data. We do this using the `INLINE` function. For example:

```
Load * Inline [
  Field1, Field2
  Value1, Value2
  Value3, Value4
];
```

This will load a table with two fields, `Field1` and `Field2`, and two rows of data.

Most of the time, this type of table is enough for what we need to do. In a few examples, where I need you to use more data than that, we will use publicly available data sources.

Who this book is for

This is not a beginner's book. This book is for anyone who has learned QlikView or Qlik Sense—either from formal training, online resources, or *QlikView 11 for Developers, Miguel García and Barry Harmsen, Packt Publishing*—and now wants to take their learning to a higher level.

Conventions

In this book, you will find a number of text styles that distinguish between different kinds of information. Here are some examples of these styles and an explanation of their meaning.

Code words in text, database table names, folder names, filenames, file extensions, pathnames, dummy URLs, user input, and Twitter handles are shown as follows: "In the `QVScriptGenTool_0_7 64Bit\Analyzer` folder there is a ZIP file called `FolderTemplate.zip`."

A block of code is set as follows:

```
Sales:
Load * INLINE [
  Country, Sales
  USA, 1000
  UK, 940
  Japan, 543
];
```

When we wish to draw your attention to a particular part of a code block, the relevant lines or items are set in bold:

```
Sales:
Load * INLINE [
  Country, Sales
  USA, 1000
  UK, 940
  Japan, 543
];
```

Any command-line input or output is written as follows:

`C:\Program Files\QlikView\qv.exe`

New terms and **important words** are shown in bold. Words that you see on the screen, for example, in menus or dialog boxes, appear in the text like this: "Click on the **Execution** tab."

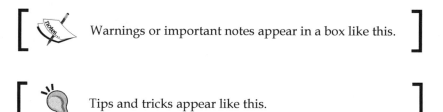

Warnings or important notes appear in a box like this.

Tips and tricks appear like this.

Reader feedback

Feedback from our readers is always welcome. Let us know what you think about this book—what you liked or disliked. Reader feedback is important for us as it helps us develop titles that you will really get the most out of.

To send us general feedback, simply e-mail `feedback@packtpub.com`, and mention the book's title in the subject of your message.

If there is a topic that you have expertise in and you are interested in either writing or contributing to a book, see our author guide at `www.packtpub.com/authors`.

Customer support

Now that you are the proud owner of a Packt book, we have a number of things to help you to get the most from your purchase.

Downloading the example code

You can download the example code files from your account at `http://www.packtpub.com` for all the Packt Publishing books you have purchased. If you purchased this book elsewhere, you can visit `http://www.packtpub.com/support` and register to have the files e-mailed directly to you.

Errata

Although we have taken every care to ensure the accuracy of our content, mistakes do happen. If you find a mistake in one of our books—maybe a mistake in the text or the code—we would be grateful if you could report this to us. By doing so, you can save other readers from frustration and help us improve subsequent versions of this book. If you find any errata, please report them by visiting `http://www.packtpub.com/submit-errata`, selecting your book, clicking on the **Errata Submission Form** link, and entering the details of your errata. Once your errata are verified, your submission will be accepted and the errata will be uploaded to our website or added to any list of existing errata under the Errata section of that title.

To view the previously submitted errata, go to `https://www.packtpub.com/books/content/support` and enter the name of the book in the search field. The required information will appear under the **Errata** section.

Piracy

Piracy of copyrighted material on the Internet is an ongoing problem across all media. At Packt, we take the protection of our copyright and licenses very seriously. If you come across any illegal copies of our works in any form on the Internet, please provide us with the location address or website name immediately so that we can pursue a remedy.

Please contact us at `copyright@packtpub.com` with a link to the suspected pirated material.

We appreciate your help in protecting our authors and our ability to bring you valuable content.

Questions

If you have a problem with any aspect of this book, you can contact us at `questions@packtpub.com`, and we will do our best to address the problem.

1
Performance Tuning and Scalability

"The way Moore's Law occurs in computing is really unprecedented in other walks of life. If the Boeing 747 obeyed Moore's Law, it would travel a million miles an hour, it would be shrunken down in size, and a trip to New York would cost about five dollars. Those enormous changes just aren't part of our everyday experience."

— Nathan Myhrvold, former Chief Technology Officer at Microsoft, 1995

The way Moore's Law has benefitted QlikView is really unprecedented amongst other BI systems.

QlikView began life in 1993 in Lund, Sweden. Originally titled "QuickView", they had to change things when they couldn't obtain a copyright on that name, and thus "QlikView" was born.

After years of steady growth, something really good happened for QlikView around 2005/2006 — the Intel x64 processors became the dominant processors in Windows servers. QlikView had, for a few years, supported the Itanium version of Windows; however, Itanium never became a dominant server processor. Intel and AMD started shipping the x64 processors in 2004 and, by 2006, most servers sold came with an x64 processor — whether the customer wanted 64-bit or not. Because the x64 processors could support either x86 or x64 versions of Windows, the customer didn't even have to know. Even those customers who purchased the x64 version of Windows 2003 didn't really know this because all of their x86 software would run just as well (perhaps with a few tweaks).

But x64 Windows was fantastic for QlikView! Any x86 process is limited to a maximum of 2 GB of physical memory. While 2 GB is quite a lot of memory, it wasn't enough to hold the volume of data that a true enterprise-class BI tool needed to handle. In fact, up until version 9 of QlikView, there was an in-built limitation of about 2 billion rows (actually, 2 to the power of 31) in the number of records that QlikView could load. On x86 processors, QlikView was really confined to the desktop.

x64 was a very different story. Early Intel implementations of x64 could address up to 64 GB of memory. More recent implementations allow up to 256 TB, although Windows Server 2012 can only address 4 TB. Memory is suddenly less of an obstacle to enterprise data volumes.

The other change that happened with processors was the introduction of multi-core architecture. At the time, it was common for a high-end server to come with 2 or 4 processors. Manufacturers came up with a method of putting multiple processors, or cores, on one physical processor. Nowadays, it is not unusual to see a server with 32 cores. High-end servers can have many, many more.

One of QlikView's design features that benefitted from this was that their calculation engine is multithreaded. That means that many of QlikView's calculations will execute across all available processor cores. Unlike many other applications, if you add more cores to your QlikView server, you will, in general, add more performance.

So, when it comes to looking at performance and scalability, very often, the first thing that people look at to improve things is to replace the hardware. This is valid of course! QlikView will almost always work better with newer, faster hardware. But before you go ripping out your racks, you should have a good idea of exactly what is going on with QlikView. Knowledge is power; it will help you tune your implementation to make the best use of the hardware that you already have in place.

The following are the topics we'll be covering in this chapter:

- Reviewing basic performance tuning techniques
- Generating test data
- Understanding how QlikView stores its data
- Looking at strategies to reduce the data size and to improve performance
- Using Direct Discovery
- Testing scalability with JMeter

Reviewing basic performance tuning techniques

There are many ways in which you may have learned to develop with QlikView. Some of them may have talked about performance and some may not have. Typically, you start to think about performance at a later stage when users start complaining about slow results from a QlikView application or when your QlikView server is regularly crashing because your applications are too big.

In this section, we are going to quickly review some basic performance tuning techniques that you should, hopefully, already be aware of. Then, we will start looking at how we can advance your knowledge to master level.

Removing unneeded data

Removing unneeded data might seem easy in theory, but sometimes it is not so easy to implement—especially when you need to negotiate with the business. However, the quickest way to improve the performance of a QlikView application is to remove data from it. If you can reduce your number of fact rows by half, you will vastly improve performance. The different options are discussed in the next sections.

Reducing the number of rows

The first option is to simply reduce the number of rows. Here we are interested in `Fact` or `Transaction` table rows—the largest tables in your data model. Reducing the number of dimension table rows rarely produces a significant performance improvement.

The easiest way to reduce the number of these rows is usually to limit the table by a value such as the date. It is always valuable to ask the question, "Do we really need all the transactions for the last 10 years?" If you can reduce this, say to 2 years, then the performance will improve significantly.

We can also choose to rethink the grain of the data—to what level of detail we hold the information. By aggregating the data to a higher level, we will often vastly reduce the number of rows.

Reducing the number of columns

The second option is to reduce the width of tables—again, especially `Fact` or `Transaction` tables. This means looking at fields that might be in your data model but do not actually get used in the application. One excellent way of establishing this is to use the **Document Analyzer** tool by Rob Wunderlich to examine your application (`http://robwunderlich.com/downloads`).

As well as other excellent uses, Rob's tool looks at multiple areas of an application to establish whether fields are being used or not. It will give you an option to view fields that are not in use and has a useful **DROP FIELD Statements** listbox from which you can copy the possible values. The following screenshot shows an example (from the default document downloadable from Rob's website):

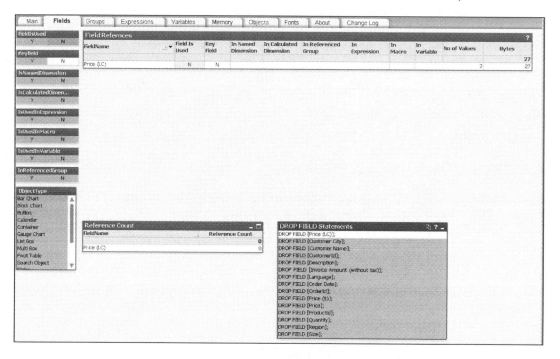

Adding these `DROP FIELD` statements into the end of a script makes it very easy to remove fields from your data model without having to dive into the middle of the script and try to remove them during the load—which could be painful.

There is a potential issue here; if you have users using collaboration objects—creating their own charts—then this tool will not detect that usage. However, if you use the `DROP FIELD` option, then it is straightforward to add a field back if a user complains that one of their charts is not working.

Of course, the best practice would be to take the pain and remove the fields from the script by either commenting them out or removing them completely from their load statements. This is more work, because you may break things and have to do additional debugging, but it will result in a better performing script.

Replacing text keys with numbers

Often, you will have a text value in a key field, for example, something like an account number that has alphanumeric characters. These are actually quite poor for performance compared to an integer value and should be replaced with numeric keys.

 There is some debate here about whether this makes a difference at all, but the effect is to do with the way the data is stored under the hood, which we will explore later. Generated numeric keys are stored slightly differently than text keys, which makes things work better.

The strategy is to leave the text value (account number) in the dimension table for use in display (if you need it!) and then use the AutoNumber function to generate a numeric value—also called a surrogate key—to associate the two tables.

For example, replace the following:

```
Account:
Load
    AccountId,
    AccountName,
    ...
From Account.qvd (QVD);

Transaction:
Load
    TransactionId,
    AccountId,
    TransactionDate,
    ...
From Transaction.qvd (QVD);
```

With the following:

```
Account:
Load
    AccountId,
```

```
    AutoNumber(AccountId) As Join_Account,
    AccountName,
    ...
From Account.qvd (QVD);

Transaction:
Load
    TransactionId,
    AutoNumber(AccountId) As Join_Account,
    TransactionDate,
    ...
From Transaction.qvd (QVD);
```

The `AccountId` field still exists in the `Account` table for display purposes, but the association is on the new numeric field, `Join_Account`.

We will see later that there is some more subtlety to this that we need to be aware of.

Resolving synthetic keys

A synthetic key, caused when tables are associated on two or more fields, actually results in a whole new data table of keys within the QlikView data model.

The following screenshot shows an example of a synthetic key using **Internal Table View** within **Table Viewer** in QlikView:

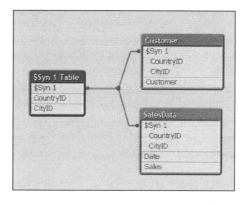

In general, it is recommended to remove synthetic keys from your data model by generating your own keys (for example, using `AutoNumber`):

```
Load
    AutoNumber(CountryID & '-' & CityID) As ClientID,
    Date,
```

```
      Sales
From Fact.qvd (qvd);
```

The following screenshot shows the same model with the synthetic key resolved using the AutoNumber method:

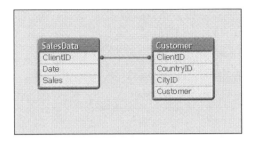

This removes additional data in the data tables (we'll cover more on this later in the chapter) and reduces the number of tables that queries have to traverse.

Reviewing the basics

So, with a basic understanding of QlikView development, you already have a good idea of how to improve performance. After reading the rest of this chapter, you will have enough information to seriously move forward and master this subject.

Generating test data

It is enormously useful to be able to quickly generate test data so that we can create QlikView applications and test different aspects of development and discover how different development methods work. By creating our own set of data, we can abstract problems away from the business issues that we are trying to solve because the data is not connected to those problems. Instead, we can resolve the technical issue underlying the business issue. Once we have resolved that issue, we will have built an understanding that allows us to more quickly resolve the real problems with the business data.

We might contemplate that if we are developers who only have access to a certain dataset, then we will only learn to solve the issues in that dataset. For true mastery, we need to be able to solve issues in many different scenarios, and the only way that we can do that is to generate our own test data to do that with.

Generating dimension values

Dimension tables will generally have lower numbers of records; there are a number of websites online that will generate this type of data for you.

For quite a while, I used `http://www.generatedata.com` to generate random data such as company names, and so on. However, in a recent blog entry by Barry Harmsen (Barry is the co-author of *QlikView 11 for Developers, Packt Publishing*) at `http://www.qlikfix.com`, he mentioned `http://www.mockaroo.com` as a resource for generating such tables.

The following screenshot demonstrates setting up a **Customer** extract in Mockaroo:

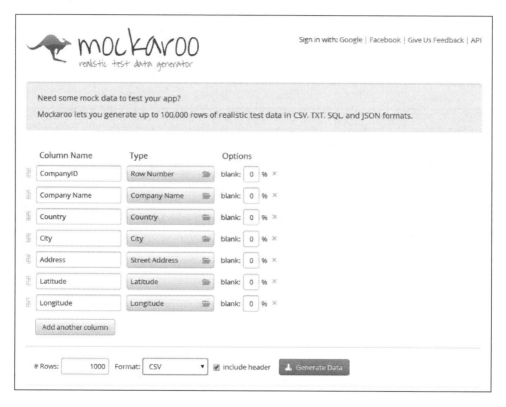

This allows us to create 1,000 customer records that we can include in our QlikView data model. The extract is in the CSV format, so it is quite straightforward to load into QlikView.

Generating fact table rows

While we might often abdicate the creation of test dimension tables to a third-party website like this, we should always try and generate the Fact table data ourselves.

A good way to do this is to simply generate rows with a combination of the AutoGenerate() and Rand() functions.

For even more advanced use cases, we can look at using statistical functions such as NORMINV to generate normal distributions. There is a good article on this written by Henric Cronström on *Qlik Design Blog* at http://community.qlik.com/blogs/qlikviewdesignblog/2013/08/26/monte-carlo-methods.

We should be aware of the AutoGenerate() function that will just simply generate empty rows of data. We can also use the Rand() function to generate a random number between 0 and 1 (it works both in charts and in the script). We can then multiply this value by another number to get various ranges of values.

In the following example, we load a previously generated set of dimension tables — Customer, Product, and Employee. We then generate a number of order header and line rows based on these dimensions, using random dates in a specified range.

First, we will load the Product table and derive a couple of mapping tables:

```
// Load my auto generated dimension files
Product:
LOAD ProductID,
     Product,
     CategoryID,
     SupplierID,
     Money#(CostPrice, '$#,##0.00', '.', ',') As CostPrice,
     Money#(SalesPrice, '$#,##0.00', '.', ',') As SalesPrice
FROM
Products.txt
(txt, utf8, embedded labels, delimiter is '\t', msq);


Product_Cost_Map:
Mapping Load
   ProductID,
   Num(CostPrice)
Resident Product;

Product_Price_Map:
Mapping Load
```

```
    ProductID,
    Num(SalesPrice)
Resident Product;
```

Now load the other dimension tables:

```
Customer:
LOAD CustomerID,
     Customer,
     City,
     Country,
     Region,
     Longitude,
     Latitude,
     Geocoordinates
FROM
Customers.txt
(txt, codepage is 1252, embedded labels, delimiter is '\t', msq);

Employee:
LOAD EmployeeID,
     Employee,
     Grade,
     SalesUnit
FROM
Employees.txt
(txt, codepage is 1252, embedded labels, delimiter is '\t', msq)
Where Match(Grade, 0, 1, 2, 3);  // Sales people
```

We will store the record counts from each table in variables:

```
// Count the ID records in each table
Let vCustCount=FieldValueCount('CustomerID');
Let vProdCount=FieldValueCount('ProductID');
Let vEmpCount=FieldValueCount('EmployeeID');
```

We now generate some date ranges to use in the data calculation algorithm:

```
// Work out the days
Let vStartYear=2009;      // Arbitrary - change if wanted
Let vEndYear=Year(Now()); // Generate up to date data
// Starting the date in April to allow
// offset year testing
Let vStartDate=Floor(MakeDate($(vStartYear),4,1));
Let vEndDate=Floor(MakeDate($(vEndYear),3,31));
Let vNumDays=vEndDate-vStartDate+1;
```

Run a number of iterations to generate data. By editing the number of iterations, we
can increase or decrease the amount of data generated:

```
// Create a loop of 10000 iterations
For i=1 to 10000

    // "A" type records are for any date/time

    // Grab a random employee and customer
    Let vRnd = Floor(Rand() * $(vEmpCount));
    Let vEID = Peek('EmployeeID', $(vRnd), 'Employee');
    Let vRnd = Floor(Rand() * $(vCustCount));
    Let vCID = Peek('CustomerID', $(vRnd), 'Customer');

    // Create a date for any Time of Day  9-5
    Let vOrderDate = $(vStartDate) + Floor(Rand() * $(vNumDays)) +
((9/24) + (Rand()/3));

    // Calculate a random freight amount
    Let vFreight = Round(Rand() * 100, 0.01);

    // Create the header record
    OrderHeader:
    Load
        'A' & $(i)      As OrderID,
        $(vOrderDate)     As OrderDate,
        $(vCID)         As CustomerID,
        $(vEID)         As EmployeeID,
        $(vFreight)      As Freight
    AutoGenerate(1);

    // Generate Order Lines

    // This factor allows us to generate a different number of
    // lines depending on the day of the week
    Let vWeekDay = Num(WeekDay($(vOrderDate)));
```

```
    Let vDateFactor = Pow(2,$(vWeekDay))*(1-(Year(Now())-
Year($(vOrderDate)))*0.05);

    // Calculate the random number of lines
    Let vPCount = Floor(Rand() * $(vDateFactor)) + 1;

    For L=1 to $(vPCount)
        // Calculate random values
        Let vQty = Floor(Rand() * (50+$(vDateFactor))) + 1;
        Let vRnd = Floor(Rand() * $(vProdCount));
        Let vPID = Peek('ProductID', $(vRnd), 'Product');
        Let vCost = ApplyMap('Product_Cost_Map', $(vPID), 1);
        Let vPrice = ApplyMap('Product_Price_Map', $(vPID), 1);

        OrderLine:
        Load
            'A' & $(i)        As OrderID,
            $(L)           As LineNo,
            $(vPID)          As ProductID,
            $(vQty)          As Quantity,
            $(vPrice)         As SalesPrice,
            $(vCost)         As SalesCost,
            $(vQty)*$(vPrice) As LineValue,
            $(vQty)*$(vCost) As LineCost
        AutoGenerate(1);

    Next

    // "B" type records are for summer peak

    // Summer Peak - Generate additional records for summer
    // months to simulate a peak trading period
    Let vY = Year($(vOrderDate));
    Let vM = Floor(Rand()*2)+7;
    Let vD = Day($(vOrderDate));
    Let vOrderDate = Floor(MakeDate($(vY),$(vM),$(vD))) + ((9/24) +
(Rand()/3));

    if Rand() > 0.8 Then

        // Grab a random employee and customer
        Let vRnd = Floor(Rand() * $(vEmpCount));
        Let vEID = Peek('EmployeeID', $(vRnd), 'Employee');
        Let vRnd = Floor(Rand() * $(vCustCount));
```

```
Let vCID = Peek('CustomerID', $(vRnd), 'Customer');

// Calculate a random freight amount
Let vFreight = Round(Rand() * 100, 0.01);
// Create the header record
OrderHeader:
Load
    'B' & $(i)        As OrderID,
    $(vOrderDate)     As OrderDate,
    $(vCID)           As CustomerID,
    $(vEID)           As EmployeeID,
    $(vFreight)       As Freight
AutoGenerate(1);

// Generate Order Lines

// This factor allows us to generate a different number of
// lines depending on the day of the week
Let vWeekDay = Num(WeekDay($(vOrderDate)));
Let vDateFactor = Pow(2,$(vWeekDay))*(1-(Year(Now())-
Year($(vOrderDate)))*0.05);

// Calculate the random number of lines
Let vPCount = Floor(Rand() * $(vDateFactor)) + 1;

For L=1 to $(vPCount)

    // Calculate random values
    Let vQty = Floor(Rand() * (50+$(vDateFactor))) + 1;
    Let vRnd = Floor(Rand() * $(vProdCount));
    Let vPID = Peek('ProductID', $(vRnd), 'Product');
    Let vCost = ApplyMap('Product_Cost_Map', $(vPID), 1);
    Let vPrice = ApplyMap('Product_Price_Map', $(vPID), 1);

    OrderLine:
    Load
        'B' & $(i)         As OrderID,
        $(L)               As LineNo,
        $(vPID)            As ProductID,
        $(vQty)            As Quantity,
        $(vPrice)          As SalesPrice,
        $(vCost)           As SalesCost,
        $(vQty)*$(vPrice) As LineValue,
        $(vQty)*$(vCost) As LineCost
    AutoGenerate(1);
```

```
      Next

   End if
Next

// Store the Generated Data to QVD
Store OrderHeader into OrderHeader.qvd;
Store OrderLine into OrderLine.qvd;
```

Barry Harmsen, co-author of *QlikView 11 for Developers, Packt Publishing*, recommends a slightly different method for generating seasonal variation. By using the `Sin()` or `Cos()` functions to generate a table containing the number of records to generate for each day, we can loop across this table and use these values to auto-generate rows for the fact table.

Understanding how QlikView stores its data

QlikView is really good at storing data. It operates on data in memory, so being able to store a lot of data in a relatively small amount of memory gives the product a great advantage—especially as Moore's Law continues to give us bigger and bigger servers.

Understanding how QlikView stores its data is fundamental in mastering QlikView development. Writing load script with this understanding will allow you to load data in the most efficient way so that you can create the best performing applications. Your users will love you.

A great primer

A great primer on how QlikView stores its data is available on *Qlik Design Blog*, written by Henric Cronström (http://community.qlik.com/blogs/qlikviewdesignblog/2012/11/20/symbol-tables-and-bit-stuffed-pointers).

Henric joined QlikView in 1994, so he knows quite a bit about exactly how it works.

Looking at things from a simple level

From a simple level, consider the following small table:

First name	Surname	Country
John	Smith	USA
Jane	Smith	USA
John	Doe	Canada

For the preceding table, QlikView will create three symbol tables like the following:

Index	Value
1010	John
1011	Jane

Index	Value
1110	Smith
1111	Doe

Index	Value
110	USA
111	Canada

And the data table will look like the following:

First name	Surname	Country
1010	1110	110
1011	1110	110
1010	1111	111

This set of tables will take up less space than the original data table for the following three reasons:

- The binary indexes are bit-stuffed in the data table—they only take up as much space as needed.
- The binary index, even though repeated, will take up less space than the text values. The Unicode text just for "USA" takes up several bytes—the binary index takes less space than that.
- Each, larger, text value is only stored once in the symbol tables.

So, to summarize, each field in the data model will be stored in a symbol table (unless, as we will see later, it is a sequential integer value) that contains the unique values and an index value. Every table that you create in the script—including any synthetic key tables—will be represented as a data table containing just the index pointers.

> Because the data table indexes are bit-stuffed, and because data is stored in bytes, adding another bit or two to the indexes may not actually increase the overall width of a data table record.

Exporting the memory statistics for a document

To help us understand what is going on in a particular QlikView document, we can export details about where all the memory is being used. This export file will tell us how much memory is being used by each field in the symbol tables, the data tables, chart objects, and so on.

Perform the following steps to export the memory statistics for a document:

1. To export the memory statistics, you need to open **Document Properties** from the **Settings** menu (*Ctrl + Alt + D*). On the **General** tab, click on the **Memory Statistics** button, as shown in the following screenshot:

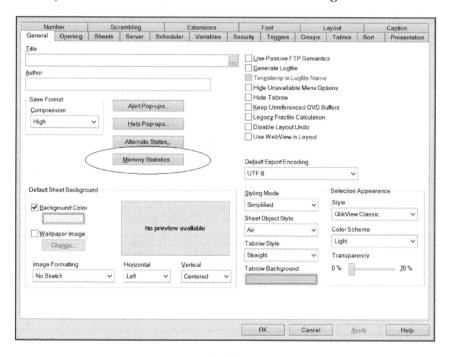

2. After you click on the button, you will be prompted to enter file information. Once you have entered the path and filename, the file will be exported. It is a tab-delimited data file:

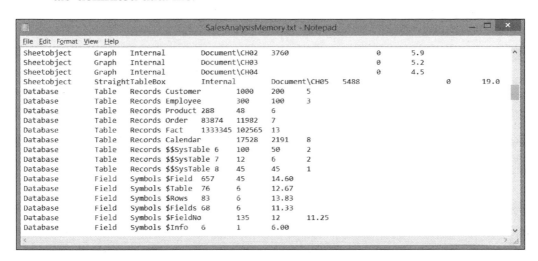

3. The easiest way to analyze this file is to import it into a new QlikView document:

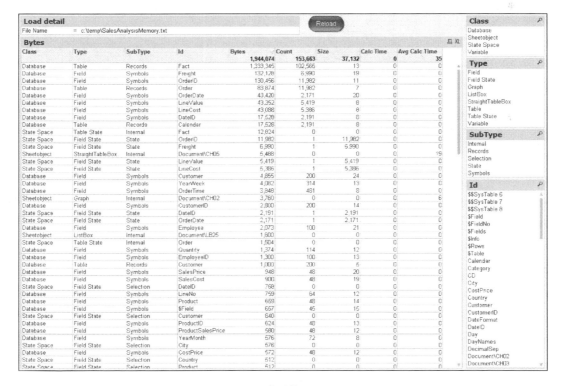

We can now see exactly how much space our data is taking up in the symbol tables and in the data tables. We can also look at chart calculation performance to see whether there are long running calculations that we need to tune. Analyzing this data will allow us to make valuable decisions about where we can improve performance in our QlikView document.

One thing that we need to be cognizant of is that the memory usage and calculation time of charts will only be available if that chart has actually been opened. The calculation time of the charts may also not be accurate as it will usually only be correct if the chart has just been opened for the first time—subsequent openings and changes of selection will most probably be calculated from the cache, and a cache execution should execute a lot quicker than a non-cached execution. Other objects may also use similar expressions, and these will therefore already be cached. We can turn the cache off—although only for testing purposes, as it can really kill performance. We will look at this in the *Testing chart performance for different load options* section.

Strategies to reduce the data size and improve performance

Using some of the test data that we have generated, or any other data that you might want, we can discover more about how QlikView handles different scenarios. Understanding these different situations will give you real mastery over data load optimization.

Optimizing field values and keys

To begin with, let's see what happens when we load two largish tables that are connected by a key. So, let's ignore the dimension tables and load the order data using a script like the following:

```
Order:
LOAD OrderID,
     OrderDate,
     CustomerID,
     EmployeeID,
     Freight
FROM
[..\Scripts\OrderHeader.qvd]
(qvd);
```

```
OrderLine:
LOAD OrderID,
     LineNo,
     ProductID,
     Quantity,
     SalesPrice,
     SalesCost,
     LineValue,
     LineCost
FROM
[..\Scripts\OrderLine.qvd]
(qvd);
```

The preceding script will result in a database memory profile that looks like the following. In the following screenshot, `Database` has been selected for `Class`:

Class	Type	SubType	Id	Bytes	Count
				1,710,383	**156,919**
Database	Table	Records	OrderLine	923,085	102,565
Database	Field	Symbols	OrderDate	346,140	11,982
Database	Field	Symbols	Freight	132,128	6,990
Database	Field	Symbols	OrderID	130,456	11,982
Database	Table	Records	Order	83,874	11,982
Database	Field	Symbols	LineValue	43,352	5,419
Database	Field	Symbols	LineCost	43,088	5,386
Database	Field	Symbols	CustomerID	2,800	200
Database	Field	Symbols	Quantity	1,374	114
Database	Field	Symbols	SalesPrice	948	48
Database	Field	Symbols	SalesCost	900	48
Database	Field	Symbols	LineNo	759	64
Database	Field	Symbols	ProductID	624	48
Database	Field	Symbols	EmployeeID	481	37
Database	Field	Symbols	$Field	174	12
Database	Field	Symbols	$FieldNo	88	8
Database	Field	Symbols	$Rows	31	2
Database	Field	Symbols	$Table	26	2
Database	Field	Symbols	$Fields	22	2
Database	Table	Records	$$SysTable 2	13	13
Database	Table	Records	$$SysTable 4	12	12
Database	Field	Symbols	$Info	6	1
Database	Table	Records	$$SysTable 3	2	2

There are some interesting readings in this table. For example, we can see that when the main data table—`OrderLine`—is stored with just its pointer records, it takes up just 923,085 bytes for 102,565 records. That is an average of only 9 bytes per record. This shows the space benefit of the bit-stuffed pointer mechanism as described in Henric's blog post.

The largest individual symbol table is the `OrderDate` field. This is very typical of a `TimeStamp` field, which will often be highly unique, have long decimal values, and have the `Dual` text value, and so often takes up a lot of memory—28 bytes per value.

The number part of a `TimeStamp` field contains an integer representing the date (number of days since 30th December 1899) and a decimal representing the time. So, let's see what happens with this field if we turn it into just an integer—a common strategy with these fields as the time portion may not be important:

```
Order:
LOAD OrderID,
     Floor(OrderDate) As DateID,
     ...
```

This changes things considerably:

Class	Type	SubType	Id	Bytes	Count
				1,381,608	147,108
Database	Table	Records	OrderLine	923,085	102,565
Database	Field	Symbols	Freight	132,128	6,990
Database	Field	Symbols	OrderID	130,456	11,982
Database	Table	Records	Order	83,874	11,982
Database	Field	Symbols	LineValue	43,352	5,419
Database	Field	Symbols	LineCost	43,088	5,386
Database	Field	Symbols	DateID	17,368	2,171
Database	Field	Symbols	CustomerID	2,800	200

The number of unique values has been vastly reduced, because the highly unique date and time values have been replaced with a much lower cardinality (2171) date integer, and the amount of memory consumed is also vastly reduced as the integer values are only taking 8 bytes instead of the 28 being taken by each value of the `TimeStamp` field.

The next field that we will pay attention to is `OrderID`. This is the key field, and key fields are always worth examining to see whether they can be improved. In our test data, the `OrderID` field is alphanumeric—this is not uncommon for such data. Alphanumeric data will tend to take up more space than numeric data, so it is a good idea to convert it to integers using the `AutoNumber` function.

`AutoNumber` accepts a text value and will return a sequential integer. If you pass the same text value, it will return the same integer. This is a great way of transforming alphanumeric ID values into integers. The code will look like the following:

```
Order:
LOAD AutoNumber(OrderID) As OrderID,
     Floor(OrderDate) As DateID,
   ...


OrderLine:
LOAD AutoNumber(OrderID) As OrderID,
     LineNo,
   ...
```

This will result in a memory profile like the following:

Database	Field	Symbols	$Table	26	2
Database	Field	Symbols	$Fields	22	2
Database	Table	Records	$$SysTable 2	13	13
Database	Table	Records	$$SysTable 4	12	12
Database	Field	Symbols	$Info	6	1
Database	Table	Records	$$SysTable 3	2	2
Database	Field	Symbols	OrderID	0	11,982

The `OrderID` field is now showing as having 0 bytes! This is quite interesting because what QlikView does with a field containing sequential integers is that it does not bother to store the value in the symbol table at all; it just uses the value as the pointer in the data table. This is a great design feature and gives us a good strategy for reducing data sizes.

We could do the same thing with the `CustomerID` and `EmployeeID` fields:

```
Order:
LOAD AutoNumber(OrderID) As OrderID,
     Floor(OrderDate) As DateID,
     AutoNumber(CustomerID) As CustomerID,
     AutoNumber(EmployeeID) As EmployeeID,
     ...
```

That has a very interesting effect on the memory profile:

Class	Type	SubType	Id	Bytes	Count
				1,345,623	**147,108**
Database	Table	Records	OrderLine	923,085	102,565
Database	Field	Symbols	Freight	132,128	6,990
Database	Field	Symbols	OrderID	95,856	11,982
Database	Table	Records	Order	83,874	11,982
Database	Field	Symbols	LineValue	43,352	5,419
Database	Field	Symbols	LineCost	43,088	5,386
Database	Field	Symbols	DateID	17,368	2,171
Database	Field	Symbols	CustomerID	1,600	200
Database	Field	Symbols	Quantity	1,374	114
Database	Field	Symbols	SalesPrice	948	48
Database	Field	Symbols	SalesCost	900	48
Database	Field	Symbols	LineNo	759	64
Database	Field	Symbols	ProductID	624	48
Database	Field	Symbols	EmployeeID	296	37
Database	Field	Symbols	$Field	171	12

Our `OrderID` field is now back in the `Symbols` table. The other two tables are still there too. So what has gone wrong?

Because we have simply used the `AutoNumber` function across each field, now none of them are perfectly sequential integers and so do not benefit from the design feature. But we can do something about this because the `AutoNumber` function accepts a second parameter—an ID—to identify different ranges of counters. So, we can rejig the script in the following manner:

```
Order:
LOAD AutoNumber(OrderID, 'Order') As OrderID,
     Floor(OrderDate) As DateID,
     AutoNumber(CustomerID, 'Customer') As CustomerID,
     AutoNumber(EmployeeID, 'Employee') As EmployeeID,
     ...


OrderLine:
LOAD AutoNumber(OrderID, 'Order') As OrderID,
     LineNo,
     ...
```

This should give us the following result:

Database	Table	Records	$$SysTable 2	13	13
Database	Table	Records	$$SysTable 4	12	12
Database	Field	Symbols	$Info	6	1
Database	Table	Records	$$SysTable 3	2	2
Database	Field	Symbols	CustomerID	0	200
Database	Field	Symbols	EmployeeID	0	37
Database	Field	Symbols	OrderID	0	11,982

This is something that you should consider for all key values, especially from a modeling best practice point of view. There are instances when you want to retain the ID value for display or search purposes. In that case, a copy of the value should be kept as a field in a dimension table and the AutoNumber function used on the key value.

 It is worth noting that it is often good to be able to see the key associations — or lack of associations — between two tables, especially when troubleshooting data issues. Because AutoNumber obfuscates the values, it makes that debugging a bit harder. Therefore, it can be a good idea to leave the application of AutoNumber until later on in the development cycle, when you are more certain of the data sources.

Optimizing data by removing keys using ApplyMap

For this example, we will use some of the associated dimension tables — Category and Product. These are loaded in the following manner:

```
Category:
LOAD CategoryID,
     Category
FROM
[..\Scripts\Categories.txt]
(txt, codepage is 1252, embedded labels, delimiter is '\t', msq);

Product:
LOAD ProductID,
     Product,
     CategoryID,
     SupplierID,
     CostPrice,
     SalesPrice
FROM
[..\Scripts\Products.txt]
(txt, codepage is 1252, embedded labels, delimiter is '\t', msq);
```

This has a small memory profile:

Class	Type	SubType	Id	Bytes	Count
				3,160	**302**
Database	Field	Symbols	Product	659	48
Database	Field	Symbols	ProductID	624	48
Database	Field	Symbols	SalesPrice	580	48
Database	Field	Symbols	CostPrice	572	48
Database	Table	Records	Product	192	48
Database	Field	Symbols	SupplierID	140	10
Database	Field	Symbols	$Field	105	7
Database	Field	Symbols	Category	67	5
Database	Field	Symbols	$FieldNo	66	6
Database	Field	Symbols	CategoryID	55	5
Database	Field	Symbols	$Table	27	2
Database	Field	Symbols	$Rows	23	2
Database	Field	Symbols	$Fields	22	2
Database	Table	Records	$$SysTable 2	8	8
Database	Table	Records	$$SysTable 4	7	7
Database	Field	Symbols	$Info	6	1
Database	Table	Records	Category	5	5
Database	Table	Records	$$SysTable 3	2	2

The best way to improve the performance of these tables is to remove the `CategoryID` field by moving the `Category` value into the `Product` table. When we have small lookup tables like this, we should always consider using `ApplyMap`:

```
Category_Map:
Mapping
LOAD CategoryID,
     Category
FROM
[..\Scripts\Categories.txt]
(txt, codepage is 1252, embedded labels, delimiter is '\t', msq);

Product:
LOAD ProductID,
     Product,
     //CategoryID,
     ApplyMap('Category_Map', CategoryID, 'Other') As Category,
     SupplierID,
     CostPrice,
     SalesPrice
FROM
[..\Scripts\Products.txt]
(txt, codepage is 1252, embedded labels, delimiter is '\t', msq);
```

By removing the Symbols table and the entry in the data table, we have reduced the amount of memory used. More importantly, we have reduced the number of joins required to answer queries based on the Category table:

Class	Type	SubType	Id	Bytes	Count
				3,044	284
Database	Field	Symbols	Product	659	48
Database	Field	Symbols	ProductID	624	48
Database	Field	Symbols	SalesPrice	580	48
Database	Field	Symbols	CostPrice	572	48
Database	Table	Records	Product	192	48
Database	Field	Symbols	SupplierID	140	10
Database	Field	Symbols	$Field	89	6
Database	Field	Symbols	Category	67	5

Optimizing performance by removing keys by joining tables

If the associated dimension table has more than two fields, it can still have its data moved into the primary dimension table by loading multiple mapping tables; this is useful if there is a possibility of many-to-many joins. You do have to consider, however, that this does make the script a little more complicated and, in many circumstances, it is a better idea to simply join the tables.

For example, suppose that we have the previously mentioned Product table and an associated Supplier table that is 3,643 bytes:

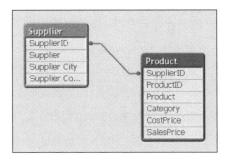

By joining the Supplier table to the Product table and then dropping SupplierID, we might reduce this down to, say, 3,499 bytes, but more importantly, we improve the query performance:

```
Join (Product)
LOAD SupplierID,
```

```
        Company As Supplier,
        ...

Drop Field SupplierID;
```

Optimizing memory by removing low cardinality fields

Joining tables together is not always the best approach from a memory point of view. It could be possible to attempt to create the ultimate joined table model of just having one table containing all values. This will work, and query performance should, in theory, be quite fast. However, the way QlikView works is the wider and longer the table you create, the wider and longer the underlying pointer data table will be. Let's consider an example.

Quite often, there will be a number of associated fields in a fact table that have a lower cardinality (smaller number of distinct values) than the main keys in the fact table. A quite common example is having date parts within the fact table. In that case, it can actually be a good idea to remove these values from the fact table and link them via a shared key. So, for example, consider we have an `Order` table loaded in the following manner:

```
Order:
LOAD AutoNumber(OrderID, 'Order') As OrderID,
     Floor(OrderDate) As DateID,
     Year(OrderDate) As Year,
     Month(OrderDate) As Month,
     Day(OrderDate) As Day,
     Date(MonthStart(OrderDate), 'YYYY-MM') As YearMonth,
     AutoNumber(CustomerID, 'Customer') As CustomerID,
     AutoNumber(EmployeeID, 'Employee') As EmployeeID,
     Freight
FROM
[..\Scripts\OrderHeader.qvd]
(qvd);
```

This will give a memory profile like the following:

Class	Type	SubType	Id	Bytes	Count
				258,644	33,524
Database	Field	Symbols	Freight	132,128	6,990
Database	Table	Records	Order	107,838	11,982
Database	Field	Symbols	DateID	17,368	2,171
Database	Field	Symbols	YearMonth	576	72
Database	Field	Symbols	Day	248	31
Database	Field	Symbols	Month	156	12
Database	Field	Symbols	$Field	115	9
Database	Field	Symbols	$FieldNo	99	9
Database	Field	Symbols	Year	54	6

We can see the values for Year, Month, and Day have a very low count. It is worth noting here that Year takes up a lot less space than Month or Day; this is because Year is just an integer and the others are Dual values that have text as well as numbers.

Let's modify the script to have the date fields in a different table in the following manner:

```
Order:
LOAD AutoNumber(OrderID, 'Order') As OrderID,
     Floor(OrderDate) As DateID,
     AutoNumber(CustomerID, 'Customer') As CustomerID,
     AutoNumber(EmployeeID, 'Employee') As EmployeeID,
     Freight
FROM
[..\Scripts\OrderHeader.qvd]
(qvd);

Calendar:
Load Distinct
     DateID,
     Date(DateID) As Date,
     Year(DateID) As Year,
     Month(DateID) As Month,
     Day(DateID) As Day,
     Date(MonthStart(DateID), 'YYYY-MM') As YearMonth
Resident
   Order;
```

We can see that there is a difference in the memory profile:

Class	Type	SubType	Id	Bytes	Count
				243,344	35,695
Database	Field	Symbols	Freight	132,128	6,990
Database	Table	Records	Order	83,874	11,982
Database	Field	Symbols	DateID	17,368	2,171
Database	Table	Records	Calendar	8,684	2,171
Database	Field	Symbols	YearMonth	576	72
Database	Field	Symbols	Day	248	31
Database	Field	Symbols	Month	156	12
Database	Field	Symbols	$Field	115	9
Database	Field	Symbols	$FieldNo	55	5
Database	Field	Symbols	Year	48	6

We have all the same symbol table values that we had before with the same memory. We do have a new data table for `Calendar`, but it is only quite small because there are only a small number of values. We have, however, made a dent in the size of the `Order` table because we have removed pointers from it. This effect will be increased as the number of rows increases in the `Order` table, whereas the number of rows in the `Calendar` table will not increase significantly over time.

Of course, because the data is now in two tables, there will be a potential downside in that joins will need to be made between the tables to answer queries. However, we should always prefer to have a smaller memory footprint. But how can we tell if there was a difference in performance?

Testing chart performance for different load options

As well as information about memory use in each data table and symbol table, we can recall that the **Memory Statistics** option will also export information about charts—both memory use and calculation time. This means that we can create a chart, especially one with multiple dimensions and expressions, and see how long the chart takes to calculate for different scenarios.

Let's load the `Order Header` and `Order Line` data with the `Calendar` information loaded inline (as in the first part of the last example) in the following manner:

```
Order:
LOAD AutoNumber(OrderID, 'Order') As OrderID,
     Floor(OrderDate) As DateID,
     Year(OrderDate) As Year,
     Month(OrderDate) As Month,
```

```
        Day(OrderDate) As Day,
        Date(MonthStart(OrderDate), 'YYYY-MM') As YearMonth,
        AutoNumber(CustomerID, 'Customer') As CustomerID,
        AutoNumber(EmployeeID, 'Employee') As EmployeeID,
        Freight
FROM
[..\Scripts\OrderHeader.qvd]
(qvd);



OrderLine:
LOAD AutoNumber(OrderID, 'Order') As OrderID,
        LineNo,
        ProductID,
        Quantity,
        SalesPrice,
        SalesCost,
        LineValue,
        LineCost
FROM
[..\Scripts\OrderLine.qvd]
(qvd);
```

Now we can add a chart to the document with several dimensions and expressions like this:

YearMonth	CustomerID	Sales $	Cost $	Margin $	Margin %	Cum. Sales $	# Orders	Product 101	Prod 102-106
		288,715,597.09	224,772,646.40	63,942,950.69	22.15%	0.00	11,982	2,209	18,782
2009-01	3	7,327.89	5,139.47	2,188.42	29.86%	7,327.89	1	0	0
2009-01	4	7,461.18	5,747.95	1,713.23	22.96%	14,789.07	1	0	0
2009-01	5	31,006.99	22,125.30	8,881.69	28.64%	45,796.06	1	0	1
2009-01	6	834.17	571.97	262.20	31.43%	46,630.23	1	0	0
2009-01	8	36,277.85	28,574.83	7,703.02	21.23%	82,908.08	2	0	1
2009-01	11	9,503.71	7,827.08	1,676.63	17.64%	92,411.79	1	0	1
2009-01	14	27,987.96	21,175.78	6,812.18	24.34%	120,399.75	2	0	1
2009-01	15	1,985.20	1,689.20	296.00	14.91%	122,384.95	1	0	0
2009-01	18	211,142.18	165,958.56	45,183.62	21.40%	333,527.13	2	2	6
2009-01	20	1,248.00	883.08	364.92	29.24%	334,775.13	1	0	0
2009-01	22	12,054.08	9,593.32	2,460.76	20.41%	346,829.21	2	1	1
2009-01	24	561.47	550.16	11.31	2.01%	347,390.68	2	0	0
2009-01	25	155.64	104.79	50.85	32.67%	347,546.32	1	0	0
2009-01	26	39,663.59	28,990.80	10,672.79	26.91%	387,209.91	3	0	1
2009-01	27	5,147.72	4,169.82	977.90	19.00%	392,357.63	1	0	1
2009-01	28	4,346.76	3,632.64	714.12	16.43%	396,704.39	1	1	0
2009-01	32	51,051.31	36,570.48	14,480.83	28.37%	447,755.70	1	0	0
2009-01	33	11,036.71	7,828.78	3,207.93	29.07%	458,792.41	1	0	2
2009-01	34	9,400.57	7,083.08	2,317.49	24.65%	468,192.98	2	0	0
2009-01	35	92,789.84	73,302.02	19,487.82	21.00%	560,982.82	2	0	4
2009-01	36	3,593.34	2,858.95	934.39	26.00%	564,576.16	1	0	0
2009-01	39	34,587.67	26,552.92	8,034.75	23.23%	599,163.83	3	1	5
2009-01	40	12,406.63	9,591.38	2,815.25	22.69%	611,570.46	1	0	0
2009-01	41	35,689.54	27,310.42	8,379.12	23.48%	647,260.00	1	0	1
2009-01	43	3,780.12	3,116.78	663.34	17.55%	651,040.12	1	0	0
2009-01	45	92,960.09	73,108.00	19,852.09	21.36%	744,000.21	2	0	5

We have used `YearMonth` and `CustomerID` as dimensions. This is deliberate because these two fields will be in separate tables once we move the calendar fields into a separate table.

The expressions that we have used are shown in the following table:

Expression Label	Expression
Sales $	Sum(LineValue)
Sales $ Color	ColorMix1(Sum(LineValue)/Max(total Aggr(Sum(LineValue), YearMonth, CustomerID)), White(), ARGB(255, 0, 128, 255))
Cost $	Sum(LineCost)
Margin $	Sum(LineValue)-Sum(LineCost)
Margin %	(Sum(LineValue)-Sum(LineCost))/Sum(LineValue)
Cum. Sales $	RangeSum(Above(Sum(LineValue),0,RowNo()))
# Orders	Count(DISTINCT OrderID)
Product 101	Sum(If(ProductID=101,1,0))
Product 102-106	Sum(If(Match(ProductID,102,103,104,105,106), 1, 0))

Turning the cache off

The cache in QlikView is enormously important. Calculations and selections are cached as you work with a QlikView document. The next time you open a chart with the same selections, the chart will not be recalculated; you will get the cached answer instead. This really speeds up QlikView performance. Even within a chart, you might have multiple expressions using the same calculation (such as dividing two expressions by each other to obtain a ratio)—the results will make use of caching.

This caching is really useful for a working document, but a pain if we want to gather statistics on one or more charts. With the cache on, we need to close a document and the QlikView desktop, reopen the document in a new QlikView instance, and open the chart. To help us test the chart performance, it can therefore be a good idea to turn off the cache.

Barry Harmsen, co-author of *QlikView 11 for Developers*, wrote a good blog entry on this recently at http://www.qlikfix.com/2014/04/15/power-qlikview-caching.

As written in the blog, we need to open the **About** view in QlikView from the **Help** menu and locate the QlikView ball:

By right-clicking on the ball, we can open the restricted **Settings** dialog where we can set the **DisableCache** value to **1** and click on the **Set** button:

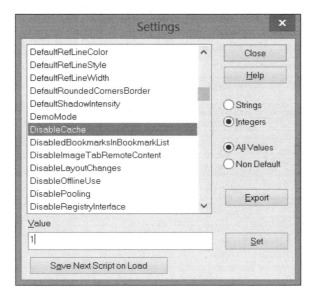

You need to close QlikView and reopen it for the change to take effect.

> Note that you need to be very careful with this dialog as you could break things in your QlikView installation. Turning off the cache is not recommended for normal use of the QlikView desktop as it can seriously interfere with the performance of QlikView. Turning off the cache to gather accurate statistics on chart performance is pretty much the only use case that one might ever come across for turning off the cache. There is a reason why it is a hidden setting!

Examining the chart calculation time for different scenarios

Now that the cache is turned off, we can open our chart and it will always calculate at the maximum time. We can then export the memory information as usual and load it into another copy of QlikView (here, the **Class** of **Sheetobject** is selected):

Class	Type	SubType	Id	Bytes	Count	Calc Time	Avg Calc Time
				2,033,840	0	265	265
Sheetobject	StraightTableBox	Internal	Document\CH01	2,033,840	0	265	265

What we could do now is make some selections and save them as bookmarks. By closing the QlikView desktop client and then reopening it, and then opening the document and running through the bookmarks, we can export the memory file and create a calculation for **Avg Calc Time**. Because there is no cache involved, this should be a valid representation.

Now, we can comment out the inline calendar and create the `Calendar` table (as we did in a previous exercise):

```
Order:
LOAD AutoNumber(OrderID, 'Order') As OrderID,
     Floor(OrderDate) As DateID,
//      Year(OrderDate) As Year,
//      Month(OrderDate) As Month,
//      Day(OrderDate) As Day,
//      Date(MonthStart(OrderDate), 'YYYY-MM') As YearMonth,
     AutoNumber(CustomerID, 'Customer') As CustomerID,
     AutoNumber(EmployeeID, 'Employee') As EmployeeID,
     Freight
FROM
[..\Scripts\OrderHeader.qvd]
(qvd);


OrderLine:
//Left Join (Order)
LOAD AutoNumber(OrderID, 'Order') As OrderID,
     LineNo,
     ProductID,
     Quantity,
     SalesPrice,
     SalesCost,
     LineValue,
     LineCost
```

```
FROM
[..\Scripts\OrderLine.qvd]
(qvd);

//exit Script;

Calendar:
Load Distinct
    DateID,
     Year(DateID) As Year,
     Month(DateID) As Month,
     Day(DateID) As Day,
     Date(MonthStart(DateID), 'YYYY-MM') As YearMonth
Resident
    Order;
```

For the dataset size that we are using, we should see no difference in calculation time between the two data structures. As previously established, the second option has a smaller in-memory data size, so that would always be the preferred option.

Optimizing performance by creating counter fields

For many years, it has been a well-established fact among QlikView consultants that a Count() function with a Distinct clause is a very expensive calculation. Over the years, I have heard that Count can be up to 1000 times more expensive than Sum. Actually, since about Version 9 of QlikView, this is no longer true, and the Count function is a lot more efficient.

 See Henric Cronström's blog entry at http://community. qlik.com/blogs/qlikviewdesignblog/2013/10/22/ a-myth-about-countdistinct for more information.

Count is still a more expensive operation, and the recommended solution is to create a counter field in the table that you wish to count, which has a value of 1. You can then sum this counter field to get the count of rows. This field can also be useful in advanced expressions like **Set Analysis**.

Using the same dataset as in the previous example, if we create a chart using similar dimensions (YearMonth and CustomerID) and the same expression for Order # as done previously:

```
Count(Distinct OrderID)
```

This gives us a chart like the following:

YearMonth	CustomerID	# Orders (Sum)
		11,982
2009-01	3	1
2009-01	4	1
2009-01	5	1
2009-01	6	1
2009-01	8	2
2009-01	11	1
2009-01	14	2
2009-01	15	1
2009-01	18	2
2009-01	20	1
2009-01	22	2
2009-01	24	2
2009-01	25	1
2009-01	26	3
2009-01	27	1
2009-01	28	1
2009-01	32	1
2009-01	33	1
2009-01	34	2
2009-01	35	2
2009-01	36	1
2009-01	39	3
2009-01	40	1
2009-01	41	1
2009-01	43	1
2009-01	45	2

After running through the same bookmarks that we created earlier, we get a set of results like the following:

Class	Type	SubType	Id	Bytes	Count	Calc Time	Avg Calc Time
				301,168	0	31	24
Sheetobject	StraightTableBox	Internal	Document\CH02	301,168	0	31	24

So, now we modify the `Order` table load as follows:

```
Order:
LOAD AutoNumber(OrderID, 'Order') As OrderID,
     1 As OrderCounter,
     Floor(OrderDate) As DateID,
     AutoNumber(CustomerID, 'Customer') As CustomerID,
     AutoNumber(EmployeeID, 'Employee') As EmployeeID,
     Freight
FROM
[..\Scripts\OrderHeader.qvd]
(qvd);
```

Once we reload, we can modify the expression for `Order #` to the following:

```
Sum(OrderCounter)
```

We close down the document, reopen it, and run through the bookmarks again. This is an example result:

Class	Type	◉ SubType	Id	Bytes	/ Count	Calc Time	Avg Calc Time
				301,104	0	16	9
Sheetobject	StraightTableBox	Internal	Document\CH02	301,104	0	16	9

And yes, we do see that there is an improvement in calculation time — it appears to be a factor of about twice as fast.

The amount of additional memory needed for this field is actually minimal. In the way we have loaded it previously, the `OrderCounter` field will add only a small amount in the symbol table and will only increase the size of the data table by a very small amount — it may, in fact, appear not to increase it at all! The only increase is in the core system tables, and this is minor.

> Recalling that data tables are bit-stuffed but stored as bytes, adding a one-bit value like this to the data table may not actually increase the number of bytes needed to store the value. At worst, only one additional byte will be needed.

In fact, we can reduce this minor change even further by making the following change:

```
. . .
Floor(1) As OrderCounter,
. . .
```

This forces the single value to be treated as a sequential integer (a sequence of one) and the value therefore isn't stored in the symbol table.

Optimizing performance by combining fact tables?

If we load all of our tables, the data structure may look something like the following:

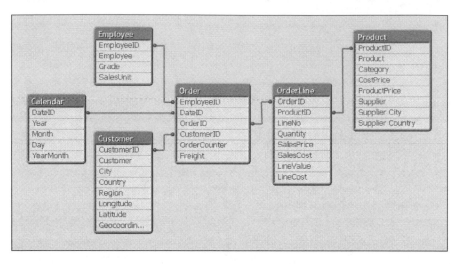

In this format, we have two fact tables — Order and OrderLine. For the small dataset that we have, we won't see any issues here. As the dataset gets larger, it is suggested that it is better to have fewer tables and fewer joins between tables. In this case, between Product and Employee, there are three joins. The best practice is to have only one fact table containing all our key fields and associated facts (measures).

In this model, most of the facts are in the OrderLine table, but there are two facts in the Order table — OrderCounter and Freight. We need to think about what we do with them. There are two options:

1. Move the EmployeeID, DateID, and CustomerID fields from the Order table into the OrderLine table. Create a script based on an agreed business rule (for example, ratio of line Quantity) to apportion the Freight value across all of the line values. The OrderCounter field is more difficult to deal with, but we could take the option of using Count(Distinct OrderID) (knowing that it is less efficient) in the front end and disposing of the OrderCounter field.

   This method is more in line with traditional data warehousing methods.

2. Move the EmployeeID, DateID, and CustomerID fields from the Order table into the OrderLine table. Leave the Order table as is, as an Order dimension table.

   This is more of a QlikView way of doing things. It works very well too.

Although we might be great fans of dimensional modeling methods (see *Chapter 2, QlikView Data Modeling*), we should also be a big fan of pragmatism and using what works.

Let's see what happens if we go for option 2. The following is the addition to the script to move the key fields:

```
// Move DateID, CustomerID and EmployeeID to OrderLine
Join (OrderLine)
Load
    OrderID,
    DateID,
    CustomerID,
    EmployeeID
Resident
    Order;

Drop Fields DateID, CustomerID, EmployeeID From Order;

// Rename the OrderLine table
RENAME Table OrderLine to Fact;
```

So, how has that worked? The table structure now looks like the following:

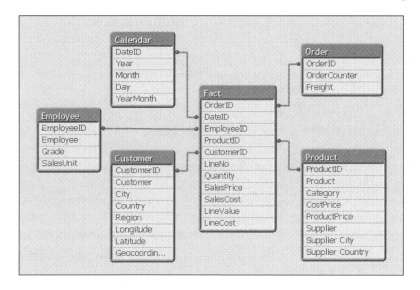

Our expectation, as we have widened the biggest data table (OrderLine) and only narrowed a smaller table (Order), is that the total memory for the document will be increased. This is confirmed by taking memory snapshots before and after the change:

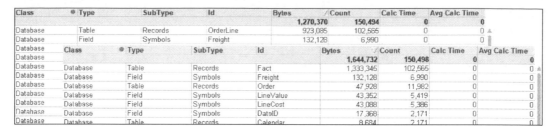

But have we improved the overall performance of the document?

To test this, we can create a new version of our original chart, except now using Customer instead of CustomerID and adding Product. This gives us fields (YearMonth, Customer, and Product) from across the dimension tables. If we use this new straight table to test the before and after state, the following is how the results might look:

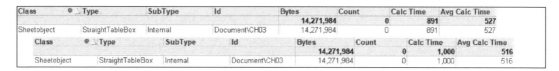

Interestingly, the average calculation has reduced slightly. This is not unexpected as we have reduced the number of joins needed across data tables.

Optimizing your numbers

QlikView has a great feature in that it can sometimes default to storing numbers as Dual values—the number along with text representing the default presentation of that number. This text is derived either by applying the default formats during load, or by the developer applying formats using functions such as Num(), Date(), Money(), or TimeStamp(). If you do apply the format functions with a format string (as the second parameter to Num, Date, and so on), the number will be stored as a Dual. If you use Num without a format string, the number will usually be stored without the text.

Thinking about it, numbers that represent facts (measures) in our fact tables will rarely need to be displayed with their default formats. They are almost always only ever going to be displayed in an aggregation in a chart and that aggregated value will have its own format. The text part is therefore superfluous and can be removed if it is there.

Let's modify our script in the following manner:

```
Order:
LOAD AutoNumber(OrderID, 'Order') As OrderID,
     Floor(1) As OrderCounter,
     Floor(OrderDate) As DateID,
     AutoNumber(CustomerID, 'Customer') As CustomerID,
     AutoNumber(EmployeeID, 'Employee') As EmployeeID,
     Num(Freight) As Freight
FROM
[..\Scripts\OrderHeader.qvd]
(qvd);


OrderLine:
LOAD AutoNumber(OrderID, 'Order') As OrderID,
     LineNo,
     ProductID,
     Num(Quantity) As Quantity,
     Num(SalesPrice) As SalesPrice,
     Num(SalesCost) As SalesCost,
     Num(LineValue) As LineValue,
     Num(LineCost) As LineCost
FROM
[..\Scripts\OrderLine.qvd]
(qvd);
```

The change in memory looks like the following:

Class	Type	SubType	Id	Bytes	Count	Calc Time	Avg Calc Time
				220,088	17,891	0	0
Database	Field	Symbols	Freight	132,128	6,990	0	0
Database	Field	Symbols	LineValue	43,352	5,419	0	0
Database	Field	Symbols	LineCost	43,088	5,386	0	0
Database	Field	Symbols	SalesPrice	948	48	0	0
Database	Field	Symbols	CostPrice	572	48	0	0

Class	Type	SubType	Id	Bytes	Count	Calc Time	Avg Calc Time
				143,316	17,891	0	0
Database	Field	Symbols	Freight	55,920	6,990	0	0
Database	Field	Symbols	LineValue	43,352	5,419	0	0
Database	Field	Symbols	LineCost	43,088	5,386	0	0
Database	Field	Symbols	CostPrice	572	48	0	0
Database	Field	Symbols	SalesPrice	384	48	0	0

We can see that there is a significant difference in the `Freight` field. The smaller `SalesPrice` field has also been reduced. However, the other numeric fields are not changed.

Some numbers have additional format strings and take up a lot of space, some don't. Looking at the numbers, we can see that the `Freight` value with the format string is taking up an average of over 18 bytes per value. When `Num` is applied, only 8 bytes are taken per value. Let's add an additional expression to the chart:

Expression label	Expression
`Avg. Bytes`	`Sum(Bytes)/Sum(Count)`

Now we have a quick indicator to see whether numeric values are storing unneeded text.

Optimizing chart calculation times

Once we have optimized our data model, we can turn our focus onto chart performance. There are a few different things that we can do to make sure that our expressions are optimal, and we can use the memory file extract to test them.

Some of the expressions will actually involve revisiting the data model. If we do, we will need to weigh up the cost of that performance with changes to memory, and so on.

It will be useful to begin with an explanation of how the QlikView calculation engine works.

The QlikView calculation engine

QlikView is very clever in how it does its calculations. As well as the data storage, as discussed earlier in this chapter, it also stores the binary state of every field and of every data table dependent on user selection—essentially, depending on the green/white/grey state of each field, it is either included or excluded. This area of storage is called the **state space** and is updated by the QlikView logical inference engine every time a selection is made. There is one bit in the state space for every value in the symbol table or row in the data table—as such, the state space is much smaller than the data itself and hence much faster to query.

There are three steps to a chart being calculated:

1. The user makes a selection, causing the logical inference engine to reset and recalculate the state space. This should be a multithreaded operation.

2. On one thread per object, the state space is queried to gather together all of the combinations of dimensions and values necessary to perform the calculation. The state space is being queried, so this is a relatively fast operation, but could be a potential bottleneck if there are many visible objects on the screen.

3. On multiple threads per object, the expression is calculated. This is where we see the cores in the task manager all go to 100 percent at the same time. Having 100 percent CPU is expected and desired because QlikView will "burst" calculations across all available processor cores, which makes this a very fast process, relative to the size and complexity of the calculation. We call it a *burst* because, except for the most complex of calculations, the 100 percent CPU should only be for a short time.

Of course, the very intelligent cache comes into play as well and everything that is calculated is stored for potential subsequent use. If the same set of selections are met (such as hitting the Back button), then the calculation is retrieved from the cache and will be almost instantaneous.

Now that we know more about how QlikView performs its calculations, we can look at a few ways that we can optimize things.

Creating flags for well-known conditions

We cannot anticipate every possible selection or query that a user might make, but there are often some quite well-known conditions that will generally be true most of the time and may be commonly used in calculations. In this example, we will look at Year-to-Date and Last Year-to-Date — commonly used on dashboards.

The following is an example of a calculation that might be used in a gauge:

```
Sum(If(YearToDate(Date), LineValue, 0))
/Sum(If(YearToDate(Date,-1), LineValue, 0))
-1
```

This uses the `YearToDate()` function to check whether the date is in the current year to date or in the year to date period for last year (using the `-1` for the offset parameter). This expression is a sum of an `if` statement, which is generally not recommended. Also, these are quite binary—a date is either in the year to date or not—so are ideal candidates for the creation of flags. We can do this in the `Calendar` table in the following script:

```
Calendar:
Load Distinct
    DateID,
    -YearToDate(DateID) As YTD_Flag,
    -YearToDate(DateID,-1) As LYTD_Flag,
    Date(DateID) As Date,
    Year(DateID) As Year,
    Month(DateID) As Month,
    Day(DateID) As Day,
    Date(MonthStart(DateID), 'YYYY-MM') As YearMonth
Resident
    Order;
```

Note the - sign before the function. This is because `YearToDate` is a Boolean function that returns either true or false, which in QlikView is represented by `-1` and `0`. If the value is in the year to date, then the function will return `-1`, so I add the - to change that to `1`. A - sign before `0` will make no difference.

In a particular test dataset, we might see an increase from 8,684 bytes to 13,026—not an unexpected increase and not significant because the `Calendar` table is relatively small. We are creating these flags to improve performance in the frontend and need to accept a small change in the data size.

The significant change comes when we change the expression in the chart to the following:

```
Sum(LineValue*YTD_Flag)/Sum(LineValue*LYTD_Flag)-1
```

In a sample dataset, we might see that the calculation reduces from, say, 46 to, say, 16—a 65 percent reduction. This calculation could also be written using **Set Analysis** as follows:

```
Sum({<YTD_Flag={1}>} LineValue)/Sum({<LYTD_Flag={1}>} LineValue)-1
```

However, this might only get a calc time of 31—only a 32.6 percent reduction. Very interesting!

If we think about it, the simple calculation of `LineValue*YTD_Flag` is going to do a multithreaded calculation using values that are derived from the small and fast in-memory state space. Both `If` and `Set Analysis` are going to add additional load to the calculation of the set of values that are going to be used in the calculation.

In this case, the flag field is in a dimension table, `Calendar`, and the value field is in the fact table. It is, of course, possible to generate the flag field in the fact table instead. In this case, the calculation is likely to run even faster, especially on very large datasets. This is because there is no join of data tables required. However, the thing to bear in mind is that the additional pointer indexes in the `Calendar` table will require relatively little space whereas the additional width of the fact table, because of the large numbers of rows, will be something to consider. However, saying that, the pointers to the flag values are very small, so you do need a really long fact table for it to make a big difference. In some cases, the additional bit necessary to store the pointer in the bit-stuffed table will not make any difference at all, and in other cases, it may add just one byte.

`Set Analysis` can be very powerful, but it is worth considering that it often has to go, depending on the formula, outside the current state space, and that will cause additional calculation to take place that may be achieved in a simpler manner by creating a flag field in the script and using it in this way. Even if you have to use `Set Analysis`, the best performing comparisons are going to be using numeric comparisons, so creating a numeric flag instead of a text value will improve the set calculation performance. For example, consider the following expression:

```
Sum({<YTD_Flag={1}>} LineValue)
```

This will execute much faster than the following expression:

```
Sum({<YTD_Flag={'Yes'}>} LineValue)
```

So, when should we use `Set Analysis` instead of multiplying by flags? Barry Harmsen has done some testing that indicates that if the dimension table is much larger relative to the fact table, then using `Set Analysis` is faster than the flag fields. The reasoning is that the multiply method will process all records (even those containing 0), so in larger tables, it has more to process. The `Set Analysis` method will first reduce the scope, and apply the calculation to that subset.

Of course, if we have to introduce more advanced logic, that might include AND/OR/NOT operations, then `Set Analysis` is the way to go—but try to use numeric flags.

Sorting for well-known conditions

Any time that you need to sort a chart or listbox, that sort needs to be calculated. Of course, a numeric sort will always be the fastest. An alphabetic sort is a lot slower, just by its nature. One of the very slowest sorts is where we want to sort by expression.

For example, let's imagine that we wish to sort our Country list by a fixed order, defined by the business. We could use a sort expression like this:

```
Match(Country,'USA','Canada','Germany','United Kingdom','China','India
','Russia','France','Ireland')
```

The problem is that this is a text comparison that will be continually evaluated. What we can do instead is to load a temporary sort table in the script. We load this towards the beginning of the script because it needs to be the initial load of the symbol table; something like the following:

```
Country_Sort:
Load * Inline [
Country
USA
Canada
Germany
United Kingdom
China
India
Russia
France
Ireland
];
```

Then, as we won't need this table in our data, we should remember to drop it at the end of the script—after the main data has been loaded:

```
Drop Table Country_Sort;
```

Now, when we use this field anywhere, we can turn off all of the sort options and use the last one—Load Order. This doesn't need to be evaluated so will always calculate quickly:

Using Direct Discovery

Traditionally, QlikView has been a totally in-memory tool. If you want to analyze any information, you need to get all of the data into memory. This has caused problems for many enterprise organizations because of the sheer size of data that they wanted to analyze. You can get quite a lot of data into QlikView—billions of rows are not uncommon on very large servers, but there is a limit. Especially in the last few years where businesses have started to take note of the buzz around Big Data, many believed that QlikView could not play in this area.

Direct Discovery was introduced with QlikView Version 11.20. In Version 11.20 SR5, it was updated with a new, more sensible syntax. This syntax is also available in Qlik Sense. What Direct Discovery does is allow a QlikView model to connect directly to a data source without having to load all of the data into memory. Instead, we load only dimension values and, when necessary, QlikView generates a query to retrieve the required results from the database.

Of course, this does have the potential to reduce some of the things that make QlikView very popular—the sub-second response to selections, for example. Every time that a user makes a selection, QlikView generates a query to pass through to the database connection. The faster the data connection, the faster the response, so a performative data warehouse is a boon for Direct Discovery. But speed is not always everything—with Direct Discovery, we can connect to any valid connection that we might normally connect to with the QlikView script; this includes ODBC connectors to Big Data sources such as Cloudera or Google.

Here we will get an introduction to using Direct Discovery, but we should read the more detailed technical details published by the Qlik Community, for example, the SR5 technical addendum at http://community.qlik.com/docs/DOC-3710.

Direct Discovery restrictions

There are a few restrictions of Direct Discovery that will probably be addressed with subsequent service releases:

- **Only one direct table is supported**: This restriction has been lifted in QlikView 11.20 SR7 and Qlik Sense 1.0. Prior to those versions, you could only have one direct query in your data model. All other tables in the data model must be in-memory.

- **Set Analysis and complex expressions not supported**: Because the query is generated on the fly, it just can't work with the likes of a Set Analysis query. Essentially, only calculations that can be performed on the source database — Sum, Count, Avg, Min, Max — will work via Direct Discovery.

- **Only SQL compliant data sources**: Direct Discovery will only work against connections that support SQL, such as ODBC, OLEDB, and custom connectors such as SAP and JDBC. Note that there are some system variables that may need to be set for some connectors, such as SAP or Google Big Query.

- **Direct fields are not supported in global search**: Global search can only operate against in-memory data.

- **Security restrictions**: Prior to QlikView 11.20 SR7 and Qlik Sense 1.0, Section Access reduction can work on the in-memory data, but will not necessarily work against the Direct table. Similarly, Loop and Reduce in Publisher won't work correctly.

- **Synthetic keys not supported**: You can only have native key associations. AutoNumber will obviously not be supported on the direct table.

- **Calculated dimensions not supported**: You can only create calculated dimensions against in-memory data.

- **Naming the Direct table**: You can't create a table alias. The table will always be called DirectTable.

It is also worth knowing that QlikView will use its cache to store the results of queries. So if you hit the Back button, the query won't be rerun against the source database. However, this may have consequences when the underlying data is updated more rapidly. There is a variable — DirectCacheSeconds — that can be set to limit the time that data is cached. This defaults to 3600 seconds.

Direct Discovery syntax

The most important statement is the opening one:

```
DIRECT QUERY
```

This tells QlikView to expect some further query components. It is similar to the SQL statement that tells QlikView to execute the subsequent query and get the results into the memory. The DIRECT QUERY is followed by:

```
DIMENSION  Dim_1, Dim_2, ..., Dim_n
```

We must have at least one dimension field. These fields will have their values loaded into a symbol table and state space. This means that they can be used as normal in listboxes, tables, charts, and so on. Typically, the DIMENSION list will be followed by:

```
MEASURE  Val_1, Val_2, ..., Val_n
```

These fields are not loaded into the data model. They can be used, however, in expressions. You can also have additional fields that are not going to be used in expressions or dimensions:

```
DETAIL  Note_1, Note_2, ..., Note_n
```

These DETAIL fields can only be used in table boxes to give additional context to other values. This is useful for text note fields.

Finally, there may be fields that you want to include in the generated SQL query but are not interested in using in the QlikView model:

```
DETACH other_1, other_2, ..., other_n
```

Finally, you can also add a limitation to your query using a standard WHERE clause:

```
WHERE x=y
```

The statement will, of course, be terminated by a semicolon.

We can also pass valid SQL syntax statements to calculate dimensions:

```
NATIVE('Valid SQL ''syntax'' in quotes') As Field_x
```

If your SQL syntax also has single quotes, then you will need to double-up on the single quotes to have it interpreted correctly.

Looking at an example Direct Query

The following is an example of a Direct Query to a SQL server database:

```
DIRECT QUERY
dimension
    OrderID,
    FLOOR(OrderDate) As DateID,
    CustomerID,
    EmployeeID,
    ProductID
measure
    Quantity,
    SalesPrice,
    LineValue,
    LineCost
detail
    Freight,
    LineNo
FROM QWT.dbo."Order_Fact";
```

This results in a table view like the following:

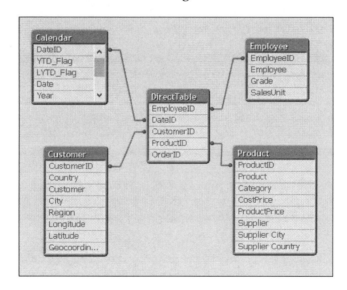

You will note that the list of fields in the table view only contains the dimension values. The measure values are not shown.

You can now go ahead and build charts mostly as normal (without, unfortunately, **Set Analysis**!), but note that you will see a lot more of the hourglass:

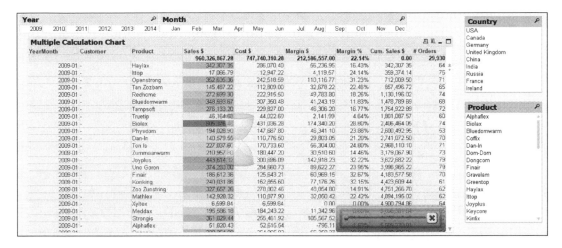

The **X** in the bottom corner of the chart can be used to cancel the execution of the direct query.

Testing scalability with JMeter

JMeter is a tool from Apache that can be used to automate web-based interactions for the purpose of testing scalability. Basically, we can use this tool to automatically connect to a QlikView application, make different selections, look at different charts, drill up and down, and repeat to test how well the application performs.

JMeter first started being used for testing QlikView about 3 years ago. At the time, while it looked like a great tool, the amount of work necessary to set it up was very off-putting.

Since then, however, the guys in the Qlik scalability center have created a set of tools that automate the configuration of JMeter, and this makes things a lot easier for us. In fact, almost anyone can set up a test—it is that easy!

Obtaining the scalability tools

The tools needed to test scalability are made available via the Qlik community. You will need to connect to the Scalability group (http://community.qlik.com/groups/qlikview-scalability).

Search in this group for "tools" and you should find the latest version. There are some documents that you will need to read through, specifically:

- Prerequisites.pdf
- QVScalabilityTools.pdf

Installing JMeter

JMeter can be obtained from the Apache website:

https://jmeter.apache.org/

However, the prerequisites documentation recommends a slightly older version of JMeter:

http://archive.apache.org/dist/jakarta/jmeter/binaries/jakarta-jmeter-2.4.zip

JMeter is a Java application, so it is also a good idea to make sure that you have the latest version of the Java runtime installed—64-bit for a 64-bit system:

http://java.com/en/download/manual.jsp

It is recommended not to unzip JMeter directly to C:\ or Program Files or other folders that may have security that reduces your access. Extract them to a folder that you have full access to. Do note the instructions in the Prerequisites.pdf file on setting heap memory sizing. To confirm that all is in order, you can try running the jmeter.bat file to open JMeter—if it works, then it means that your Java and other dependencies should be installed correctly.

Microsoft .Net 4.0 should also be installed on the machine. This can be downloaded from Microsoft. However, it should already be installed if you have QlikView Server components on the machine.

Installing the scalability tools

Depending on your system, you may find that the ZIP file that you download has its status set to **Blocked**. In this case, you need to right-click on the file, open the properties, and click on the **Unblock** button:

If you don't, you may find that the file appears to unzip successfully, but the executables will not run. You might see an error like this in the Windows Application Event Log:

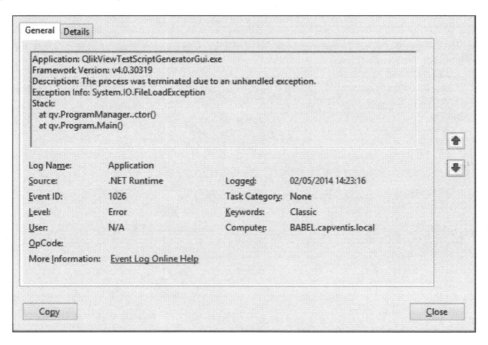

After you have made sure that the ZIP file is unblocked, you can extract the scalability tools to a folder on your system. Follow the instructions in the `Prerequisites.pdf` file to change the configuration.

Hitting *Start* + *R* and then typing `perfmon` will allow you to run the **Performance Monitor** tool to import the profile as set out in the documentation.

About the scalability tools

The toolset consists of the following separate parts:

- **Script generator**: Used to generate the JMeter script
- **Script executor**: Executes the generated script
- **Analyzer**: A QlikView document that reads various logs to give you results

Running an example execution

Running a session is actually quite straightforward, and a lot easier than having to craft the script by hand.

There are a couple of steps that we need to do before we can generate a test script:

1. We need to open the target application in QlikView desktop and extract the layout information:

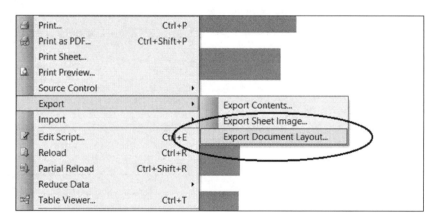

This exports all of the information about the document, including all of the objects, into XML files that can be imported into the script generator. This is how the script generator finds out about sheets and objects that it can use.

2. Copy the `AjaxZfc` URL for the application. We need to give this information to the script builder so that it knows how to connect to the application:

3. Clear the existing log files from the QVS. These files will be in the `ProgramData\QlikTech\QlikViewServer` folder. Stop the QlikView Server Service and then archive or delete the `Performance*.log`, `Audit*.log`, `Events*.log`, and `Sessions*.log` files. When you restart the service, new ones will start to be created:

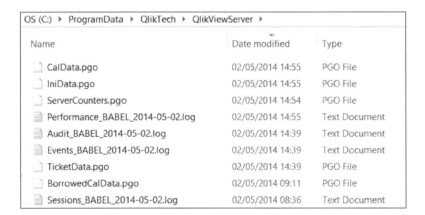

 Note that you should be careful not to delete the PGO files in the same folders—these are copies of the server's license information files.

4. Start the Performance Monitor using the template that you configured earlier. Double-check that it starts to create content in the folder (for example, `C:\PerfLogs\Admin\New Data Collector Set\QlikView Performance Monitor`).

Once those steps have been completed, we can go ahead and create a script:

1. Execute the script generator by running
   `QlikViewTestScriptGeneratorGui.exe` from the `ScriptGenerator` folder.

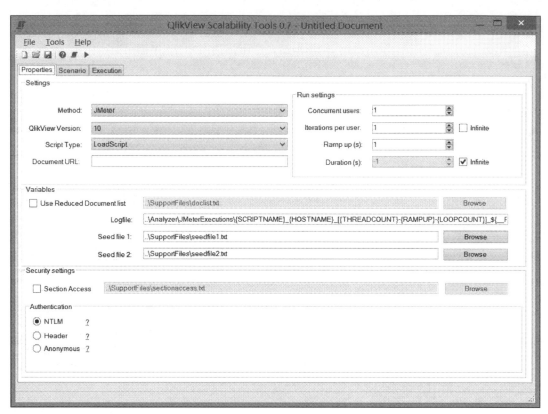

2. There are some properties that we need to set on this page:

Property	Value
QlikView version	11.
Document URL	Paste the URL that you recorded earlier.
Security settings	Choose the right authentication mechanism for your QlikView server (more details discussed later).
Concurrent users	How many users you want to run concurrently.
Iterations per user	How many times each user will run through the scenario. If you set this to **Infinite**, you need to specify a **Duration** below.
Ramp up	What time should there be before all users are logged in. 1 means that all users start together.

Property	Value
Duration	How long the test should be run for. If you set this to **Infinite** then you must set a number of **Iterations per user** above it.

If you use NTLM, then you cannot use more than one concurrent user. This is because the NTLM option will execute under the profile of the user running the application and each concurrent user will therefore attempt to log in with the same credentials. QVS does not allow this so each concurrent user will actually end up killing each other's sessions.

If you want to simulate more than one user, then you can turn on Header authentication in the QVWS configuration and make use of the `userpw.txt` file to add a list of users. The QVS will need to be in DMS mode to support this. Also bear in mind that you will need to have an appropriate number of licenses available to support the number of users that you want to test with.

3. Save the document in the `ScriptGenerator\SourceXMLs` folder. Note that you should not use spaces or non-alphanumeric characters in the XML filename. It is a good idea to make the filename descriptive as you might use it again and again.

4. Click the **Scenario** tab. Click the **Browse** button and navigate to the folder where you save the document layout information earlier. Save the template (it's always a good idea to save continually as you go along). Change the **Timer Delay Min** to 30 and the **Max** to 120:

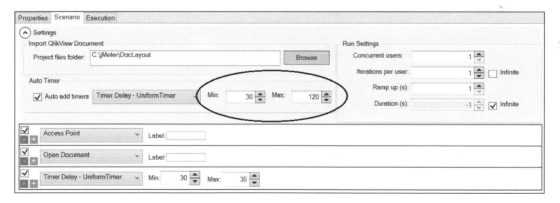

This setting specifies the range of delay between different actions. We should always allow an appropriate minimum to make sure that the application can update correctly after an action. The random variation between the minimum and maximum settings gives a simulation of user thinking time.

5. By default, there are three default actions—open AccessPoint, open the document, and then a timer delay. Click on the green + button on the left-hand side of the bottom timer delay action to add a new action below it. Two new actions will be added—an unspecified **Choose Action** one and a timer delay containing the settings that we specified above. The **Auto add timers** checkbox means that a timer delay will be automatically added every time we add a new action.

6. Build up a scenario by adding appropriate actions:

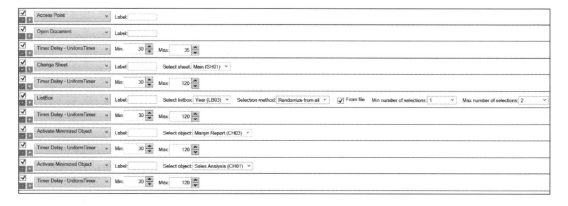

Remember to keep saving as you go along.

7. Click on the **Execution** tab. Click on **Yes** in answer to the **Add to execution** prompt. Expand the **Settings** option and click on **Browse** to select the JMeter path:

When you click on **OK**, you will be prompted on whether to save this setting permanently or not. You can click on **OK** in response to this message:

1. Right-click on the script name and select **Open in JMeter**:

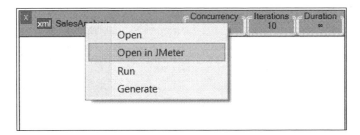

2. Click on **OK** on **OutputPopupForm**. When JMeter opens, note the entries that have been created in the test plan by the script generator.

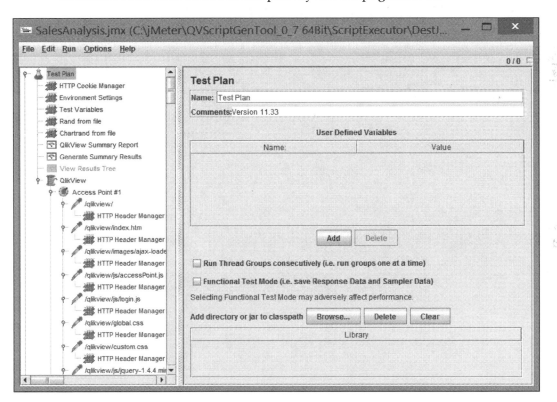

3. Close JMeter. Back in the script generator, right-click on the script again and select **Run** from the menu. The **Summary** tab appears, indicating that the script is executing:

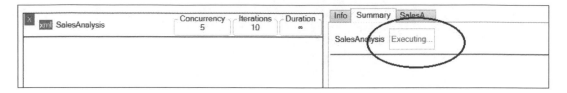

Once you have executed a test, you will want to analyze the results. The scalability tools come with a couple of QVW files to help you out here. There are a couple of steps that you need to go through to gather all the files together first:

1. In the `QVScriptGenTool_0_7 64Bit\Analyzer` folder, there is a ZIP file called `FolderTemplate.zip`. Extract the `FolderTemplate` folder out of the ZIP file and rename it to match the name of your analysis task—for example, `SalesAnalysis`. Within this folder, there are four subfolders that you need to populate with data:

Subfolder	Data source
EventLogs	These are the QVS event logs—`Events_servername_*.log`
JMeterLogs	These are the JMeter execution logs that should be in `QVScriptGenTool_0_7 64Bit\Analyzer\ JMeterExecutions`
ServerLogs	These are the CSV files created—`SERVERNAME_Processes*.csv`
SessionLogs	These are the QVS session logs—`Sessions_servername_*.log`

2. Open the `QVD Generator.qvw` file using QlikView Desktop. Set the correct name for the subfolder that you have just created:

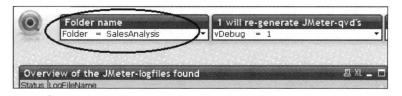

3. Reload the document.

4. Once the document has reloaded, manually edit the name of the server using the input fields in each row of the table:

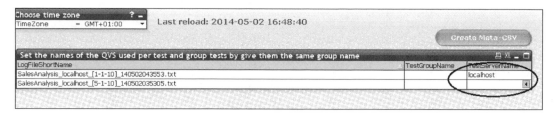

5. Once you have entered the data, click on the **Create Meta-CSV** button. You can then close the QVD Generator.

6. Open the SC_Results - DemoTest.qvw file and save it as a new file with an appropriate name—for example, SC_Results - SalesAnalysis.qvw. Change the **Folder Name** variable as before and reload.

Now you can start to analyze your server's performance during the tests:

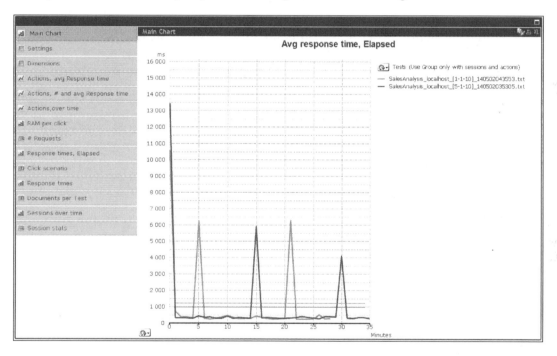

Because you can run multiple iterations of the test, with different parameters, you can use the tool to run comparisons to see changes. These can also be scheduled from the command line to run on a regular basis.

One thing that these JMeter scripts can be used for is a process called "warming the cache". If you have a very large QlikView document, it can take a long time to load into memory and create the user cache. For the first users to connect to the document in the morning, they may have a very poor experience while waiting for the document to open— they may even time out. Subsequent users will get the benefit of these user actions. However, if you have a scheduled task to execute a JMeter task, you can take the pain away from those first users because the cache will already be established for them when they get to work.

Summary

There has been a lot of information in this chapter, and I hope that you have been able to follow it well.

We started by reviewing some basic performance improvement techniques that you should already have been aware of, but you might not think about. Knowing these techniques is important and is the beginning of your path to mastering how to create performative QlikView applications.

We then looked at methods of generating test data that can be used to help you hone your skills.

Understanding how QlikView stores its data is a real requisite for any developer who wants to achieve mastery of this subject. Learning how to export memory statistics is a great step forward to learn how to achieve great things with performance and scalability.

We looked at different strategies for reducing the memory profile of a QlikView application and improving the performance of charts.

By this stage, you should have a great start in understanding how to create really performative applications.

When it gets to the stage where there is just too much data for QlikView to manage in-memory, we have seen that we can use a hybrid approach where some of the data is in-memory and some of the data is still in a database, and we can query that data on the fly using Direct Discovery.

Finally, we looked at how we can use JMeter to test our applications with some real-world scenarios using multiple users and repetitions to really hammer an application and confirm that it will work on the hardware that is in place.

Having worked through this chapter, you should have a great understanding of how to create scalable applications that perform really well for your users. You are starting to become a QlikView master!

In the next chapter, we will learn about best practices in modeling data and how that applies to QlikView.

QlikView Data Modeling

2

"It is a capital mistake to theorize before one has data. Insensibly one begins to twist facts to suit theories, instead of theories to suit facts."

— *Sherlock Holmes (Arthur Conan Doyle), A Scandal in Bohemia*

In data warehousing and business intelligence, there are many approaches to data modeling. We hear of personalities such as Bill Inmon and Ralph Kimball. We talk of normalization and dimensional modeling. But we also might have heard about how QlikView can cut across all of this—we don't need to worry about data warehousing; we just load in all the data from source systems and start clicking. Right?

Well, that might be right if you want to load just a very quick application directly from the data source and aren't too worried about performance or maintainability. However, the dynamic nature of the QlikView script does not mean that we should throw out all of the best practices in data warehouse design that have been established over the course of many years.

In this chapter, we are going to look at the best practices around QlikView data modeling. As revealed in the previous chapter, this does not always mean the best performing data model. But there are many reasons why we should use these best practices, and these will become clear over the course of this chapter and the next.

The following are the topics we'll be covering in this chapter:

- Reviewing basic data modeling
- Dimensional data modeling
- Handling slowly changing dimensions
- Dealing with multiple fact tables in one model

Reviewing basic data modeling

If you have attended QlikView training courses and done some work with QlikView modeling, there are a few things that you will know about, but I will review them just to be sure that we are all on the same page.

Associating data

QlikView uses an associative model to connect data rather than a join model. A join model is the traditional approach to data queries. In the join model, you craft a SQL query across multiple tables in the database, telling the **database management system (DBMS)** how those tables should be joined—whether left, inner, outer, and so on. The DBMS might have a system in place to optimize the performance of those queries. Each query tends to be run in isolation, returning a result set that can be either further explored—Excel pivot tables are a common use case here—or used to build a final report. Queries might have parameters to enable different reports to be executed, but each execution is still in isolation. In fact, it is the approach that underlies many implementations of a "semantic layer" that many of the "stack" BI vendors implement in their products. Users are isolated from having to build the queries—they are built and executed by the BI system—but each query is still an isolated event.

In the associative model, all the fields in the data model have a logical association with every other field in the data model. This association means that when a user makes a selection, the inference engine can quickly resolve which values are still valid—possible values—and which values are excluded. The user can continue to make selections, clear selections, and make new selections, and the engine will continue to present the correct results from the logical inference of those selections. The user's queries tend to be more natural and it allows them to answer questions as they occur.

It is important to realize that just putting a traditional join model database into memory, as many vendors have started to do, will not deliver the same interactive associative experience to users. The user will probably get faster running queries, but they will still be isolated queries.

Saying that, however, just because QlikView has a great associative model technology, you still need to build the right data model to be able to give users the answers that they don't know and are looking for, even before they have asked for them!

Automatically associating tables

We should know that QlikView will automatically associate two data tables based on both tables containing one or more fields that match exactly in both name and case. QlikView fields and table names are always case sensitive—Field1 does not match to FIELD1 or field1.

Suppose that we run a very simple load statement such as the following:

```
Customer:
Load * Inline [
CustomerID, Customer
1, Customer A
2, Customer B
];

Sales:
Load * Inline [
Date, CustomerID, Value
2014-05-12, 1, 100
2014-05-12, 2, 200
2014-05-12, 1, 100
];
```

This will result in an association that looks like the following:

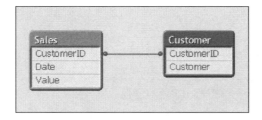

If you read the previous chapter, you will know that this will generate two data tables containing pointer indexes that point to several symbol tables for the data containing the unique values.

Understanding synthetic keys

A **synthetic key** is QlikView's method of associating two tables that have more than one field in common. Before we discuss the merits of them, let's first understand exactly what is happening with them.

For example, consider the following simple piece of script:

```
Budget:
Load * Inline [
CustomerID, Year, BudgetValue
1, 2013, 10000
2, 2013, 15000
1, 2014, 12000
2, 2014, 17500
];

Sales:
Load * Inline [
Date, Year, CustomerID, Value
2013-01-12, 2013, 1, 100
2013-02-25, 2013, 2, 200
2013-02-28, 2013, 1, 100
2013-04-04, 2013, 1, 100
2013-06-21, 2013, 2, 200
2013-08-02, 2013, 1, 100
2014-05-12, 2014, 1, 100
2014-05-12, 2014, 2, 200
2014-05-12, 2014, 1, 100
];
```

This will produce an **Internal Table View** like the following:

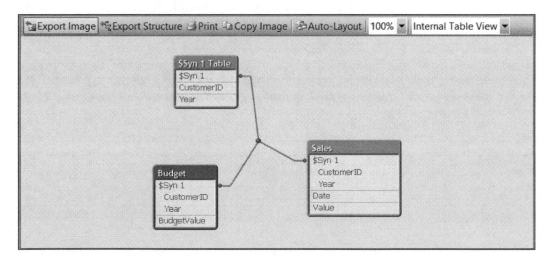

It is worth noting that QlikView can also represent this as a **Source Table View**, showing the association in a more logical, database way, like the following:

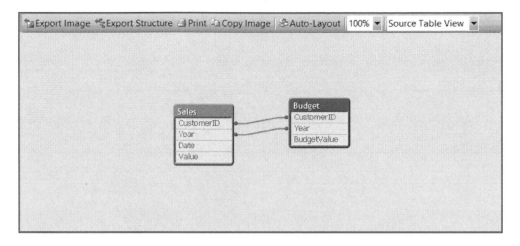

To be honest, I never use this view, but I can understand why some people, especially those transitioning from a SQL background, might feel comfortable with it. I would urge you to get more comfortable with **Internal Table View** because it is more reflective of what is happening internally in QlikView.

We can see from **Internal Table View** that QlikView has moved the common fields into a new table, **$Syn 1 Table**, that contains all the valid combinations of the values. The values have been replaced in the original tables with a derived composite key, or surrogate key, that is associated with **$Syn 1 Table**.

To me, this is perfectly sensible data modeling. When we look at our options later on in the chapter, we will begin to recognize this approach as **Link Table** modeling. There are, however, some scare stories about using synthetic keys. In fact, in the documentation, it is recommended that you remove them. The following is quoted from *QlikView Reference Manual*:

> *When the number of composite keys increases, depending on data amounts, table structure and other factors, QlikView may or may not handle them gracefully. QlikView may end up using excessive amounts of time and/or memory. Unfortunately, the actual limitations are virtually impossible to predict, which leaves only trial and error as a practical method to determine them.*
>
> *An overall analysis of the intended table structure by the application designer. is recommended, including the following:*

Forming your own non-composite keys, typically using string concatenation inside an AutoNumber script function.

Making sure only the necessary fields connect. If, for example, a date is used as a key, make sure not to load e.g. year, month or day_of_month from more than one internal table.

The important thing to look at here is that it says, "When the number of composite keys increases…"—this is important because you should understand that a synthetic key is not necessarily a bad thing in itself. However, having too many of them is, to me, a sign of a poor data modeling effort. I would not, for example, like to see a table viewer looking like the following:

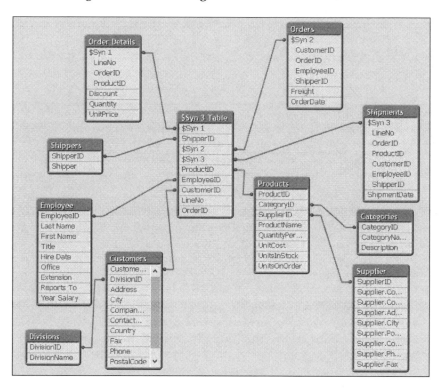

There have been some interesting discussions about this subject in the Qlik community. John Witherspoon, a long time contributor to the community, wrote a good piece entitled *Should we stop worrying and love the Synthetic Key* (http://community.qlik.com/thread/10279).

Of course, Henric Cronström has a good opinion on this subject as well, and has relayed it in *Qlik Design Blog* at http://community.qlik.com/blogs/qlikviewdesignblog/2013/04/16/synthetic-keys.

My opinion is similar to Henric's. I like to see any synthetic keys resolved in the data model. I find them a little untidy and a little bit lazy. However, there is no reason to spend many hours resolving them if you have better things to do and there are no issues in your document.

Creating composite keys

One of the methods used to resolve synthetic keys is to create your own composite key. A composite key is a field that is composed of several other field values. There are a number of ways of doing this, which we will examine in the next sections.

Using string concatenation

The very simplest way of creating a composite key is to simply concatenate all the values together using the & operator. If we were to revisit the previously used script and apply this, our script might now look like the following:

```
Budget:
Load
    CustomerID & Year as BudgetKey,
    BudgetValue
Inline [
CustomerID, Year, BudgetValue
1, 2013, 10000
2, 2013, 15000
1, 2014, 12000
2, 2014, 17500
];

Sales:
Load
    Date,
    Year,
    CustomerID,
    CustomerID & Year as BudgetKey,
    Value
Inline [
Date, Year, CustomerID, Value
2013-01-12, 2013, 1, 100
2013-02-25, 2013, 2, 200
2013-02-28, 2013, 1, 100
2013-04-04, 2013, 1, 100
2013-06-21, 2013, 2, 200
2013-08-02, 2013, 1, 100
```

```
2014-05-12, 2014, 1, 100
2014-05-12, 2014, 2, 200
2014-05-12, 2014, 1, 100
];
```

When we reload this code, the table viewer will look like the following screenshot:

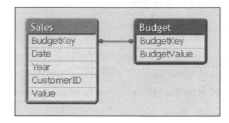

The synthetic key no longer exists and everything looks a lot neater.

 We will ignore any potential data issues with this particular dataset for now — we will cover more on that later in this chapter.

To see the composite key in action, I like to use a table box with values from both tables, just to see that the association works:

CustomerID	Year	Value	BudgetKey	BudgetValue
1	2013	100	12013	10000
1	2014	100	12014	12000
2	2013	200	22013	15000
2	2014	200	22014	17500

A table box works very well for this use case. I utilize them all the time when testing key associations like this. It is almost the only time that I use table boxes these days! In a normal user interface, a table box can be useful to display transaction-level information, but you can also use a straight table for this and have far more control with the chart than with the table. Totals, set analyses in expressions, and visual cues are all things that you can have in a straight table that you can't have in a table box.

We need to concern ourselves with key collision potentials; in this case, the key value of **12013**, composed of the **CustomerID** value of **1** and the **Year** value of **2013**. Let's imagine a further set of values where the **CustomerID** value is **120** and the **Year** value is **13**. That would cause a problem because both combinations would be **12013**. For that reason, and this should be considered a best practice, I would prefer to see an additional piece of text added between the two keys like the following:

```
    ...
    CustomerID & '-' & Year as BudgetKey,
    ...
```

If we do that, then the first set of values would give a key of **1-2013** and the second would give a key of **120-13**—there would no longer be a concern about key collision. The text that you use as the separator can be anything—characters such as the hyphen, underscore, and vertical bar are all commonly used.

 Note that if you use keys like this in calculations or Dollar-sign Expansion (which would not be a good practice), then a hyphen could be interpreted as a minus sign. We shouldn't really use keys like that though.

Using one of the Hash functions

A **Hash** function takes the number of fields as a parameter and creates a fixed length string representing the hash of those values. The length of the string, and hence the possibility of having key collisions, is determined by the hash bit length. There are the following three functions:

- `Hash128()`
- `Hash160()`
- `Hash256()`

The number at the end of the function name (`128`, `160`, or `256`) represents the number of bits that will be used for the hash string. We don't really need to worry too much about the potential for key collision—in his blog post on the subject, Barry Harmsen, co-author of *QlikView 11 for Developers, Packt Publishing*, worked out that the chance of a collision using `Hash128()` was one in 680 million (`http://www.qlikfix.com/2014/03/11/hash-functions-collisions/`).

Of course, if you do have a large dataset where that risk becomes greater, then using the `Hash256()` function instead will reduce the possibility to, effectively, zero. Of course, a longer hash key will take up more space.

If we were to use a Hash function in our script, it would look like the following:

```
    Budget:
    Load
        Hash128(CustomerID, Year) as BudgetKey,
        BudgetValue
        ...
```

```
Sales:
Load
    Date,
    Year,
    CustomerID,
    Hash128(CustomerID, Year) as BudgetKey,
    Value
    ...
```

Notice that the function just takes a list of field values. The Hash functions are deterministic—if you pass the same values to the function, you will get the same hash value returned. However, as well as having the same values, the order that the fields are passed in the function must also be identical.

This load will produce values that look like the following in my table box:

CustomerID	Year	Value	BudgetKey	BudgetValue
1	2013	100	DYL1<51`_X(R6[2_R8#>50	10000
1	2014	100	HBFK;#0]KWHI;T<V^SI>5(	12000
2	2013	200	H8L0(A@3FW8N%C=3G8+>5$	15000
2	2014	200	L!FJ'/?02XXD*<G*SSQ>5,	17500

The other thing that is important to know about the Hash functions is that their deterministic nature should transcend different reloads on different machines. If you run the same script as I did, on the same version of QlikView, you should get the same result.

Using the AutoNumber function

One of the problems with both of the two previously mentioned approaches is that the keys that are generated are string values and, as we saw in the previous chapter, they will take up a lot of space. It is far more efficient to use integer keys—and especially sequential integer keys (because they are not stored in the symbol tables). The AutoNumber function will do that for us.

The AutoNumber function will accept a string value and return an integer. How it works is that during the brief lifetime of a load script execution, QlikView maintains an internal database to store the passed string values. If you pass exactly the same value, then you will get exactly the same integer returned. It can be said to be deterministic (given the same input, you will get the same output), but only within the current execution of the script.

This last point is important to note. If I pass "XXX" and get a return of 999 today, I cannot guarantee that "XXX" will return 999 tomorrow. The internal database is created anew at each execution of the script, and so the integer that is returned depends on the values that are passed during the load. It is quite likely that tomorrow's dataset will have different values in different orders so will return different integers.

AutoNumber will accept two possible parameters—a text value and an AutoID. This AutoID is a descriptor of what list of sequential integers will be used, so we can see that we have multiple internal databases, each with its own set of sequential integers. You should always use an AutoID with the AutoNumber function.

When creating a composite key, we combine the AutoNumber function with the string concatenation that we used previously.

There is a "hybrid" function of AutoNumber and Hash (128 and 256) that will generate the hash value and then use that string in the AutoNumber calculation. This is useful, but it does not have the facility to pass the AutoID.

If we modify our script to use AutoNumber, then it should look something like the following:

```
Budget:
Load
   Year, CustomerID,
   AutoNumber(CustomerID & '-' & Year, 'Budget') as BudgetKey,
   BudgetValue
   ...


Sales:
Load
   Date,
   Year,
   CustomerID,
   AutoNumber(CustomerID & '-' & Year, 'Budget') as BudgetKey,
   Value
   ...
```

The table box will look like the following:

CustomerID	Year	Value	BudgetKey	BudgetValue
1	2013	100	1	10000
1	2014	100	3	12000
2	2013	200	2	15000
2	2014	200	4	17500

We now have a sequential integer key instead of the text values.

One thing that is interesting to point out is that the string values for keys make it easy to see the lineage of a key—you can discern the different parts of the key. I will often keep the keys as strings during a development cycle just for this reason. Then, when moving to production, I will change them to use AutoNumber.

Realizing that facts are calculated at the level of their table

One thing that new QlikView developers, especially those with a SQL background, have difficulty grasping is that when QlikView performs a calculation, it performs it at the correct level for the table in which the fact exists. Now, I know what I just wrote might not make any sense, but let me illustrate it with an example.

If I have an OrderHeader table and an OrderLine table in SQL Server, I might load them into QlikView using the following script:

```
OrderHeader:
LOAD OrderID,
   OrderDate,
   CustomerID,
   EmployeeID,
   Freight;
SQL SELECT *
FROM QVTraining.dbo.OrderHeader;

OrderLine:
LOAD OrderID,
   "LineNo",
   ProductID,
   Quantity,
   SalesPrice,
   SalesCost,
   LineValue,
   LineCost;
SQL SELECT *
FROM QVTraining.dbo.OrderLine;
```

Note that there are facts here at different levels. In the `OrderLine` table, we have the `LineValue` and `LineCost` facts. In the `OrderHeader` table, we have the `Freight` fact.

If I want to look at the total sales and total freights by a customer, I could create a chart like the following:

Dimension	Total Freight Expression	Total Sales Expression
CustomerID	Sum(Freight)	Sum(LineValue)

This would produce a straight table that looks as follows:

CustomerID	Total Freight	Total Sales
	1,498,116.84	998,296,382.35
1001	7,630.71	3,360,064.06
1002	7,916.07	4,639,691.47
1003	8,188.87	4,963,990.16
1004	7,879.04	5,678,877.59
1005	7,413.66	3,827,835.46
1006	7,856.24	5,470,773.01
1007	7,843.42	4,819,726.77
1008	7,295.45	4,360,783.45
1009	7,110.83	4,509,171.42
1010	7,406.63	5,519,946.07
1011	7,324.32	5,066,749.68
1012	6,653.31	4,068,364.91
1013	7,207.09	4,704,212.66
1014	7,562.32	4,808,996.39
1015	6,999.62	4,725,484.66
1016	7,629.47	5,446,577.47
1017	8,447.81	5,128,596.12

Now, this is actually correct. The total freights and sales values are correctly stated for each customer. The values have been correctly calculated at the level that they exist in the data model.

If I were to do something similar in SQL, I might create a query like the following:

```
SELECT
    OH.CustomerID,
    CAST(Sum(OH.Freight) As money) As [Total Freight],
    CAST(SUM(OL.LineValue) As money) As [Total Sales]
FROM OrderHeader OH
INNER JOIN OrderLine OL
ON OH.OrderID=OL.OrderID
GROUP BY OH.CustomerID
ORDER BY 1
```

The result might look like the following screenshot:

	CustomerID	Total Freight	Total Sales
1	1001	55790.16	3360064.06
2	1002	92202.98	4639691.47
3	1003	80287.23	4963990.16
4	1004	93817.77	5678877.59
5	1005	77836.41	3827835.46
6	1006	96574.37	5470773.01
7	1007	95090.42	4819726.77
8	1008	69295.74	4360783.45
9	1009	81225.48	4509171.42
10	1010	92216.97	5519946.07
11	1011	77006.00	5066749.68
12	1012	77694.56	4068364.91
13	1013	82742.20	4704212.66
14	1014	99173.56	4808996.39
15	1015	82172.07	4725484.66

We can see that the sales values match with QlikView, but the freight values are totally overstated. This is because the freight values have been brought down a level and are being totaled with the same freight value repeated for every line in the one order. If the freight value was $10 for an order and there were 10 order lines, QlikView would report a correct freight value of $10 while the SQL query would give us an incorrect value of $100.

This is really important for us to know about when we come to data modeling. We need to be careful with this. In this instance, if a user were to drill into a particular product, the freight total will still be reported at $10. It is always worth checking with the business whether they need those facts to be moved down a level and apportioned based on a business rule.

Joining data

As part of basic training, you should have been introduced to the concepts of join, concatenate, and `ApplyMap`. You may have also heard of functions such as `Join` and `Keep`. Hopefully, you have a good idea of what each does, but I feel that it is important to review them here so that we all know what is happening when we use these functions and what the advantages and disadvantages are of using the functions in different scenarios.

Understanding Join and Keep

Even though the QlikView data model is an associative one, we can still use joins in the script to bring different tables together into one. This is something that you will do a lot when data modeling, so it is important to understand.

As with SQL, we can perform inner, left, right, and outer joins. We execute the joins in a logically similar way to SQL, except that instead of loading the multiple tables together in one statement, we load the data in two or more statements, separated by `Join` statements. I will explain this using some simple data examples.

Inner joins

An **inner join** will join two tables together based on matches across common key values. If there are rows in either table where there are no matches, then those rows will no longer exist in the final combined table. The following is an example load:

```
Table1:
Load * Inline [
FieldA, FieldB, FieldC
1, A, 1A
2, B, 2B
3, C, 3C
];

Inner Join (Table1)
Load * Inline [
FieldA, FieldD, FieldE
2, X, 2X
3, Y, 3Y
4, Z, 4Z
];
```

This will result in a single table with five fields and two rows that looks like the following:

FieldA	FieldB	FieldC	FieldD	FieldE
2	B	2B	X	2X
3	C	3C	Y	3Y

I describe an inner join as destructive because it will remove rows from either table. Because of this, you need to think carefully about its use.

Note that in all the examples of Join, we will use the option to include the table name — as in Join (TableName) — as a parameter to Join. If you don't include it, then the join will be assumed to be to the last loaded table. It is always be best practice to explicitly state it.

Left and right joins

I use left joins quite frequently, but rarely a right one. Which is which? Well, the first table that you load is the left table. The second table that you use the Join statement on is the right table.

The left join will keep all records in the left, or first, table and will join any matching rows from the right table. If there are rows in the right table that do not match, they will be discarded. The right join is the exact opposite. As such, these joins are also destructive as you can lose rows from one of the tables.

We will use the previous example script and change Inner to Left:

```
. . .
Left Join (Table1)
. . .
```

This results in a table that looks like the following:

FieldA	FieldB	FieldC	FieldD	FieldE
1	A	1A	-	-
2	B	2B	X	2X
3	C	3C	Y	3Y

Note that the first row has been retained from the left table, despite there being no matches. However, FieldD and FieldE in that row are null.

Changing from Left to Right will result in the following table:

FieldA	FieldB	FieldC	FieldD	FieldE
2	B	2B	X	2X
3	C	3C	Y	3Y
4	-	-	Z	4Z

In this case, the row from the left table has been discarded while the unmatched row from the right table is retained with null values.

Outer joins

An **outer join** will retain all the rows from all the tables. Matching rows will have all their values populated whereas unmatched rows will have null values in the appropriate fields.

For example, if we replace the `Left` or `Right` join in the previous script with the word `Outer`, then we will get a table similar to the following:

FieldA	FieldB	FieldC	FieldD	FieldE
1	A	1A	-	-
2	B	2B	X	2X
3	C	3C	Y	3Y
4	-	-	Z	4Z

 The keyword `Outer` is not mandatory. This means that `Outer Join (Table1)` and `Join (Table1)` are the same join.

Cartesian joins

For newbie QlikView developers who have come from the world of SQL, it can be a struggle to understand that you don't get to tell QlikView which fields it should be joining on. You will also notice that you don't need to tell QlikView anything about the datatypes of the joining fields.

This is because QlikView has a simple rule on the join—if you have fields with the same field names, just as with the associative logic, then these will be used to join. So you do have some control over this because you can rename fields in both tables as you are loading them.

The datatype issue is even easier to explain—QlikView essentially doesn't do datatypes. Most data in QlikView is represented by a **dual**—a combination of formatted text and a numeric value. If there is a number in the dual, then QlikView uses this to make the join—even if the format of the text is different.

But what happens if you don't have any fields to join on between the two tables? What we get in that scenario is a **Cartesian join**—the product of both tables. Let's have a look at an example:

```
Rene:
Load * Inline [
Field1, Field2
1, A
2, B
3, C
];
```

```
Join (Rene)
Load * Inline [
Field3, Field4
4, X
5, Y
6, Z
];
```

This results in a table like the following:

Field1	Field2	Field3	Field4
1	A	4	X
1	A	5	Y
1	A	6	Z
2	B	4	X
2	B	5	Y
2	B	6	Z
3	C	4	X
3	C	5	Y
3	C	6	Z

We can see that every row in the first table has been matched with each row in the second table.

Now this is something that you will have to watch out for because even with moderately sized datasets, a Cartesian join will cause a huge increase in the number of final rows. For example, having a Cartesian join between two tables with 100,000 rows each will result in a joined table with 10,000,000,000 rows! This issue quite often arises if you rename a field in one table and then forget to change the field in a joined table.

Saying that though, there are some circumstances where a Cartesian product is a desired result. There are some situations where I might want to have every value in one table matched with every value in another. An example of this might be where I match every account number that I have in the system with every date in the calendar so that I can calculate a daily balance, whether there were any transactions on that day or not.

Understanding the effect of duplicate key values on joins

If you have some understanding of joins, you will be aware that when one of the tables has rows with duplicate values of the join key—which is common with primary to foreign key joins—then the resultant table will also have multiple rows. A quick example to illustrate this is as follows:

```
Dimension:
Load * Inline [
```

```
KeyField, DimensionValue
1, One
2, Two
3, Three
];

Left Join (Dimension)
Load * Inline [
KeyField, Value
1, 100
2, 200
3, 301
3, 302
];
```

This will result in a table like the following:

KeyField	DimensionValue	Value
1	One	100
2	Two	200
3	Three	301
3	Three	302

We have two rows for the KeyField value 3. This is expected. We do need to be careful though that this situation does not arise when joining data to a fact table. If we join additional tables to a fact table, and that generates additional rows in the fact table, then all of your calculations on those values can no longer be relied on as there are duplicates. This is definitely something that you need to be aware of when data modeling.

What if there are duplicate key values in both tables? For example, suppose that the first table looked like the following:

```
Dimension:
Load * Inline [
KeyField, DimensionValue
1, One
2, Two
3, Three.1
3, Three.2
3, Three.3
];
```

This will lead us to a table that looks like the following:

KeyField	DimensionValue	Value
1	One	100
2	Two	200
3	Three.1	301
3	Three.1	302
3	Three.2	301
3	Three.2	302
3	Three.3	301
3	Three.3	302

The resulting number of rows is the product of the number of keys in each table. This is something that I have seen happen in the field and something that you really need to look out for. The symptoms will be a far-longer-than-expected load time and large amounts of memory consumed. Have a look at this, perhaps silly, example:

```
BigSillyTable:
Load
    Floor(Rand()*5) As Key1,
    Rand()*1000 As Value1
Autogenerate(1000);

Join
Load
    Floor(Rand()*5) As Key1,
    Rand()*1000 As Value2
AutoGenerate(1000);
```

There are only 1,000 rows in each table with a low cardinality key that is duplicated (so there is an average of 200 rows per key). The resulting table will have approximately 200,000 rows!

This may seem a bit silly, but I have come across something similar.

Understanding Keep

The Keep syntax is quite interesting. It operates in a similar way to one of the destructive joins—it must take an inner, left, or right keyword—that means it will remove appropriate rows from the tables where there are no matches. However, it then leaves the tables as separate entities instead of joining them together into one.

As a use case, consider what might happen if you have a list of account numbers loaded and then used left Keep to load a transaction table. You would be left with the account and transaction tables as separate entities, but the transaction table would only contain rows where there was a matching row in the account table.

Concatenating rows

Concatenation in QlikView is quite similar to the Union All function in SQL (we can make it like a simple union by using the Distinct keyword when loading the tables). As with many things in QlikView, it is a little easier to implement than a union, in that you don't have to always ensure that both tables being concatenated have the same number of fields. If you concatenate tables with different numbers of fields, QlikView will go ahead and add any additional fields and populate nulls into any fields that didn't already have values. It is useful to review some of the aspects of Concatenate because we use it very often in data modeling.

Reviewing Concatenate

If you have come across concatenation before, you should be aware that QlikView will automatically concatenate tables based on both tables having the exact same number of fields and having all fields with the same names (case sensitive). For example, consider the following load statements:

```
Table1:
Load * Inline [
A, B, C
1, 2, 3
4, 5, 6
];

Table2:
Load * Inline [
A, C, B
7, 8, 9
10, 11, 12
];
```

This will not actually end with two tables. Instead, we will have one table, Table1, with four rows:

A	B	C
1	2	3
4	5	6
7	9	8
10	12	11

If the two tables do not have identical fields, then we can force the concatenation to happen using the Concatenate keyword:

```
Table:
Load * Inline [
A, B, C
1, 2, 3
4, 5, 6
];

Concatenate (Table1)
Load * Inline [
A, C
7, 8
10, 11
];
```

This will result in a table like the following:

A	B	C
1	2	3
4	5	6
7	-	8
10	-	11

You will notice that the rows where there were no values for field **B** have been populated with null.

There is also a NoConcatenate keyword that might be useful for us to know about. It stops a table being concatenated, even if it has the same field names as an existing table. Several times, I have loaded a table in a script only to have it completely disappear. After several frustrating minutes debugging, I discovered that I have named the fields the same as an existing table — which causes automatic concatenation. My table hadn't really disappeared, the values had just been concatenated to the existing table.

Differentiating Concatenate and Join

Sometimes it can be difficult to understand what the effective difference is between Concatenate and Join and when we should use either of them. So, let's look at a couple of examples that will help us understand the differences.

Here are a couple of tables:

Key	Value1
1	100
2	200
3	300

Key	Value2
1	1000
2	2000
3	3000

Now, if I load these tables with Concatenate, I will get a resulting table that looks like the following:

Key	Value1	Value2
1	100	-
1	-	1000
2	200	-
2	-	2000
3	300	-
3	-	3000

If I loaded this table with Join, the result looks like the following:

Key	Value1	Value2
1	100	1000
2	200	2000
3	300	3000

We will have a longer data table with Concatenate, but the symbol tables will be identical. In fact, the results when we come to use these values in a chart will actually be identical! All the QlikView functions that we use most of the time, such as Sum, Count, Avg, and so on, will ignore the null values, so we will get the same results using both datasets.

So, when we have a 1:1 match between tables like this, both Join and Concatenate will give us effectively the same result. However, if there is not a 1:1 match—where there are multiple key values in one or more of the tables—then Join will not produce the correct result, but Concatenate will. This is an important consideration when it comes to dealing with multiple fact tables, as we will see later.

It is worth considering that if you need to calculate something like *Value1/Value2* on every line, then they will need to be matched with Join (or ApplyMap as discussed in the following section).

Mapping data with ApplyMap

This is one of my favorite functions in QlikView — I use it all the time. It is extremely versatile in moving data from one place to another and enriching or cleansing data. Let's review some of the functionality of this very useful tool.

Reviewing the basic functionality of ApplyMap

The basic function of `ApplyMap` is to move data — usually text data — from a mapping table into a dimension table. This is a very normal operation in dimensional modeling. Transactional databases tend to be populated by a lot of mapping tables — tables that just have a key value and a text value.

The first thing that we need to have for `ApplyMap` is to load the mapping table of values to map from. There are a few rules for this table that we should know:

- A mapping table is loaded with a normal `Load` statement that is preceded by a `Mapping` statement.
- The mapping table can only have two columns.
- The names of the columns are not important — only the order that the columns are loaded is important:
  - The first column is the mapping lookup value
  - The second column is the mapping return value
- The mapping table does not survive past the end of the script. Once the script has loaded, all mapping tables are removed from memory.
- There is effectively no limit on the number of rows in the mapping table. I have used mapping tables with millions of rows.
- Mapping tables must be loaded in the script before they are called via `ApplyMap`. This should be obvious, but I have seen some confusion around it.

As an example, consider the following table:

```
Mapping_Table:
Mapping
Load * Inline [
LookupID, LookupValue
1, First
2, Second
3, Third
];
```

There are a couple of things to note. First, let's look at the table alias—`Mapping_Table`. This will be used later in the `ApplyMap` function call (and we always need to explicitly name our mapping tables—this is, of course, best practice for all tables). The second thing to note is the names of the columns. I have just used a generic `LookupID` and `LookupValue`. These are not important. I don't expect them to associate to anything in my main data model. Even if they did accidentally have the same name as a field in my data model, there is no issue as the mapping table doesn't associate and doesn't survive the end of the script load anyway.

So, I am going to pass a value to the `ApplyMap` function—in this case, hopefully, either 1, 2, or 3—and expect to get back one of the text values—First, Second, or Third.

In the last sentence, I did say, "hopefully." This is another great thing about `ApplyMap`, in that we can handle situations where the passed ID value does not exist; we can specify a default value.

Let's look at an example of using the mentioned map:

```
Table:
Load
    ID,
    Name,
    ApplyMap('Mapping_Table', PositionID, 'Other') As Position
Inline [
ID, Name, PositionID
101, Joe, 1
102, Jane, 2
103, Tom, 3
104, Mika, 4
];
```

In the `ApplyMap` function, we have used the `Mapping_Table` table alias of our mapping table—note that we pass this value, in this case, as a string literal. We are passing the ID to be looked up from the data—`PositionID`—which will contain one of 1, 2, 3, or 4. Finally, we pass a third parameter (which is optional) to specify what the return value should be if there is no match on the IDs.

Note that you don't always have to pass a string literal—anything that returns a string that matches to a previously loaded mapping table will work.

This load will result in the following table:

ID	Name	Position
101	Joe	First
102	Jane	Second
103	Tom	Third
104	Mika	Other

We can see that **Joe**, **Jane**, and **Tom** were successfully mapped to the correct position, whereas **Mika**, whose ID was **104**, did not have a matching value in the mapping table so ended up with **Other** as the position value.

Mapping numbers

Something that many people don't think about, but which works very well, is to use the mapping functionality to move a number from one place to another. As an example, imagine that I had a product cost table in my database that stored the averaged cost for each product per month. I want to use this value in my fact table to calculate a margin amount per line. My mapping load may look something like the following:

```
Product_Cost_Map:
Mapping Load
    Floor(MonthStart(CostMonth)) & '-' & ProductID As LookupID,
    [Cost Value] As LookupValue;
SQL SELECT * From [Monthly Product Cost];
```

A good thing to note here is that we are using a composite key for the lookup ID. This is quite common and never an issue—as long as you use the exact same syntax and value types in the ApplyMap call.

 Recall that the Floor function will take any numeric value, remove any decimal part—without rounding—and return just the integer part. The MonthStart function will always return the first of the month for any date passed to it.

Once we have this table loaded—and, depending on the database, this could have millions of rows—then we can use it in the fact table load. It will look something like this:

```
Fact:
Load
   ...
   SalesDate,
```

```
        ProductID,
        Quantity,
        ApplyMap('Product_Cost_Map', Floor(MonthStart(SalesDate)) & '-'
                & ProductID,0)
                *Quantity As LineCost,
    . . .
```

In this case, we use the `MonthStart` function on the sales date and combine it with `ProductID` to create the composite key.

Here, we also use a default value of 0—if we can't locate the date and product combination in the mapping table, then we should use 0. We could, instead, use another mapping to get a default value:

```
    Fact:
    Load
        . . .
        SalesDate,
        ProductID,
        Quantity,
        ApplyMap('Product_Cost_Map',
                Floor(MonthStart(SalesDate)) & '-' & ProductID,
                ApplyMap('Default_Cost_Map', ProductID, 0))
                *Quantity As LineCost,
        . . .
```

So, we can see that we can nest `ApplyMap` calls to achieve the logic that we need.

Using ApplyMap instead of Join with duplicate rows

We saw earlier in the discussion on joins that where there are rows with duplicate join IDs in one (or both) of the tables, the join will result in more rows in the joined table. This is often an undesired result—especially if you are joining a dimension value to a fact table. Creating additional rows in the fact table will result in incorrect results.

There are a number of ways of making sure that the dimension table that you join to the fact table will only have one row joined and not cause this problem. However, I often just use `ApplyMap` in this situation and make sure that the values that I want to be joined are sorted to the top. This is because in a mapping table, if there are duplicate key values, only the first row containing that key will be used.

As an example, I have modified the earlier basic example:

```
    Mapping_Table:
    Mapping
    Load * Inline [
```

```
LookupID, LookupValue
1, First
2, Second.1
2, Second.2
3, Third.1
3, Third.2
3, Third.3
];
```

We can see that there are now duplicate values for the 2 and 3 keys. When we load the table as before, we will get this result:

ID	Name	Position
101	Joe	First
102	Jane	Second.1
103	Tom	Third.1
104	Mika	Other

We can see that the additional rows with the duplicate keys are completely ignored and only the first row containing the key is used. Therefore, if we make sure that the rows are loaded in the order that we want—by whatever order by clause we need to construct—we can just use ApplyMap to move the data into the fact table. We will be sure that no additional rows can possibly be created as they might be with Join.

Dimensional data modeling

There are several methodologies for implementing a data warehouse or data mart that might be useful to consider when implementing QlikView in an organization. However, for me, the best approach is dimensional modeling—often called **Kimball dimensional modeling**—as proposed by Ralph Kimball and Margy Ross in the book *The Data Warehouse Toolkit*, *John Wiley & Sons*, now available in its third edition.

Some other methodologies, most noticeably that proposed by Bill Inmon, offer a "top-down" approach to data warehousing whereby a normalized data model is built that spans the entire enterprise, then data marts are built off this to support lines of business or specific business processes. Now, QlikView can sit very readily in this model as the data mart tool, feeding off the **Enterprise Data Warehouse** (**EDW**). However, QlikView cannot implement the normalized EDW.

In my opinion, Kimball dimensional modeling, on the other hand, is right up QlikView's street. In fact, I would suggest that you can build almost all elements of this type of data warehouse using just QlikView! The difference is that Kimball's approach is more "bottom-up"—the data marts (in our case, QlikView applications) are built first and then they can be combined to build a bigger data warehouse. Also, with this approach, we can build a data framework that power users can make use of to build their own analyses, beyond what might be achievable with other tools.

In this chapter, I am going to talk about some of the concepts of Kimball dimensional modeling, but I will not be going into deep detail on Kimball's concepts. I will describe the concept at a high level and then go in to detail on how that can be applied from a QlikView point of view. To find out more information on Kimball dimensional modeling, I recommend the following:

- Buy and read *The Data Warehouse Toolkit*
- Check out the Kimball Group's online resources at `http://www.kimballgroup.com/data-warehouse-business-intelligence-resources`

There are some key fundamental concepts that we should understand about dimensional modeling. You may already be familiar with some of the terminology. Ralph Kimball didn't create the concepts of facts and dimensions, and you will come across those terms in many contexts. However, he has created a solid methodology for modeling data in multiple different scenarios.

Differentiating between facts and dimensions

Essentially, facts are numbers. They are numbers that we will add up, average, count, or apply some other calculation to. For example, sales value, sales quantity, and monthly balance are all facts.

Dimensions are the values that give context to our facts. So, customer or product are both examples of dimensions. Date is also a good example of a dimension—almost every fact that you will come across will have a date context.

We store dimensions in a table of attributes. For example, a customer table might have attributes of name, city, or country. A date table will have attributes such as year, month, quarter, and week.

We will store one or many facts in a table along with the keys to associate them to the dimensions. An example of a row in a sales fact table might look like the following:

RowID	DateID	CustomerID	ProductID	StoreID	Quantity	Sales Value	Sales Cost	Sales Margin
2345	20140520	2340000563	1929	34	20	120.00	100.00	20.00

What this row of data tells us is that on a particular date, in a particular store, a particular customer purchased 20 units of a particular product that had a sales value of $120.00. We can find out what product was sold by looking for **ProductID** 1929 in the `Product` dimension table.

Of course, this is not a normal query! Typically, we might start by selecting a store and then that would select for us all the fact rows that are associated with that row. We then have a calculation to add up all the sales values from that set of rows to give us the total sales for that store.

Understanding the grain

The single row in the previous fact table represents the **grain** of the data—the lowest level—that we are going to report on. Typically, for best results, you want the grain to be the lowest transaction level. In this case, it might not be. This customer might have bought the same product several times on the same day, so this row would actually represent an aggregated view of the data. If we added in a new field for, say, transaction number or perhaps transaction time, then we would increase the number of rows in the fact table, lowering the level of the data and changing the grain.

When we are designing the model, we need to understand what grain we want the data to be at. The business requirement will define the grain for us—if it is important for us to know the times of transactions, then we may want to have the grain at a lower level. If not, then a higher level is good. Of course, we need to consider that part of the joy of QlikView is to answer those questions that haven't been asked, so we may need to consider that, while the business does not need that grain now, they will perhaps need it in the future. We also need to balance that against the number of transaction rows in the fact table, which will be the primary driver of the size of our in-memory document and the speed of results for our users.

Understanding star schemas

Once we have loaded the fact table and the four dimension tables discussed previously, our schema might look something like the following:

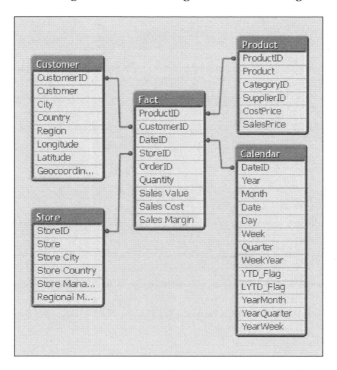

This structure, with one fact table and several dimension tables, with the dimensions all being at one level, is a classic **star schema**.

If we look at the `Product` table here, we will note that there is a `CategoryID` field and a `SupplierID` field. This would lead us to understand that there is additional data available for `Category` and `Supplier` that we could load and end up with a schema like the following:

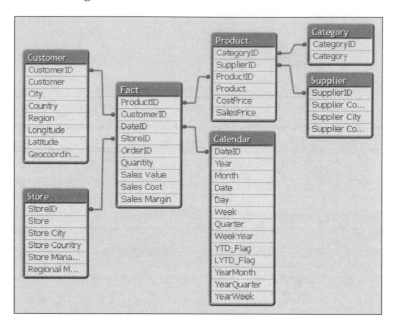

This is no longer a "pure" star schema. As we add tables in this way, the schema starts to become more like a snowflake than a star—it is called a **snowflake** schema.

We discussed in the previous chapter about the potential issues in having many tables in a schema because of the number of joins across data tables. It is important for us to understand that it isn't necessary for the snowflake to remain and that we should actually move the data from the `Category` and `Supplier` tables into the `Product` table, returning to the star schema. This is not just for QlikView; it is as recommended by Kimball. Of course, we don't always have to be perfect and pragmatism should be applied.

By joining the category and supplier information into the `Product` table, we will restore the star schema and, from a QlikView point of view, probably improve performance of queries. The `Product` table will be widened, and hence the underlying data table would increase in width also, but we also have the option of dropping the `CategoryID` and `SupplierID` fields so it probably will not have a very large increase in size. As dimension tables are, generally, relatively smaller than the fact tables, any additional width in the data table will not unduly increase the size of the overall document in memory.

Summing with facts

There are some complications with facts when it comes to the types of calculations that we can perform on them. The most basic calculation that we can do with any fact is to add up the values in that field using the Sum function. But not all facts will work correctly in all circumstances.

Luckily, most facts will probably be fully **additive**. This means that we can perform a Sum function using that field and we will get a sensible and correct answer no matter what context we apply—no matter what selections we make or charts we use that calculation in. For example, the Sales Value field is usually going to be additive across all dimensions and give us a correct answer as we make different selections.

Some facts are only **semi-additive**. These facts can be summed, but only across some of the dimensions. For other dimensions, it does not make sense to sum them, for example, a monthly balance field. It makes sense to select a month and then sum these balances across accounts, territories, cities, and so on, but it doesn't make sense at all to sum a balance across months. If the balance in my checking account is about $100 at the end of every month, it doesn't mean that it will be $1,200 at the end of the year (though I really wish it did!).

Yet other facts won't be additive at all. These are called **non-additive** facts. Any ratio or percent value would not be additive. For example, if we stored the sales margin percent (the sales margin divided by the sales value) in the fact table, then this could not be sensibly added up in any way. If possible, we shouldn't have such ratios in the fact table and should, instead, always retain the original additive facts. It is perfectly sensible to calculate a margin percent expression like this in QlikView:

```
Sum([Sales Margin])/Sum([Sales Value])
```

Because both of the facts involved are additive, the expression will calculate correctly across all dimensions.

Discovering more about facts

There are a few different types of fact tables that we will encounter reasonably regularly. These are as follows:

- Transaction
- Periodic snapshot
- Factless

The following sections give a brief description of these and how you may need to deal with them in QlikView.

Transaction fact tables

The **transaction fact table** is by far the most common type that you will encounter. At the lowest grain, each row in the table represents one event that has happened; for example, a sale of a particular product in a particular store to a particular customer at a particular time by a particular operator at a particular till. Another example might be the scanning of a product as it is placed into a pick basket in a warehouse automated pick system.

Each of these is an atomic event—it is the lowest level of detail that we can have about the process in question. It also gives us more flexibility from a QlikView point of view in that we can calculate our results over many different dimensions.

Because this transaction represents one event, there are generally relatively few facts associated with it. We might, for example, just have quantity and value. If the system gives us the information, we might also have cost and perhaps a derived margin, but that would be all.

Periodic snapshot fact tables

We can, as we have already discussed, aggregate transactions to a higher level. If the retailer does not care about which customer bought a product or at what till, we might remove the customer, till, time, and operator from the transaction and then roll up the values to just date, store, and product, summing up the facts appropriately.

Often, this is done for a performance benefit because less rows will equal less memory used by QlikView. However, when we change the grain and reduce the number of dimensions, we also have the opportunity to add other facts to the table from other events. For example, retailers often throw out unsaleable items—this is called **waste**. This event would also have a date, store, and product associated with it so we could join the two fact tables to create a new, wider fact table. Any other events in the store that have a date and product associated with them could equally be joined in.

The fact tables are called **periodic snapshot** fact tables. Usually they have a period associated with them such as a particular day or rolled up to week or month.

In the previous example, the periodic snapshot table will have the same structure as a transaction fact table and it is fair to say that it still counts as a transaction fact table for modeling purposes. The facts are rolled up from the underlying facts and can be treated the same. However, there are periodic snapshot tables that will represent the end of period position for a value—for example, an account balance or an inventory level—and we need to be careful with these because the facts will be semi-additive.

Factless fact tables

There are fact tables that record an atomic event that doesn't have any particular amount or other measure associated with it. For example, many retailers will have a person on the shop floor who has the task of wandering around checking for empty shelves. If they find a shelf where all the stock has been sold, they scan the product bar code off the shelf and this goes into the backend system. This "gap count" just records the date, time, shelf number, and product. There is no quantity or value involved.

Quite often, we will create a fact—usually just with a value of 1—to be used in calculations.

Dealing with nulls in fact tables in QlikView

Because QlikView isn't too hung up on referential integrity of data, we as designers should always be thinking about it because we shouldn't really allow a disconnect between dimension tables and fact tables. Null values in fact fields are not a problem for QlikView. They will get completely ignored in the majority of calculations, and this is the correct behavior that we want.

Null values in dimension keys are a different matter. QlikView will allow them, but this causes us a problem when it comes to charts. Let's look at a very simple example:

```
Dimension:
Load * Inline [
CustomerID, Customer, Country
1, Customer A, USA
2, Customer B, USA
3, Customer C, UK
4, Customer D, UK
];

Fact:
Load
*
Inline [
Date, CustomerID, Sales Value
2014-01-01, 1, 100
2014-01-01, 2, 100
2014-01-01, 3, 100
2014-01-01, 4, 100
2014-01-01, , 100
2014-01-02, 1, 100
2014-01-02, 2, 100
2014-01-02, 4, 100
];
```

Note that this inline statement won't actually produce a null value; it will instead produce a zero length string. However, this is good enough for the example.

If we create a chart for the sum of sales value by country, it will look like the following:

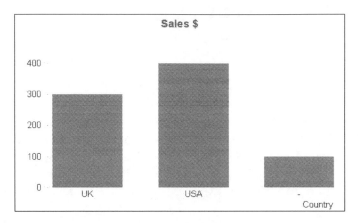

We have a bar that shows an amount associated with a null value. We can't select this bar to find out any other information. I can't drill down to discover the transactions that are not associated to a country.

The way to handle this is to actually create an additional row in the dimension table with a default value and key that we can use in the fact table:

```
Dimension:
Load * Inline [
CustomerID, Customer, Country
0, Missing, Missing
1, Customer A, USA
2, Customer B, USA
3, Customer C, UK
4, Customer D, UK
];

Fact:
Load
    Date,
```

```
    If(Len(CustomerID)=0, 0, CustomerID) As CustomerID,
    [Sales Value]
Inline [
Date, CustomerID, Sales Value
2014-01-01, 1, 100
2014-01-01, 2, 100
2014-01-01, 3, 100
2014-01-01, 4, 100
2014-01-01, , 100
2014-01-02, 1, 100
2014-01-02, 2, 100
2014-01-02, 4, 100
];
```

We now have a value in the Country field that we can drill into to discover fact table rows that do not have a customer key:

There may actually be cases where the key is not missing but is just not applicable. In that case, we can add an additional "Not Applicable" row to the dimension table to handle that situation.

Designing dimension tables

We have a good idea now about fact tables, but we have only briefly talked about the dimension tables that create the context for the facts.

Denormalizing dimensions and conformed dimensions

We discussed star schemas previously, and we discussed that snowflake schemas are not ideal for QlikView and also not recommended by Kimball.

Snowflaking dimensions is akin to the normalization process that is used to design transactional databases. While it may be appropriate for transactional databases, where insert speed is the most important thing, it is not appropriate for reporting databases, where retrieval speed is the most important thing. So denormalizing the dimension tables, by joining the lower level tables back into the main table (joining category and supplier into product in the previous example), is the most efficient method—and this applies for QlikView as well as any database warehouse.

There is another excellent reason for creating a single table to represent a dimension. We are generally not going to build only one QlikView document. We will probably have many business processes or areas that we will want to cover with our applications. These QlikView documents might share dimensions, for example, both a sales and a purchases application will have a product dimension. Depending on the organization, the product that you buy might be the same as the products that you sell. Therefore, it makes sense to build one product dimension, store it to QVD, and then use it in any documents that need it.

Dimensions created that will be shared across multiple dimensional models are called **conformed dimensions**.

Understanding surrogate keys

In Kimball dimensional modeling, there is the concept of replacing the original primary key values of dimensions, in both the dimension and fact tables, with a sequential integer value. This should especially be the case where the primary key is made up of multiple key values.

We should recognize this immediately in QlikView as we already discussed it in *Chapter 1, Performance Tuning and Scalability*—we use the **AutoNumber** function to create a numeric key to associate the dimension with the fact table.

If necessary, we can retain the original key values in the dimension table so that they can be queried, but we do not need to retain those values in the fact table.

Dealing with missing or late arriving dimension values

A late arriving dimension value is a value that does not make it into the dimension table at the time that we load the information into QlikView. Usually, this is a timing issue. The symptoms are the same as if the dimension value doesn't exist at all—we are going to have a referential integrity issue.

Let's look at a quick example:

```
Dimension:
Load * Inline [
CustomerID, Customer, Country
1, Customer A, USA
2, Customer B, USA
3, Customer C, UK
4, Customer D, UK
];

Fact:
Load * Inline [
Date, CustomerID, Sales Value
2014-01-01, 1, 100
2014-01-01, 2, 100
2014-01-01, 3, 100
2014-01-01, 4, 100
2014-01-01, 5, 100
2014-01-02, 1, 100
2014-01-02, 2, 100
2014-01-02, 4, 100
];
```

We can see that we have four rows in the dimension table, but we have five distinct key values in the fact table. We need to add additional rows to the dimension table derived from the fact table:

```
Concatenate (Dimension)
Load Distinct
    CustomerID,
    'Missing ' & CustomerID As Customer,
    'Missing ' & CustomerID As Country
Resident
    Fact
Where Len(Lookup('CustomerID', 'CustomerID', CustomerID,
'Dimension'))=0;
```

You might wonder why I am not using a `Not Exists` function here. `Exists` will check in the symbol table to see whether a value has already been loaded. We only have one symbol table per field and, in this case, both tables have the same field name — `CustomerID` — and hence will have the same symbol table. Because the fact table has been loaded, the symbol table will be fully loaded with all of the available values, so a `Not Exists` function will never return true and no additional values will be loaded.

Defining Kimball's four-step dimensional design process

Now that we know a bit more about the definitions around facts and dimensions, we can talk about Kimball's dimensional design process. This, as a basic tenet, can be applied to almost every QlikView application that you might build.

The four steps are as follows:

- Select the business process
- Declare the grain
- Identify the dimensions
- Identify the facts

Selecting the business process

There are often two ways that developers choose to pick the subject of their QlikView documents. One is line-of-business — for example, Sales, HR, Finance, and so on. The other is by business process. A **business process** is a set of activities that a business performs that may generate a set of metrics, for example, process orders, ship orders, or order stock. Each process will generate one set of facts.

The difference between a line-of-business application and a process-based application is sometimes so subtle that you'll feel there isn't really a difference at all! This is especially true where the identified line-of-business appears to only really have one process within an organization.

Take selling for example. In some organizations, the only thing that is important about selling is the taking orders process. If you are asked to build a sales application for that organization, the line-of-business and the process will be the same. In other organizations, however, they will also be looking for information on customer and prospect contacts — visits, phone calls, and so on.

The line-of-business application will probably want to try and load the facts from both processes so as to compare them and answer business questions about the relationship between visits and orders. The process-based application will tend to just focus on the one set of facts.

In a "pure" Kimball dimensional model, we focus on the process model and one fact table. Where we are building a more line-of-business application with multiple fact tables, we should apply this four step sequence for each process. We will discuss later how we handle a QlikView model with multiple fact tables.

So, the first step is to select that business process.

Declaring the grain

We have already learned what is meant by grain—the level of detail in the fact table. By declaring the grain, we are specifying what level of aggregation we want to deal with.

In almost every situation, the best choice of grain is the atomic choice—the transactional data at the lowest level of detail. Going atomic means that our users can slice and dice the information by whatever dimensions they want. By making a choice to aggregate the fact table, we remove some choice from the user. For example, if we aggregate the retail sales to day, store, and product, we remove the ability of the users to interrogate the data by till, operator, or time of day.

Identifying the dimensions

The dimensions that will be used will pretty much fall out of grain declaration. The complication here is where we are doing a line-of-business app; while we are doing this step by step for one process at a time, we need to be aware of those dimensions that are shared, and we should be sure to have a conformed dimension.

Identifying the facts

We need to specify what facts—what numbers in the data—we are going to use. We also need to think about any derived facts that might be necessary. For example, if we have a quantity and price, do we need to derive the line value?

Learning some useful reusable dimension methods

There are a couple of things that you will come up against repeatedly in creating QlikView documents. One that you will pretty much use in all QlikView documents is the creation of a calendar dimension. Another, that you might not use in every application but will come in useful, is dealing with hierarchies. Lastly, we will look at the practice of creating dimensional facts.

Creating a calendar dimension

Almost every fact table that we will come across will have a date of some sort—at least one, there may be more. Quite often, the source system that we will be extracting the data from may have a calendar table that we can use as the dimension table, but sometimes it doesn't and we need to derive one ourselves.

The basic idea of creating a calendar dimension is to first establish the bounds—what are the earliest and latest dates that should be included. Once we have that, we can generate a row for every date between those bounds (inclusive) and use QlikView functions to derive the date parts—year, month, week, and so on.

In training, you may have come across some methods to establish the minimum and maximum values of the date by querying the fact table. For example, you may have seen something like the following:

```
MinMaxDates:
Load
   Min(OrderDate) As MinDate,
   Max(OrderDate) As MaxDate
Resident
   Fact;

Let vStartDate=Peek('MinDate');
Let vEndDate=Peek('MaxDate');

Drop Table MinMaxDates;
```

There are some problems with this method, so I rarely use it outside the classroom.

One of them is that once you get past a million fact table records, the time taken to calculate the min and max values becomes more and more perceptible and unacceptable in a well-designed script.

However, for me, the main issue is that it is a pointless exercise. The minimum date will rarely, if ever, change—it is a well-known value and can therefore be stated in the script without having to try and calculate it every time. The maximum date, depending on the business, is almost always going to be today, yesterday, or some derivation thereof. Therefore, it is easily calculable without having to scan down through a data table. My calendar script is almost always going to start off something like the following:

```
Let vStartDate=Floor(MakeDate(2009,1,1));
Let vEndDate=Floor(Today());
Let vDiff=vEndDate-vStartDate+1;
```

So, I am stating that the first date for my data is January 1, 2009. The end date is today. When working with dates, I will always transform them to integer values, especially when used with variables. Integers are a lot easier to deal with. I will also always calculate the number of dates that I will need in my calendar as the last date minus the first date plus 1. The rest of my script might look like the following:

```
Calendar:
Load *,
    Date(MonthStart(DateID), 'YYYY-MM') As YearMonth,
    Year & '-' & Quarter As YearQuarter,
    WeekYear & '-' & Num(Week, '00') As YearWeek;
Load
    DateID,
    Year(DateID) As Year,
    Month(DateID) As Month,
    Date(DateID) As Date,
    Day(DateID) As Day,
    Week(DateID) As Week,
    'Q' & Ceil(Month(DateID)/3) As Quarter,
    WeekYear(DateID) As WeekYear,
    -Year2Date(DateID) As YTD_Flag,
    -Year2Date(DateID, -1) As LYTD_Flag;
Load
    RecNo()-1+$(vStartDate) As DateID
AutoGenerate($(vDiff));
```

There are a couple of preceding loads here, which I quite like to use to make scripts more readable. If you haven't come across preceding loads, any load statement that is just a list of field names and functions, terminated with a semicolon, will load its data from the next statement down in the script.

In this case, at the bottom of the pile is an `AutoGenerate` function that will generate the required number of rows. We use a calculation based on the current record number and the start date to calculate the correct date that we should use. The preceding load directly above it will create all the date parts—year, month, week, and so on, and a couple of year-to-date flags that we can use in calculations. The topmost preceding load will use fields created in the middle part to create additional fields.

If you really need a script to derive the calendar table from the data, I can highly recommend the script published on the Qlik community website by Torben Seebach from itelligence in Denmark at `http://community.qlik.com/docs/DOC-6662`.

Unwrapping hierarchies

Way back in the day, there was a piece of script going around that would unwrap a hierarchical relationship in data. It was the most complicated piece of script that you could imagine—but it worked. It was so popular that Qlik decided to create new functions in QlikView to do the operation. There are two—`Hierarchy` and `HierarchyBelongsTo`.

Creating leaves with Hierarchy

The `Hierarchy` function will unwrap the hierarchy and create multiple leaf nodes for each level of the hierarchy. Let's create a very simple hierarchical table:

```
Load * Inline [
NodeID, Location, ParentID
1, World,
2, EMEA, 1
3, Americas, 1
4, AsiaPac, 1
5, USA, 3
6, Canada, 3
7, Brazil, 3
8, UK, 2
9, Germany, 2
10, France, 2
11, China, 4
12, Japan, 4
13, New York, 5
14, Texas, 5
15, California, 5
```

```
16, London, 8
17, Greater Manchester, 8
18, Manchester, 17
19, Bavaria, 9
20, Munich, 19
21, New York, 13
22, Heuston, 14
23, San Francisco, 15
];
```

Each row has a node key, a name, and a parent key that refers to the node key of the level above. So, USA's parent key is 3, which refers to the node key of the Americas.

The first three parameters of the Hierarchy function are mandatory. The other parameters are optional. The parameters are as follows:

Parameter	Description
NodeID	This is the unique key for each row in the input table.
ParentID	This is the key that refers to the parent's node key.
NodeName	This is the field that has the name of the node.
ParentName	If we want to create a new field to store the name of the node's parent, we can pass a string value here (that means the text is passed in single quotes).
PathSource	If we want a path field—a single field containing the full hierarchical path—then we need to tell the functions which field contains the text. Usually, this will be the same as the NodeName field, and if you leave it blank, then the NodeName field will be used.
PathName	Again, if we want a path field, we need to specify a name for it—this is a string value, so the text must be in single quotes.
PathDelimiter	For the path field, this specifies the value that should separate each of the values—a string value in single quotes.
Depth	We can have a field created to store the level in the hierarchy. We pass the desired name of the new field as a string value in single quote marks.

We don't need to have the path or the depth fields created, but they can be useful to have.

To change the preceding table into a full hierarchy, we add the `Hierarchy` statement above the `Load` statement:

```
Hierarchy(NodeID, ParentID, Location, 'Parent Location', 'Location',
'PathName', '~', 'Depth')
Load * Inline [
...
```

This will produce a table that looks like the following:

NodeID	Location	ParentID	Location1	Location2	Location3	Location4	Location5	Parent Location	PathName	Depth
1	World		World	-	-	-		-	World	1
2	EMEA	1	World	EMEA	-	-	-	World	World~EMEA	2
3	Americas	1	World	Americas	-	-	-	World	World~Americas	2
4	AsiaPac	1	World	AsiaPac	-	-	-	World	World~AsiaPac	2
5	USA	3	World	Americas	USA	-	-	Americas	World~Americas~USA	3
6	Canada	3	World	Americas	Canada	-	-	Americas	World~Americas~Canada	3
7	Brazil	3	World	Americas	Brazil	-	-	Americas	World~Americas~Brazil	3
8	UK	2	World	EMEA	UK	-	-	EMEA	World~EMEA~UK	3
9	Germany	2	World	EMEA	Germany	-	-	EMEA	World~EMEA~Germany	3
10	France	2	World	EMEA	France	-	-	EMEA	World~EMEA~France	3
11	China	4	World	AsiaPac	China	-	-	AsiaPac	World~AsiaPac~China	3
12	Japan	4	World	AsiaPac	Japan	-	-	AsiaPac	World~AsiaPac~Japan	3
13	New York	5	World	Americas	USA	New York	-	USA	World~Americas~USA~N..	4
14	Texas	5	World	Americas	USA	Texas	-	USA	World~Americas~USA~T..	4
15	California	5	World	Americas	USA	California	-	USA	World~Americas~USA~C..	4
16	London	8	World	EMEA	UK	London	-	UK	World~EMEA~UK~London	4
17	Greater Manc..	8	World	EMEA	UK	Greater Manch..	-	UK	World~EMEA~UK~Greater..	4
18	Manchester	17	World	EMEA	UK	Greater Manch..	Manchester	Greater Manchester	World~EMEA~UK~Greater..	5
19	Bavaria	9	World	EMEA	Germany	Bavaria	-	Germany	World~EMEA~Germany~..	4
20	Munich	19	World	EMEA	Germany	Bavaria	Munich	Bavaria	World~EMEA~Germany~..	5
21	New York	13	World	Americas	USA	New York	New York	New York	World~Americas~USA~N..	5
22	Heuston	14	World	Americas	USA	Texas	Heuston	Texas	World~Americas~USA~T..	5
23	San Francisco	15	World	Americas	USA	California	San Francisco	California	World~Americas~USA~C..	5

If the `PathName` field is added as a listbox, the **Show as TreeView** option can be specified on the **General** properties tab:

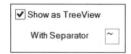

With this option turned on, the listbox will be presented in a tree view:

Creating parent associations with HierarchyBelongsTo

The HierarchyBelongsTo function is slightly different in that it unwraps the link from parent to child and makes it navigable in QlikView. Each child node is associated with its parent, grandparent, and so on. We can also create a field to capture the depth difference between node and ancestor.

The parameters are as follows—only the DepthDiff parameter is optional:

Parameter	Description
NodeID	This is the unique key for each row in the input table.
ParentID	This is the key that refers to the parent's node key.
NodeName	This is the field that has the name of the node.
AncestorID	This is a string value, passed in single quote marks, to specify a name for the field to store the ancestor key.
AncestorName	This is a string value, passed in single quote marks, to specify a name for the field to store the name of the ancestor.
DepthDiff	If you want this field created, pass a string value, in single quote marks, for the name that you want for the field.

Taking the inline table of the previous locations, we can replace the Hierarchy function with a HierarchyBelongsTo function as shown:

```
HierarchyBelongsTo (NodeID, ParentID, Location, 'AncestorID',
'AncestorName', 'DepthDiff')
Load * Inline [
...
```

Then, we will obtain a table that looks like the following:

NodeID	Location	AncestorID	AncestorName	DepthDiff
1	World	1	World	0
2	EMEA	1	World	1
2	EMEA	2	EMEA	0
3	Americas	1	World	1
3	Americas	3	Americas	0
4	AsiaPac	1	World	1
4	AsiaPac	4	AsiaPac	0
5	USA	1	World	2
5	USA	3	Americas	1
5	USA	5	USA	0
6	Canada	1	World	2
6	Canada	3	Americas	1
6	Canada	6	Canada	0
7	Brazil	1	World	2
7	Brazil	3	Americas	1
7	Brazil	7	Brazil	0
8	UK	1	World	2
8	UK	2	EMEA	1
8	UK	8	UK	0
9	Germany	1	World	2
9	Germany	2	EMEA	1
9	Germany	9	Germany	0
10	France	1	World	2
10	France	2	EMEA	1
10	France	10	France	0
11	China	1	World	2
11	China	4	AsiaPac	1
11	China	11	China	0
12	Japan	1	World	2
12	Japan	4	AsiaPac	1
12	Japan	12	Japan	0
13	New York	1	World	3
13	New York	3	Americas	2
13	New York	5	USA	1

This table has all the nodes associated to their parents and vice versa.

Creating dimensional facts

Most of the facts that we deal with in the fact table are numbers that we will calculate and recalculate based on a user's selections. It can sometimes be useful for us to precalculate some values in the script that are less dependent on other dimensions and store them in the dimension table. Some examples are:

- Customer balance
- Number of orders this year
- Number of orders last year
- Current stock quantity

These values should all be calculable from the fact table, but having them precalculated in the dimension table means that performance can be improved. Having them in the dimension table also makes them easier to use as dimension type values—we can query and group by them.

Creating these facts in the script is as simple as loading and grouping from the fact table, for example:

```
Left Join (Customer)
Load
    CustomerID,
    Count(OrderID) As [Orders This Year],
    Sum([Line Value]) As [Sales This Year]
Resident Fact
Where Year(OrderDate)=Year(Today())
Group by CustomerID;
```

Handling slowly changing dimensions

For many dimensions, we are not usually worried about changes being made in the underlying system. If a salesperson gets married and their surname changes from "Smith" to "Jones," we just reload the QlikView document and the new surname will appear in the selectors. However, if the same person changes from the inside sales team to the northwest sales team, just updating the data means that sales attributed to that salesperson will no longer get attributed to the correct team.

These changes to the dimensions do not happen very frequently and are called **slowly changing dimensions (SCDs)**. Kimball defines eight different methods of handling SCDs, from Type 0 to Type 7. The first example discussed previously, the change of surname, is an example of Type 1—simply update the value (Type 0 says to use the original value). The second change, where the sales team is updated, should be handled by Type 2—add a new row to the dimension table. Type 1 and Type 2 will be, by far, the most common ways of handling SCDs.

For a full list of the SCD handling types with descriptions, see *The Data Warehouse Toolkit* or go to `http://www.kimballgroup.com/data-warehouse-business-intelligence-resources/kimball-techniques/dimensional-modeling-techniques/`.

The rest of this section will talk about Type 2. If we are lucky, either the underlying dataset or the ETL that loads the data warehouse where we are getting our data from will already record start and end dates for the validity of the records, for example, something like the following:

SalesPersonID	Name	Territory	From	To
1	Joe Bloggs	NE	01/01/2009	
2	Jane Doe	Inside	01/01/2009	12/31/2013
2	Jane Doe	NW	01/01/2014	

Let's discuss different methods of how we can handle this.

Taking the most recently changed record using FirstSortedValue

The first method that can be used is just to transform the Type 2 data into Type 1 data and treat it as if the additional records were just updates.

We can use a function in QlikView called `FirstSortedValue`. The function can be used within a `Group By` load expression and will return the first value of a field based on the grouped fields and a sort field. Let's look at an example, just using the three rows mentioned previously:

```
Data:
Load * Inline [
SalesPersonID, Name, Territory, From, To
1, Joe Bloggs, NE, 2009-01-01,
2, Jane Doe, Inside, 2009-01-01, 2013-12-31
2, Jane Doe, NW, 2014-01-01,
];

Inner Join (Data)
Load
    SalesPersonID,
    FirstSortedValue(Distinct Territory, -From, 1) As Territory
Resident
    Data
Group by SalesPersonID;
```

The magic is in the `FirstSortedValue` function. The parameters are as follows:

Parameter	Meaning
`Distinct`	When you sort the values in a dataset, it is possible that there might be more than one row with the same sort. The default functionality is to return a null value in this case. When we specify `Distinct`, one of the values will be returned, although we can only assume that the value returned will be based on load order.
`Territory`	This is the field value that we want to be returned after the sort is performed.
`-From`	This is the field (in this case a date field) that defines the sort order. Sort order is lowest to highest. By adding a minus sign before the field name, we change the sort order to highest to lowest—this is what we want in this case because we want the latest date.
`1`	This is an optional parameter and `1` is the default value. This specifies which row we want after the values are sorted.

The result of this join is shown in the following table:

SalesPer...	Name	Territory	From
1	Joe Bloggs	NE	2009-01-01
2	Jane Doe	NW	2014-01-01

Of course, this is not what we really want in this situation, and we need to look at further alternatives.

Using IntervalMatch with SCDs

QlikView has a great function called `IntervalMatch` that works very well in situations where we have start and end dates and we want to match this to a dimension such as a calendar.

To see it in action, let's load some data. First, we will load the tables as separate entities. We should create a unique key in the salesperson table to associate into the fact table. We also need to back-fill the `To` date with a value if it is blank—we will use today's date:

```
SalesPerson:
Load
    AutoNumber(SalesPersonID & '-' & Territory & '-' & From, 'SP') As
SP_ID,
    SalesPersonID,
    Name,
```

```
      Territory,
      From,
      If(Len(To)=0, Today(), To) As To
Inline [
SalesPersonID, Name, Territory, From, To
1, Joe Bloggs, NE, 2009-01-01,
2, Jane Doe, Inside, 2009-01-01, 2013-12-31
2, Jane Doe, NW, 2014-01-01,
];

Fact:
Load * Inline [
OrderDate, SalesPersonID, Sales Value
2013-01-01, 1, 100
2013-02-01, 2, 100
2014-01-01, 1, 100
2014-02-01, 2, 100
];
```

Now, this will create a false association:

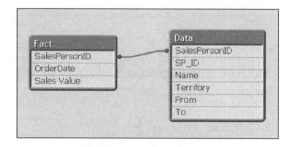

If we do a calculation based on the **Sales Person** column, we will actually get the correct result:

Sales Person	Sales $
	400
Jane Doe	200
Joe Bloggs	200

However, if we calculate on **Territory**, the result is incorrect:

Territory	Sales $
	400
Inside	200
NE	200
NW	200

The result actually doesn't look like it makes any sense—although it is perfectly logical if we think about it.

At this stage, we can introduce `IntervalMatch`:

```
LinkTable:
IntervalMatch(OrderDate, SalesPersonID)
Load
    From,
    To,
    SalesPersonID
Resident
    SalesPerson;
```

This will create a table, called `LinkTable`, with four fields—`OrderDate`, `SalesPersonID`, `From`, and `To`—containing the logical association between the order date, sales person, and the from and to dates.

Now, we are not finished because we also have a synthetic key that we should remove. What we need to do is join the `SP_ID` field from the salesperson table into this link table and then we can join `OrderDate`, `SalesPersonID`, and `SP_ID` from the link table into the fact table. Once that is done, we can drop the link table and also drop `SalesPersonID` from the fact table (as the association will be on `SP_ID`).

This will look like the following:

```
Left Join (LinkTable)
Load
    From,
    To,
    SalesPersonID,
    SP_ID
Resident
    SalesPerson;

Left Join (Fact)
Load
    OrderDate,
    SalesPersonID,
    SP_ID
Resident
    LinkTable;

Drop Table LinkTable;
Drop Field SalesPersonID From Fact;
```

The resulting table structure will look like the following:

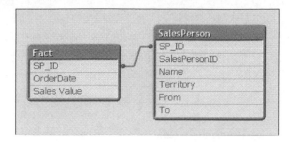

The straight table of sales by territory will now look like the following:

Territory	Sales $
	400
Inside	100
NW	100
NE	200

Using hash to manage from/to dates

The from/to dates that we have in the data source should hopefully be managed by either the source application or an ETL tool. However, sometimes QlikView is the ETL tool, and we need to manage those from/to dates as best we can.

One method we can do is to load the data with a hash key (see *Using one of the Hash functions* earlier in this chapter) that encapsulates all the field values in each row. We can then store the data to QVD. Using this key, we should be able to detect when the data changes. If it changes, we can then load the new data and add to the data in the QVD.

We can load the initial set of data, with an initial start date, in the following manner:

```
SalesPerson:
LOAD
    Hash256(SalesPersonID, Name, Territory) As HashKey,
    SalesPersonID,
    Name,
    Territory,
    '2009-01-01' As From
FROM
[..\Scripts\SalesPersonList_Initial.txt]
```

```
(txt, codepage is 1252, embedded labels, delimiter is ',', msq);

Store SalesPerson into SalesPerson.QVD;
```

Now, once we have the QVD built, we can have a daily reload process that loads the QVD, loads the current salesperson file, and compares for hashes that don't already exist. If there are a few that don't exist, we can add them with today as the From date in the following manner:

```
SalesPerson_Temp:
LOAD HashKey,
    SalesPersonID,
    Name,
    Territory,
    From
FROM
SalesPerson.QVD
(qvd);

Concatenate (SalesPerson_Temp)
LOAD
    Hash256(SalesPersonID, Name, Territory) As HashKey,
    SalesPersonID,
    Name,
    Territory,
    Date(Today(), 'YYYY-MM-DD') As From
FROM
[..\Scripts\SalesPersonList_Current.txt]
(txt, codepage is 1252, embedded labels, delimiter is ',', msq)
Where Not Exists(HashKey, Hash256(SalesPersonID, Name, Territory));

Store SalesPerson_Temp into SalesPerson.QVD;
```

As long as the data in the current dataset doesn't change, the existing QVD will stay the same. If it does change, the new or updated rows will be added to the QVD.

 If we are using QlikView data files to store slowly changing dimensions in this way, we need to be aware that QVDs are not considered to be a resilient persistent storage method. Appropriate backups need to be put in place because if you lose these QVDs, then you lose the change information.

Now, you may have noticed that I have called the table `SalesPerson_Temp`. This is because I am not finished with it yet. I need to now calculate the `To` date. I can do this by sorting the list by salesperson and date, with the date in descending order—that means that the first row for each salesperson will be the most recent date and therefore the `To` date will be today. On subsequent rows, the `To` date will be the previous row's `From` date minus one day:

```
SalesPerson:
Load
   SalesPersonID,
   Name,
   Territory,
   From,
   Date(If(Previous(SalesPersonID)<>SalesPersonID,
       Today(),
       Previous(From)-1), 'YYYY-MM-DD') As To
Resident
   SalesPerson_Temp
Order by SalesPersonID, From Desc;

Drop Table SalesPerson_Temp;
```

Now, we have our table with to/from dates that we can use with an interval match as demonstrated in the previous section.

Dealing with multiple fact tables in one model

In data models designed around business processes, we will often have just one source fact table. If we have additional fact tables, they tend to be at a similar grain to the main fact table, which is easier to deal with. Line-of-business documents may have fact tables from lots of different sources that are not at the same grain level at all, but we are still asked to deal with creating the associations. There are, of course, several methods to deal with this scenario.

Joining the fact tables together

If the fact tables have an identical grain, with the exact same set of primary keys, then it is valid to join, using a full outer join, the two tables together. Consider the following example:

```
Fact:
Load * Inline [
Date, Store, Product, Sales Value
2014-01-01, 1, 1, 100
2014-01-01, 2, 1, 99
2014-01-01, 1, 2, 111
2014-01-01, 2, 2, 97
2014-01-02, 1, 1, 101
2014-01-02, 2, 1, 98
2014-01-02, 1, 2, 112
2014-01-02, 2, 2, 95
];

Join (Fact)
Load * Inline [
Date, Store, Product, Waste Value
2014-01-01, 1, 1, 20
2014-01-01, 2, 1, 10
2014-01-02, 2, 2, 11
2014-01-03, 2, 1, 5
];
```

This will produce a table that looks like the following:

Date	Store	Product	Sales Value	Waste Value
2014-01-01	1	1	100	20
2014-01-01	1	2	111	-
2014-01-01	2	1	99	10
2014-01-01	2	2	97	-
2014-01-02	1	1	101	-
2014-01-02	1	2	112	-
2014-01-02	2	1	98	-
2014-01-02	2	2	95	11
2014-01-03	2	1	-	5

We know from our previous discussion about null values in fact tables that QlikView will perfectly handle these values for all calculations.

Concatenating fact tables

Concatenation of tables instead of joining them is often a go-to strategy for the creation of combined fact tables. It works well because logically we end up with the same result as joining. Also, if there is any suspicion that there are duplicate keys (so, in our example, two or more rows for the same date, `Store` and `Product` — which may be valid), then concatenation will still work where a join will not. In the previous example, if we were to concatenate rather than join, then the table would look like the following:

Date	Store	Product	Sales Value	Waste Value
2014-01-01	1	1	100	-
2014-01-01	1	1	-	20
2014-01-01	1	2	111	-
2014-01-01	2	1	99	-
2014-01-01	2	1	-	10
2014-01-01	2	2	97	-
2014-01-02	1	1	101	-
2014-01-02	1	2	112	-
2014-01-02	2	1	98	-
2014-01-02	2	2	95	-
2014-01-02	2	2	-	11
2014-01-03	2	1	-	5

One thing that we need to consider is that this table is longer than the previous one while still being as wide. Therefore, it will take up more space in memory.

It can also work to concatenate fact tables that have a different grain. In that case, it is a good idea to populate the key values that are missing with a key value pointing to the "not applicable" value in the dimension, as we discussed earlier.

Changing the grain of a fact table

We mentioned previously that we can reduce the granularity of a fact table by aggregating the facts to a smaller subset of dimensions — for example, removing transaction time and aggregating to transaction date. There may be other occasions, and good business reasons, where you have a fact table at one grain and want to make it more granular to match with another fact table. For example, suppose that I have sales data by date and have budget data by week; I may want to split the budget down to the day level to give me more granularity in my day-by-day analysis.

Imagine a scenario where we are going to load the weekly budget but we want to apportion that over the days in a different ratio—to reflect general trading conditions. The percentages that we want per day are as follows:

Day	Percentage
Monday	10%
Tuesday	13%
Wednesday	15%
Thursday	17%
Friday	20%
Saturday	25%
Sunday	0%

We can load a mapping table with this information and then use that to calculate the correct daily value:

```
Budget_Day_Percent:
Mapping Load * Inline [
Day, Percentage
0, .10
1, .13
2, .15
3, .17
4, .20
5, .25
6, 0
];

Budget:
Load
    YearWeek,
    Store,
    Product,
    [Budget Value] As WeekBudget
From Budget.qvd (QVD);

Left Join (Budget)
Load
    YearWeek,
    Date
From Calendar.qvd (QVD);
```

```
Left Join (Budget)
Load
    Date,
    Store,
    Product,
    WeekBudget
       * ApplyMap('Budget_Day_Percent', WeekDay(Date), 0)
       As [Budget Value]
Resident
    Budget;

Drop Field WeekBudget;
```

Linking fact tables of different grains

If the fact tables have different grains, especially where they have quite different dimension keys, only sharing a few, it often doesn't make sense to concatenate them—we just create a wide and long fact table that has many null values. In that case, it makes more sense to create a link table to associate the two tables.

A link table is pretty much exactly like a synthetic key table, except that we are controlling the creation of composite keys. There are a couple of simple rules for the creation of link tables:

- Create a key in each fact table that will associate the rows in the fact table to the link table. This will mostly be a combination of the keys that we are going to use in the link table using AutoNumber.
- Use a mixture of concatenation and joins to create the link table.
- Drop the key fields that have been added to the link table from the fact tables.

I did once have a different approach to this, using primary keys for each fact table, but the preceding approach is far simpler.

Let's look at an example. We will return to retail sales and budgets, but this time we will have very different grains that are not easily changeable. We will have a date, store, and product, but the sales information will be down to till, operator, and time. There is very little chance of us manipulating the budget data down to this level.

Now, it is valid to concatenate these tables as we discussed earlier. Once you have used both techniques a number of times, you will be able to make a good judgment of which one to use on a case-by-case basis. Most often, the overriding consideration should be memory size and lower memory equals lower cache and better performance for more users.

The following is the example load:

```
Sales:
LOAD
    AutoNumber(Floor(Date) & '-' & Store & '-' & Product, 'SB_Link') As
SB_Link,
    *
INLINE [
  Date, Store, Product, Till, Operator, Time, Sales Quantity, Sales
Value
  2014-01-01, 1, 1, 1, 1, 09:00:00, 1, 12.12
  2014-01-01, 1, 2, 1, 1, 09:01:30, 2, 3.33
  2014-01-01, 2, 1, 3, 5, 10:11:01, 4, 17.88
  2014-01-01, 2, 2, 5, 5, 12:02:22, 1, 1.70
];


Budget:
LOAD
    AutoNumber(Floor(Date) & '-' & Store & '-' & Product, 'SB_Link') As
SB_Link,
    *
INLINE [
  Date, Store, Product, Budget Value
  2014-01-01, 1, 1, 20.00
  2014-01-01, 1, 2, 3.00
  2014-01-01, 2, 1, 20.00
  2014-01-01, 2, 2, 3.00
];

Link_Table:
Load Distinct
    SB_Link,
    Date,
    Store,
    Product
Resident
    Sales;

Join (Link_Table)
Load Distinct
    SB_Link,
    Date,
    Store,
```

```
    Product
Resident
    Budget;

Drop Fields Date, Store, Product From Sales;
Drop Fields Date, Store, Product From Budget;
```

This will produce a model like the following:

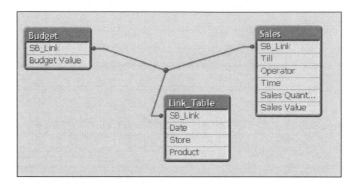

In this case, we happen to have all the fields that we are using in the link table in both tables. What happens if we have a different table in the mix that only has two of those fields? For example, if we have a table containing the current stock levels for each product by store, we can add this to the link table in the following manner:

```
Store_Stock:
Load
    AutoNumber(Store & '-' & Product, 'SS_Link') As SS_Link,
    *
Inline [
Store, Product, Stock Level
1, 1, 12.00
1, 2, 2.00
2, 1, 6.00
2, 2, 2.00
];

Join (Link_Table)
Load Distinct
    SS_Link,
    Store,
    Product
Resident
    Store_Stock;

Drop Fields Store, Product from Store_Stock;
```

The data model will now look like the following:

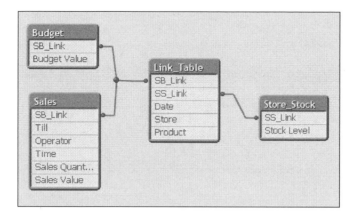

We can continue to add keys to this table like this—either joining or concatenating. We can also, if necessary, build two or three link tables and then concatenate them together at the end.

Drilling across with document chaining

One of the basics of dimensional modeling is the ability to drill between models to answer questions. There are a few situations in QlikView that make this an important consideration, for example:

- We might have multiple data models, with some shared dimensions, that might be difficult technically, or even excluded by license, to associate within one QlikView document.

- Most analysis for most users can be performed on an aggregated, low-memory-footprint data model, but for some users on some occasions, they need to drill down to a lower level of detail.

- In some situations, the number of applications is not a consideration, and we create multiple applications within different business areas but want users to have some options to link between them.

QlikView handles this quite well with the document chaining function. As with any other system where you need to drill across, the ability to do so is entirely dependent on the use of conformed dimensions.

To enable document chaining with the ability to drill across, we need to add an action to a suitable object (button, text object, gauge chart, or line object) with an **External** action type of **Open QlikView Document**. We can see the settings for this in the following screenshot:

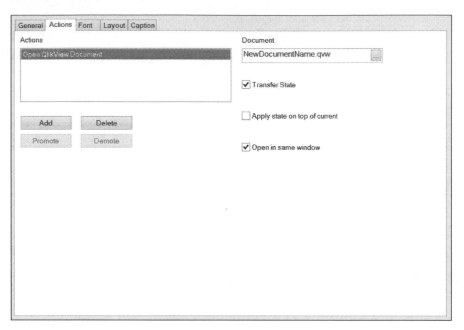

The **Transfer State** option will pass the current selections from this QlikView document to the document being opened. This is based on field name and the values. This is why it is important to use conformed dimensions because they ensure that both the field names and field values are the same between all the documents that are sharing those dimensions.

Summary

This chapter has had a lot of really important information. We started by reviewing what you should already know about associating data. You learned important information about keys and autonumbering and the level of calculations used in QlikView. We also reviewed the different methods of stitching data together—join, concatenate, and mapping.

We then moved on to talk about dimensional data modeling, fact and dimension tables, and best practices from Ralph Kimball. You learned how to handle SCDs and multiple fact tables and how to drill across tables.

The previous chapter dealt with loading data for performance. The next chapter will help us continue our learning of how best to load data, building QVD layers, to support a dimensional modeling approach.

3
Best Practices for Loading Data

"Data! Data! Data!" he cried impatiently. "I can't make bricks without clay."

— Sherlock Holmes (Arthur Conan Doyle), The Adventure of the Copper Beeches

In this chapter, beginners to QlikView development will be shown how to connect to different data sources with the QlikView script, load tables of data, transform that data, and create charts and other objects. However, in the real world of QlikView application development, it will be very rare that you will create an application that contains the whole process, from data source to final visualizations, within one QlikView document.

Extract, transform, and load (ETL) is a standard process within data warehousing; moving and transforming data from different data locations into the final dimensional model tables.

In this chapter, we will be looking at creating best practice ETL techniques using QlikView tools. Initially, we will look at how to do this using the QlikView script. At the end of this chapter, we will look at using QlikView's graphical ETL tool — **Expressor** — to provision data for QlikView.

These are the topics that will be covered in this chapter:

- Reviewing data load and storage concepts
- Understanding why to use an ETL approach
- Using an ETL approach to create QVD data layers

- Mastering loading techniques:
    - Incremental load
    - Partial load
    - Binary load

- Using QlikView Expressor for ETL

Reviewing data loading concepts

There are a few things that we need to remind ourselves of before we can fully grasp the concepts covered in this chapter.

Getting data from anywhere

QlikView is data-agnostic. It doesn't care where the data comes from, all QlikView cares about is whether the data is numeric or alphanumeric, and if it is numeric, does it have an alphanumeric representation that needs to be stored. Hence, for practical discussion purposes, there are only two datatypes in QlikView—numeric and dual.

> QlikView does actually recognize both integer and float values and stores them accordingly, with floats taking up more storage bytes. If the numeric values have a format, then they are stored as duals— with the number and the formatted string stored together. The Floor function will not only remove decimals from a number, leaving just an integer, but it will also remove any formatting so it will reduce the amount of space needed to store the values.

This is sometimes difficult for people coming from a database world, where there can be great difficulty in moving data from one place to another. Database ETL designers will have to worry about whether the source data is one length of string versus the target. In QlikView, we need not worry; it is just going to be text.

There are sometimes issues due to this, such as when there is an ambiguity about what the data is, but it does save a lot of time. This is especially true when we need to bring data together from multiple data sources. We may have sales information coming from an ERP system, user information coming from an HR system, and customer contact information coming from a CRM system. Then, add to that budget information from Excel. Because we don't care about the strict datatypes, QlikView can handle all of this data easily. We can start building our applications and delivering results very quickly.

One of the reasons that QlikView can be better than traditional reporting solutions is that QlikView takes a snapshot of the data into the memory and users will query that snapshot. This takes a load off the core systems because the users' queries are not continually running against a production database. However, to make this an even better situation, we need to make sure that QlikView plays nicely with the database and we are not attempting to load 20 million transaction records every 30 minutes. That is behavior that makes us very unpopular with DBAs very quickly.

The data-from-anywhere ability of QlikView is also a great advantage over many other systems, where you might be limited to only connecting to one data source at a time and are forced to write ETL to move other data sources into the common source. Some other systems have the ability to combine data from multiple sources, but often not in such a straightforward way. One of the reasons ETL has developed as a software category is the ability to report on data from multiple sources. Companies had no option but to move the data into a central warehouse where reports could be run. There are, of course, some very good techniques and practices that have come out of ETL processing that we can apply to QlikView implementations—techniques that will save us from the wrath of the DBA!

Loading data from QlikView

One technique that is often quickly forgotten by QlikView developers, if they ever knew about it in the first place, is the BINARY load. This statement will load all of the data of a QlikView file (.qvw) into another—the data tables, symbol tables, and so forth. Once they have been loaded into the new file, you can use it as is, add additional data, remove and reload tables, or perform any other processing that you want.

Because you are loading another file's data tables, symbol tables, and other tables into a new file, there is one restriction in that the BINARY statement must be the very first statement in the script, as shown in the following screenshot:

```
Main | Connection | SubRoutine | Inline Table | DIMS | Fact | Info
 1   BINARY ..\Apps\DailySales.qvw;
 2
 3   SET ThousandSep=',';
 4   SET DecimalSep='.';
 5   SET MoneyThousandSep=',';
 6   SET MoneyDecimalSep='.';
 7   SET MoneyFormat='€#,##0.00;-€#,##0.00';
 8   SET TimeFormat='hh:mm:ss';
 9   SET DateFormat='DD/MM/YYYY';
10   SET TimestampFormat='DD/MM/YYYY hh:mm:ss[.f
11   SET MonthNames='Jan;Feb;Mar;Apr;May;Jun;Jul
12   SET DayNames='Mon;Tue;Wed;Thu;Fri;Sat;Sun';
13
```

Using this technique, you might have a chain of binary loading documents, each one loading from the one before, but then adding some new data or even removing rows or whole tables, to make it more unique. Another use case is to have completely different documents from a frontend visualization point of view, with different audiences, that share the same data model—one document can load the data while the other documents simply binary load from the original.

Loading similar files with concatenation

We already talked about automatic and manual concatenation in the *Joining data* section *Chapter 2, QlikView Data Modeling*. We will recall that if two tables with the same number of identically named fields are loaded, then QlikView will automatically concatenate those tables.

If we load data from file-based sources using wildcards in the filenames, QlikView will attempt to load each of the matching files. As long as the files contain the same set of fields, the rows in each file will be automatically concatenated, for example:

```
Load Field1, Field2, Field3
From File*.txt (txt, utf8, embedded labels, delimiter is ',',
  msq);
```

As long as every file that matches the wildcard `File*.txt` contains the three fields listed, they will all be concatenated.

> The wildcards available are the standard Windows ones—`*` to represent zero or many characters and `?` to represent just one character.

Loading dissimilar files with Concatenate and For Each

So, if similar files can be loaded using a simple wildcard, what if there are differences, perhaps even just a field or two, but you would still like to concatenate the fields? This might be a common use case if you are loading files that have been generated over time but have had new fields added to them during that period. The older files won't have the fields, so rather than try and retro-fit those files, we can handle them like this:

```
// Assign a variable with blank text
Set vConcatenateOrders='';
FOR Each vFilename in FileList('c:\Data\Filter*.txt')
  Orders:
```

```
$(vConcatenateOrders)
LOAD *
FROM
$(vFilename)
(txt, utf8, embedded labels, delimiter is ',', msq);
// Update the variable with a concatenate statement
Set vConcatenateOrders='Concatenate  (Orders)';

Next
```

The `For Each` statement combined with the `FileList` function will loop through all of the values that are returned by the file specification. The full absolute path (for example, `C:\Data\OrderExport2.csv`) will be assigned to the `vFilename` variable.

> There is also a function called `DirList` that will return a list of folders. Both `FileList` and `DirList` will return their values in dictionary order.

Understanding QlikView Data files

A **QlikView Data (QVD)** file is a file format that QlikView uses to store a table of data to disk. Only one table can be stored in each QVD file.

A QVD contains three parts:

- An XML header, which describes the data contained in the QVD. This XML file also contains useful information about the date and time that the QVD was created, the name of the document that created the QVD file, the name of the table in QlikView, and lineage information about where the data originated from—which database queries or table files made up the table in QlikView before the data was stored to QVD.

- The symbol tables for each field in the data in a byte-stuffed format. Byte stuffing helps remove potentially illegal characters from the data. Although this can increase the size of the stored data over the original data, it is usually not significant for symbol tables.

- A bit-stuffed data table is a table of index pointers that points to the symbol table values (as we discussed in *Chapter 1, Performance Tuning and Scalability*).

So, basically the QVD file is an on-disk representation of how that data is stored in memory. For this reason, loading data from a QVD file back into memory is very fast. In fact, if you do no transformation to the data in the load script, then the load is essentially straight from disk into memory. This is the fastest way of getting a single table of data into QlikView.

Even if you need to transform the data, or use `where` clauses, the data load is still very fast—as fast as from any other table files. There are a couple of operations that can be performed on a QVD that do not interfere with the fastest, most optimized load:

- Rename fields using `As`
- A `Where` clause using a single `Exists`

Storing tables to QVD

When we have loaded data into a table, we can store that table to an external file using the `Store` command. The basic syntax of the command is like this:

```
Store TableName into path_to_file (format);
```

This is the syntax that would be used 99 times out of 100. There is a slightly more advanced syntax, where we can specify the fields to be stored:

```
Store Field1, Field2, Field3 from TableName into path_to_file (format)
```

The path will be any valid absolute, relative, or UNC path to the file that you wish to create. The format is one of three values:

Format	Description
qvd	This creates a file of type QVD as described previously.
txt	This creates a comma-separated Unicode text file.
qvx	An XML-based table format that QlikView can read. Because this is an open format, it is often used by third-party organizations to export data to be loaded into QlikView.

If the format is omitted, `qvd` will be used. Because of that, you will usually see `Store` statements without the format specified. A best practice would be to always include the format, even if it is QVD.

Some examples of valid `Store` statements are:

```
Store Sales into D:\QlikView\QVD\Sales.qvd;
Store OrderID, OrderDate, CustomerID, ProductID, SalesValue
From Sales into ..\QVD\Sales.qvd (qvd);
Store Customer into \\qvserver\data\Customer.qvx (qvx);
Store Product into ..\csv\Product.csv (txt);
```

Using QVD files

One of the things that new developers often ask about QVDs is, "why?". They wonder why they need to use QVDs. They know that they can connect to a database and read data and they feel that they can do that again and again and don't see any reason why they need to bother writing the data to a QVD file first. There are, however, several very good reasons to store data in QVDs:

- Speeding up loads by storing data that doesn't change, or doesn't change very frequently. Loading data from a database is relatively much slower than loading data from a local QVD. For example, if you have 2-year-old transactions, that won't change; you could have those in QVDs, and then load newer transactions from the database and concatenate the two sets of data. Of course, this also reduces the load on the database server because we are only looking for relatively few rows of data on each SQL call.

- Combining data from multiple different sources. For example, we could have a new ERP system in place but we also want to add in sales information from an old system. If we keep the old data in QVD, we don't need to have the old database online, so it can be decommissioned.

- Incremental load is the ultimate use of QVDs to load transactional information in the minimum amount of time possible. Basically, we load only the newest data from the database, combine with the older data from locally stored QVDs, and then update the QVDs.

 There is an excellent section on this in both the QlikView Reference Manual and in the QlikView Help file—search for `Using QVD Files for Incremental Load`. We will run through an example of this later in this chapter.

- As discussed in *Chapter 2, QlikView Data Modeling*, dimensional modeling approaches say that we should use conformed dimensions where dimensions are shared across different models. This is an excellent use of QVDs—we create the QVD once and then can share it across many QlikView documents. Even if we are not following a strict dimensional modeling approach, we can still use QVDs to reuse data in more than one application.

- Implementing data quality when preparing data for users. A cleaned set of QVD files, that are centrally created and controlled, can be provisioned for users with confidence that data is correct.

Just from a development point of view, you will find that you are performing reloads again and again as you are perfecting your data model. If you are reloading from a slow database connection, this can be painful. If you create local QVDs, then your development efforts will proceed a lot faster.

Understanding why you should use an ETL approach

Hopefully, from the preceding section, you might start to see why the majority of expert QlikView developers use some kind of an ETL approach to data loading using QVDs.

There are several advantages to using an ETL approach to just load all the data directly from data sources, such as:

- Speeding up overall data loading and reducing of load on database servers by archiving data to QVD

- Reusing extracted data in multiple documents

- Applying common business rules across multiple documents: one version of the truth

- Creating conformed dimensions across multiple business processes, supporting a dimensional modeling approach

- Provisioning a data layer that allows QlikView users to self-serve, without it being necessary to have database skills

Speeding up overall data loading

As mentioned in the previous section, it doesn't make sense to constantly load data from a database that doesn't change. It makes much more sense for the data that doesn't change to be stored locally in QVD files, and then we only need to go to the database server for the data that has changed since the last time that we queried for it.

This approach makes your network engineers and DBAs very happy because the database isn't over-taxed and the amount of network traffic is reduced.

As data volumes increase, it often becomes critical to make sure that reloads are as short as possible so as to fit inside a reload window. By having as much of the data as possible stored locally on the QlikView server in QVD files, we can make sure that we have the shortest reload times possible.

Reusing extracted data in multiple documents

It is not uncommon for the same data table to be used in many places. For example, you may have a staff list that is extracted from an HR system but is used right across all areas of the business. You may also have a global calendar table, which will be used by almost every application, which can be loaded from the finance system.

By extracting the data once into QVD, you are, again, reducing network traffic and database load. If this data is not updated on a very frequent basis, it is also not necessary to re-extract that from the database frequently during the day to feed into a more real-time application. A table like the calendar might only be refreshed monthly.

 Real time means different things to different people, but I would define it as the periodicity of the reload that gives the business the information that it needs to make decisions now. For some businesses that demand a refresh every minute, for others, once a week will do.

Applying common business rules across multiple documents

From a *one version of the truth* point of view, it is critical that measures are calculated the same way across all documents that use them. If two people use different calculations for, say, margin, then they will get different answers and drive, potentially, different actions.

By using an ETL approach, the same calculation can be used to feed the same measure to multiple fact tables, which helps ensure that the same result is obtained across the business.

Creating conformed dimensions

Conformed dimensions are a fundamental of dimensional modeling. What this means is that we create one dimensional table to represent the same entity across the entire business.

For example, we sell a product to customers, our sales people visit prospects, and we order from suppliers. All of these are examples of organizations. By creating a single organization dimension that can be shared across multiple dimensional models, we can gain insight that would otherwise be difficult to achieve.

In the Kimball dimensional modeling approach, there is a technique called the Enterprise Data Warehouse Bus Architecture that helps you identify dimensions that will be shared across multiple models. For more information, see *The Data Warehouse Toolkit* by Ralph Kimball and Margy Ross or their website:

```
http://www.kimballgroup.com/data-warehouse-business-intelligence-
resources/kimball-techniques/kimball-data-warehouse-bus-architecture/
```

Provisioning a self-service data layer

By adopting an ETL approach, we can make our fact table and dimension table QVDs available for users to load into QlikView to create their own analyses, without having to have any database expertise or database connection credentials.

In fact, you can create a QlikView application that will create a script that will read the appropriate QVDs for a process into a new QlikView application, which means your power users do not even have to have any QlikView scripting knowledge.

Using an ETL approach to create QVD data layers

We now know that there are very good reasons for adopting an ETL approach to loading data in QlikView. Now we need to learn how we should go about implementing the approach.

Each part—Extract, Transform, and Load—has its own set of recommendations because each part has a very different function.

Essentially, the approach looks like this:

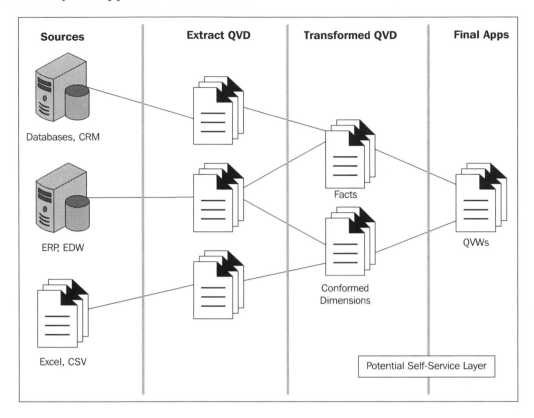

The approach can be explained as follows:

1. Extract the data from data sources into QVDs.
2. Transform the data from the initial QVDs into transformed fact tables and conformed dimensions.
3. Load the transformed QVDs into the final applications.

The final two layers, the transformed QVDs and the final applications, become potential sources for a user's self-service. We can have confidence that users who load data from these layers will be getting access to clean, governed data.

Creating a StoreAndDrop subroutine

When we are loading data to create QVDs, we will end up calling the `Store` statement quite frequently. Also, we tend to drop tables once we have stored them as we don't need that data in the QVW file that has created them. So, we will also call the `Drop` statement quite often.

Anytime that we do something quite frequently in the script, it is a good idea to put that into a subroutine that we can call. Here is an example of a script that will perform the `Store` and the `Drop` operations:

```
Sub StoreAndDrop(vTableName, vPrefix, vQVDFolder)
  Store [$(vTableName)] into
    [$(vQVDFolder)\$(vPrefix)$(vTableName).qvd];
  Drop Table [$(vTableName)];
End Sub
```

The subroutine gets passed the name of the table that we want to store, a prefix that we might want to add to the QVD files, and a folder that we want to put the files in—again, this is absolute, relative, or UNC.

Here are some examples of calling this subroutine:

```
Call StoreAndDrop('Table1', 'E_', 'C:\Temp');
Call StoreAndDrop('Table2', 'EX_', '.\');
```

This is an example of a function that you might want to have in an external text file that can be included in all of your scripts, the advantage being that we can have a central place for the maintenance and support of functions.

To include an external file, you would have a statement like this (this one can be created by using the menu in the script editor—**Insert | Include Statement**):

```
$(Include=..\scripts\storeanddrop.qvs);
```

Now, there is a slight problem with this directive in that if the file doesn't exist or there is some other problem reading the file, QlikView will then just ignore the directive (silent fail). Therefore, we should probably think about modifying the statement to read as follows:

```
$(Must_Include=..\scripts\storeanddrop.qvs);
```

This will throw an error in the script if there is a problem reading the file—which we probably want to have happen. The script failure will throw an error on the desktop or cause an automated task to fail on the server—unless we are handling the error using the `ErrorMode` and `ScriptError` variables.

Extracting data

The goal of extracting data is to connect to our database or other sources, and move the required data from source to QVD as quickly as possible. To this end, we will do basically no transformation of the data at all.

Creating an extractor folder structure

To keep things well organized, we should adopt a practice of keeping to a folder structure for our extraction files and the QVDs that they generate.

Within our `Extractors` folder, there should be a subfolder for each data source. For example, we will have a subfolder for our `Sales Database` and `HR System`. We might also have a subfolder for a set of budget files that are stored in Excel somewhere. We will very often have a `Shared` subfolder that will contain useful scripts and QVDs that will be shared across multiple sources. For example, we might store our `StoreAndDrop` script in the `Shared` subfolder structure. Our folder structure may look like the following screenshot:

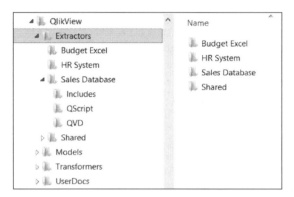

It is worth noting that if there was only going to be one budget Excel file and it is related to sales, it is perfectly correct to do the practical thing and handle it alongside the other sales data instead of creating a separate set of folders.

Unless an Excel file requires a load process such as `CrossTable`, I probably wouldn't create a QVD from it at all. The overhead counteracts any benefits.

Within each subfolder, there will be three new subfolders:

Subfolder	Purpose
Includes	This folder will hold `include` text files containing a QlikView script. A common use of such files is to store connection strings or variable declarations that might be shared across multiple files. By keeping such information in a separate `include` file, we can quickly change values without having to edit multiple QVWs.
QScript	This folder will hold either QVW files that will be executed by a server/publisher reload task or text files (usually with a QVS extension) containing a script that we will run via a publisher task. In either case, the purpose of the script will be to connect to the data sources, load the data, and store the data into QVD files.
QVD	The destination folder for the data generated by the scripts.

Differentiating types of scripts

While all extractor scripts will connect to a data source, load the data, then store to QVD, there are some logical differences based on the way that they will operate and the frequency that they will be executed. The following table describes this:

Script type	Description
Low frequency	The data that is being loaded does not change frequently or at all. Therefore, there is little point in refreshing the QVD on a very frequent (for example, daily) basis. A good example of this might be a calendar table, which we can use to calculate many years into the past and many years into the future. Another example may be a department structure that doesn't really change very frequently. We can refresh the QVD every so often, automatically or manually, but not frequently. The complexity of the script is irrelevant because it runs so infrequently.
Simple, high frequency	Common for dimensional data, we will connect to the data source, load the data, and store straight to QVD with little or no additional calculation. We will do this frequently because we need to make sure that any changes in such data are reflected in the models. However, the size of these dimension tables (relatively small compared to the fact tables) means that loading the entire table every time is not unfeasible.

Script type	Description
Complex, high frequency	Usually applied to fact tables where loading the entire table every time is unfeasible, we need to apply additional logic so as to only load from the database those records that we need to get now. We will then combine those records with records that we already have in a QVD so as to create the final extract QVD.

It is important to analyze your loads for these characteristics because you need to appropriately combine or split scripts based on when you should be performing reloads. It is pointless, for example, to include a low frequency script along with a high frequency script in the one script module. Also, it would be good practice to have your simple scripts in a separate module to your complex scripts.

In an environment where there are data batch jobs running—for example, data warehouse ETL processes or financial account processing—we are often limited in our Qlik reloads to a certain time window. In those circumstances, we need to be even more certain that we are not loading unnecessary data.

Executing the extractors

Execution of the extractors should be very straightforward. Each of the scripts will connect to the data source, load the data, and write the data to a QVD in the QVD folder. At the end of execution, you should have an up-to-date set of QVDs for that data source, ready for transformations.

As a best practice, it is a good idea to also adopt a naming convention for the QVD files that are produced. It can be a good idea to prefix the files with a letter or abbreviation—such as E_ or EX_—so as to quickly distinguish an extractor QVD from any other. Including the table name in the filename is mandatory. Adding the data source or abbreviation would also be a good step, for example:

```
E_SalesData_Customer.qvd
```

Transforming data

The transformation step is where all the magic happens. We will take QVD data (and possibly simple Excel data) and transform that data into conformed dimensions and fact tables.

Creating a transformer and model folder structure

When transforming, we are going to make use of two folder structures. One will hold the transformation scripts and include files that will actually perform the transformations. The other folder structure will hold the QVDs that are output from those transformations. The reason we split into `Transformers` and `Models` is that, in theory, we should only have one transformer that creates a QVD, such as a conformed dimension, but that QVD may need to be written out to more than one `Model` subfolder.

The subfolders under `Transformers` and `Models` should be based on the modeling that you have performed in advance—either process or line-of-business based. Have a look at the following screenshot:

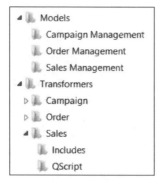

 It is worth remembering that when we are using a structured folder arrangement like this, then we should use relative paths in our script so that we can move files from development servers, where we will have established identical paths, to test or production servers without having to change the script.

Executing transformers

The only rule that we can specify about execution of transformers is that they need to be appropriately scheduled after the extractors that create the QVDs that the transformers depend on. Other than that, we will be applying different business rules to that data and those rules are context-specific.

This is a good point to add a reminder that when creating surrogate keys using the AutoNumber function, the keys generated can only be relied upon within the same script. We can't create surrogate keys in a QVD in one script and expect them to match surrogate keys created in a different script, even if the original keys were identical. We can, however, use a function such as Hash256 to create consistent surrogate keys between different loads, remembering to apply AutoNumber on them when loading data into the final application.

It is a good practice to apply a naming convention to the files that are generated in the Models folders. A common convention is to apply a prefix of FACT_ to a fact table and DIM_ to a dimension table. A source name would not be appropriate here as there may be multiple sources, so just the prefix plus the table name will suffice, for example:

```
FACT_Sales.qvd;
DIM_Organization.qvd;
DIM_Calendar.qvd;
```

For operational reasons, you may wish to partition your fact tables, so a partition indicator would be appropriate:

```
FACT_Sales_2012.qvd;
FACT_Sales_2013.qvd;
FACT_Sales_2014.qvd;
```

Loading data

If the transformation step has been carried out correctly, there should be very little to do in the UserApp folder other than to load the QVDs.

Creating a UserApp folder structure

As with the other operations, it is a best practice to create a UserApp folder structure with a subfolder structure that represents either the business process or line-of-business for the apps within it.

This whole UserApp folder can be mounted on a QlikView server, or each subfolder could be mounted separately.

Executing the load step

The load step could be as simple as the following:

```
LOAD * FROM ..\Models\Campaign Management\FACT_Sales.qvd (QVD);
LOAD * FROM ..\Models\Campaign Management\DIM_Organization.qvd (QVD);
LOAD * FROM ..\Models\Campaign Management\DIM_Calendar.qvd (QVD);
```

If the transformation step has been correctly implemented, then the tables should load (optimized load) and all the tables should be associated correctly with no synthetic keys.

The one allowable transformation (which does cause an unoptimized load) that might be performed in this step is the use of the AutoNumber function to generate surrogate keys. Using it at this stage will ensure that the generated keys will associate correctly as they are all being generated within the same script.

Mastering loading techniques

There are a few techniques for data loading that you need to spend some time learning to be a true master of the subject. We will have a look at some examples of them in this section.

It has already been mentioned that there is an excellent article on incremental load in both the help file and the reference manual. We will work through some examples here to help give you a good grounding in the subject. We will also look at a couple of other load techniques that will be very useful in your arsenal—binary load and partial load.

Loading data incrementally

The basic process of an incremental load is to have most of the data stored in QVDs on the server and then connect to the database to just obtain those records that are needed to update the QVDs to be concurrent.

Thinking about this, there must be a few pieces that are needed before we can implement the strategy:

- There will need to be an initial load of the data. This may be a complete load of the data table into one QVD or it may be a partitioned load of the data in several QVD files based on, most likely, a date field.

- We will need to be able to establish which field in the data identifies new or updated records. If the data is transactional, with only new rows being ever added, a sequential ID field will work for this purpose. A create date can also be used. However, if the data might be modified, we will need to have a date field that stores the modified date and time.

- We need to have a primary key for the data stored. We can use this value in an Exists clause or we can use it with joins to the source data to handle deletions.

- We will need to establish a way of storing the last time that we ran the extraction process. I like to use a variable for this as their values will persist with a given QVW file. However, we can also add some resilience by storing the value to a QVD.

Note that because we are using QVD files to persist data, it is a good idea to ensure that those QVD files are backed up on a regular basis. Although they can, in theory, be recreated from the original data source, it may be a lot quicker to just restore the files from an archive. In the case where the original data is no longer available, backup becomes even more critical.

Establishing the script for the basic process

The script for the basic process will be as follows:

1. Establish the date and time that the extraction was last run:

```
// When was the last load?

// Do we have a value in our variable?
If Len('$(vLastExtractionDate)')=0 Then

  // Do we have a QVD with the date?
  Let vFileLen=FileSize('..\QVD\Sales.Transactions.
LastQVDExtractionDate.qvd');
  if Len('$(vFileLen)')=0 Then
    // Set the last extraction date to an arbitrary date.
    // For example, the first day of this year
    Let vLastExtractionDate=
        TimeStamp(YearStart(Today()), 'YYYYMMDD HH:mm:ss');
  Else
    LastExtraction:
    Load
      LastExtractionDate
    From
```

```
            [..\QVD\Sales.Transactions.LastQVDExtractionDate.qvd] (QVD);

        Let vLastExtractionDate=Peek('LastExtractionDate');

        Drop Table LastExtraction;

        // It is possible that there was no date in the file
        if Len('$(vLastExtractionDate)')=0 Then
          Let vLastExtractionDate=YearStart(Today());
        End if
      End if

    End if
```

2. Record the current date and time:

```
    // Record the current date and time
    Let vCurrentExtractionDate=TimeStamp(Now(), 'YYYYMMDD HH:mm:ss');
```

3. Extract the records from the database where the modified date lies between the two dates:

```
    // Load the modified records
    Orders:
    LOAD OrderID,
         OrderDate,
         CustomerID,
         EmployeeID,
         Freight;
    SQL SELECT *
    FROM QVTraining.dbo.OrderHeader
    Where OrderDate >= '$(vLastExtractionDate)'
    and OrderDate < '$(vCurrentExtractionDate)';
```

4. Concatenate data from the stored QVD—if it exists—where we have not already loaded that row:

```
    // Concatenate QVD data - if it exists
    Let vFileLen=FileSize('..\QVD\E_Sales.Transactions.qvd');
    // Note that if the file doesn't exists, vFileLen will be blank
    If Len('$(vFileLen)')>0 Then

      Concatenate (Orders)
      Load *
      From
```

```
        [..\QVD\Sales.Transactions.LastQVDExtractionDate.qvd] (QVD)
        Where Not Exists(OrderID);

    End if
```

5. Store the entire table back to the QVD:

```
    // Store the data back to the QVD
    Store Orders into [..\QVD\E_Sales.Transactions.qvd] (QVD);

    Drop Table Orders;
```

6. Update the date and time for the last extraction:

```
    // Update the Last Extract date
    Let vLastExtractionDate=vCurrentExtractionDate;

    // Persist the value to QVD
    LastExtraction:
    Load
      '$(vLastExtractionDate)' As LastExtractionDate
    AutoGenerate(1);

    Store LastExtraction into [..\QVD\Sales.Transactions.
    LastQVDExtractionDate.qvd] (QVD);

    Drop Table LastExtraction;
```

Running an incremental load when data is only added

In many transactional systems, rows are only allowed to be added to the system. This is true for many bookkeeping systems. If you make a mistake, you are not allowed to edit or delete the row: you need to add a new transaction to correct the error.

In that case, our basic process is actually too complex. It will work perfectly as it is, but we can modify it to remove the Not Exists clause when loading the QVD. In theory, the QVD should never contain records that we have loaded within the date range. However, in the real world, it is always better to leave the check in place—Exists does not impact an optimized load from the QVD.

Loading incrementally when data might be modified

Other systems allow users to make adjustments directly to the transactional data. If they do, they will usually (although not universally!) have a field that contains the timestamp for when the modification was made.

In this case, our basic script should work perfectly. You just need to modify the extraction query and make sure that you include a `where` clause on the field that contains the modified date.

Handling deletions from the source system

It could be possible that the system that you are reading data from may allow transaction rows to be deleted. The problem for us is that we may have one of the deleted rows already stored in our QVD and we will get no indication (because there can be no modified date on a deleted row!) that the row is gone.

In that situation, we will add an `Inner Join` load of the primary key value from the data source, just after we have concatenated the rows from the QVD to the modified rows, but just before we store the data to QVD. The `Inner Join` load will remove any rows from the in-memory table that do not exist in the data source. We can then store the table to file and the deleted rows will no longer exist, for example:

```
// Check for deleted records
Inner Join (Orders)
SQL SELECT OrderID
FROM QVTraining.dbo.OrderHeader
Where OrderDate >= '20140101';
```

Note that there is a date on this. We are assuming here that previous years' data is stored in separate QVD files, so we would not be modifying this.

Handling situations where there is no modify date

Handling situations when there is no modify date present is tricky and you will need to utilize the assistance of the local DBA or application developer. Often the system will keep a log of changes and you may be able to query this log to obtain a list of the primary keys for the records that have changed in the period since the last extraction.

If there is no such set of records, you may be able to get the DBA or developer to create a database trigger that creates a separate record in a table when a row is inserted or modified. You can then query this table to obtain your list of primary keys.

Whatever the situation, there is often some kind of solution available.

Partially reloading only one part of the data model

Partial reload in QlikView is a very useful feature. It allows us to either completely replace a whole table in the data model or add new rows to a table, without modifying the data in any of the other tables. This can be used to really speed up data loads for more real-time applications.

A partial reload can be executed from the **File** menu in QlikView desktop, or by selecting the **Partial** checkbox when configuring the reload schedule in QlikView Server or publisher. When the partial reload is executed, it will completely ignore tables that are loaded normally and will not modify them in any way. However, tables that have a load statement prefixed with the `Replace` or `Add` keyword will be modified. During a normal reload, these keywords are ignored.

> Mapping tables will have been removed from the original data after the load, so if we are going to use them in the partial load, we will also need to reload them with the `Replace` keyword.

Replacing a table

To completely replace a whole table, we put the `Replace` keyword before the load statement for that table, for example:

```
Orders:
Replace
Load *
From [..\QVD\Orders.qvd] (QVD);
```

In this case, we assume that the QVD has already been updated (perhaps using the incremental load process) and we need to replace the whole table.

Adding new rows to a table

We can also add new rows to a table without having to remove the table. By placing the `Add` keyword before the load statement, we can leave what we have already loaded and then just add new rows. This can be an effective method of running incremental loads:

```
Orders:
Add
LOAD OrderID,
     OrderDate,
```

```
        CustomerID,
        EmployeeID,
        Freight;
SQL SELECT *
FROM QVTraining.dbo.OrderHeader
Where OrderDate>'$(vLastReloadTime)';
// Update the last reload time
Let vLastReloadTime=Timestamp(Now(), 'YYYYMMDD HH:mm:ss');
```

Managing script execution in partial reloads

In the last example, the final step was to update a variable. We may notice, however, that there was no option to say whether this should happen if the load is a partial load or a normal reload. All such assignments will happen either way. We can, however, manage this process by using the `IsPartialReload` function, which returns `true` or `false`, depending on the reload type:

```
If IsPartialReload() Then
  // Do partial reload stuff
Else
  // Do normal reload stuff
End if
```

Loading the content of another QVW

We can extract the entire contents of one QVW into another using a process called `Binary` load. The `Binary` statement takes the path to a QlikView QVW file and loads all of the data tables, symbol tables, and so forth into the loading document.

Because this process essentially creates a new data model in the loading document, there is a rule about `Binary`, in that it must be the very first statement executed in the script. Also, we can have only one `Binary` statement in any one application.

Once the `Binary` load has completed, you can then add additional script to do whatever you need to do. For example, you may wish to add a new table. Another thing that you may want to do is extract tables from the original data into QVD files. You may also want to drop tables.

One use case that I have for this is for the creation of several documents that have an identical data model but will have different UIs. You may want to give a more structured UI with locked down ability to add new objects, or export data, to one set of users, while giving a different UI with full collaboration and export to another set of users.

Henric Cronström from Qlik has written an excellent blog post on how the cache in QlikView Server works that indicates that because the QlikView Server cache is global, there are actually cache efficiencies that mean that this approach is not necessarily a bad thing for your server:

```
http://community.qlik.com/blogs/qlikviewdesignblog/2014/04/14/the-
qlikview-cache
```

Using QlikView Expressor for ETL

In June 2012, Qlik announced the purchase of Expressor Software. The press release talked about a **metadata intelligence** solution for data lineage and data governance, but what exactly is this product?

There are a couple of parts to the technology that are interesting. The main business of Expressor Software was the creation of an ETL tool that could connect to multiple different data sources, read data, and write it out to different locations. As part of this, they happened to create connectors that could connect to QlikView files—QVW, QVD, and QVX—and read both data and metadata from those files. They also created connectors to write out data in QVX format. Obviously, they felt that the QlikView market was worth going after.

Almost as a side effect, they were able to create the genesis of what is today the QlikView Governance Dashboard. Using their technology, they were able to connect to QlikView files and read enough metadata to create a full governance solution about a QlikView implementation. This was actually a big deal because governance was something that Qlik was getting beaten about with by competitors. Now there was an effective solution—Qlik liked it so much, they bought the company.

Introducing Expressor

Expressor is actually formed of three major components:

- **Studio**: This is the desktop tool used to build the ETL packages.
- **Data integration engine**: This is a GUI-free service that actually runs the packages, either on demand or on a schedule (it is a special version of this engine that is used by the Governance Dashboard).
- **Repository**: This is a source repository based on the subversion versioning and revision control system. This allows multiple developers to work on the same project.

As an ETL tool, Expressor Studio is quite intuitive for those who have experience with other ETL tools. It has some differences but many similarities.

Most ETL tools will have some kind of scripting/development language to enable the building of business rules to be applied to data during the transformation stage. With Expressor, that language is Lua:

```
http://www.lua.org
```

One thing that Expressor has, that makes it different, is its ability to partition data on the fly during data loads and make the data loading process multithreaded. Most Qlik developers will be familiar with data being loaded and processed one row at a time. Expressor will intelligently partition the entire load into separate sets of rows and then load each of these partitions simultaneously. This can make a huge impact on data load times, significantly reducing them.

Understanding why to use Expressor for ETL

Why, when QlikView and Qlik Sense already have a rich and powerful scripted ETL ability (as we have seen already), would we consider using Expressor instead?

The very simple answer is, control. By using Expressor or any other ETL tool to create the QVD or QVX data model layer, we are taking control of the data provisioning and centrally controlling it. Policies and security are put in place to make sure that QlikView users, no matter what ability, cannot get enterprise data other than via the QlikView data layer.

This could be seen as a downside by QlikView developers, who may be anxious to get applications built and deployed. However, granting such access to the enterprise data systems is not seen as a good practice in data governance. We extract the data, apply common business rules, and deploy the QlikView data layer from a central tool.

We can still, probably, make the argument that the data layer could still be provisioned using QlikView. However, there are still very good reasons to use Expressor instead:

- **It isn't QlikView**: The people who will be responsible for provisioning the data layer may not be QlikView developers. If they are experienced database developers, then they will be much more comfortable with Expressor than with QlikView scripts.
- **Speed**: The ability to automatically partition data loads and run multithreaded data loads make Expressor extremely quick for getting data.
- **Repository**: This helps in allowing multiple users to work on the same projects and gives versioning control to projects.

When reading on further, it will be useful to have a copy of Expressor installed on your workstation. The installation is very straightforward and the application will run, without license, on Windows 7 and 8 desktops.

Understanding workspaces, libraries, projects, and artifacts

Within QlikView Expressor, we will partition our own work into different organization units to better manage what we are doing. The terminology is very different from QlikView, so we need to understand that now.

Creating a workspace

A workspace is a collection of related projects. As with most things in this regard, there are no hard-and-fast rules about how many workspaces you need to create. Some organizations may have one. Others have one for every project. The norm is somewhere in between the two. We will probably have a workspace for related areas of ETL—perhaps by line-of-business or by data source.

There are two types of workspaces—standalone and repository. A standalone workspace will be stored locally on the developer's workstation. The repository workstation is stored in the Expressor repository. A standalone workspace can be converted to a repository workspace.

When we first open QlikView Expressor, we are presented with some options for workspaces:

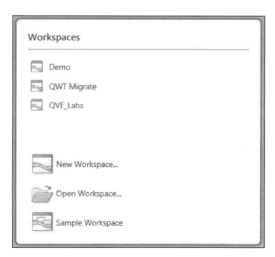

When we select the **New Workspace…** option, we are presented with the following screen:

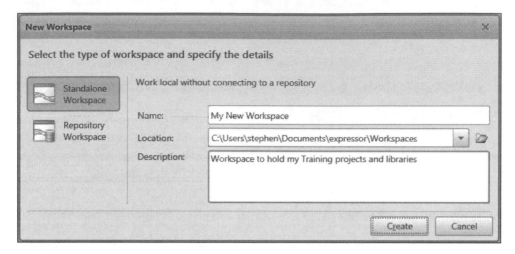

We can pick that our new workspace is either **Standalone Workspace** or **Repository Workspace**. If we select **Standalone Workspace**, we can specify the path to where the workspace will be stored. If we select **Repository Workspace**, we will give the connection information to where the repository is stored.

The repository is an Expressor implementation of the Subversion versioning system. This will be available with an Expressor server and is useful for multideveloper environments.

> Anyone who has used Subversion may note that the default port that Expressor uses is 53690, whereas the default Subversion port is 3690. Note that you should not update the version of svn that Expressor uses to the latest version available as you will probably break the repository.

Managing extensions

In QlikView Expressor, extensions are code libraries that allow Expressor to read and write to different file types and databases. There are some extensions that are installed out-of-box (such as the **QlikView Extension**), but we need to make sure that they are enabled. We need to access the **Manage Extensions…** option from the **Desktop** menu:

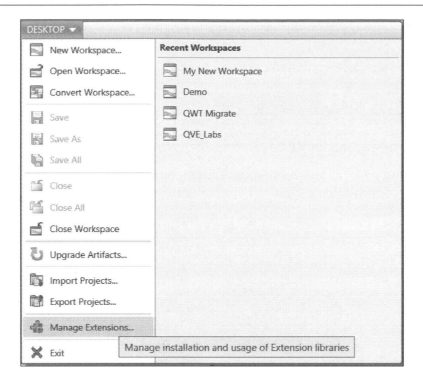

When we select the menu option, the **Manage Extensions** dialog opens:

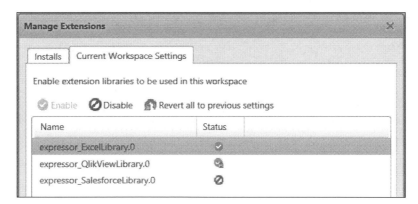

Within this window, we can use the **Current Workspace Settings** tab to enable or disable extensions. We can use the **Installs** tab to install a new extension or uninstall an existing one.

Working with libraries and projects

Basically, a library and a project are the same thing. Both of them are storage locations for other objects, such as data flows, connection information, and so forth. The only difference is that a library cannot contain a deployment package—only a project can produce one of these packages for the integration engine.

A library is used to hold objects, or artifacts as they are called in Expressor, which will be shared among other projects.

To add a new project or library, you can select the **Project** or **Library** buttons on the ribbon bar or you can right-click on the workspace name:

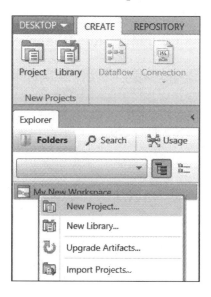

To add either, we just need fill in a name and description in the dialog and click on the **Create** button:

Note that the name of the project, as with all other artifacts, cannot have spaces in it. It can only consist of letters, numbers, and the underscore symbol. It must begin with a letter.

Understanding artifacts

When we create the project, we will see several folders—one for each of the types of artifact that may make up our project:

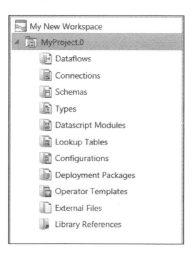

The different artifacts are as follows:

Artifact	Description
Dataflows	A **Dataflow** artifact is the actual flow of data, in one or more steps, that is the actual ETL process. They are defined via a drag-and-drop visual interface.
Connections	The **Connections** artifacts tell Expressor how to connect to the data. We can have file connections—basically a path to a folder, database connections, or QVX connector connections—a connection to a package that will generate a QVX.
Schemas	**Schemas** map the source or target data to the datatypes that are understood by Expressor. They may encapsulate transformations.
Types	The **Types** artifact will contain semantic type information about data. We have two types of semantic type, atomic—mapping data type and constraints for one piece of data, and composite—essentially mapping an entity of atomic types.

Artifact	Description
Datascript Modules	The artifacts will contain Lua functions that can be called from transformation scripts or can be used to implement a custom data read.
Lookup Tables	Not dissimilar to mapping tables in QlikView, these are locally stored tables that we can use to map values as part of a transformation.
Configurations	**Configurations** can contain multiple parameters that we can then use throughout the other artifacts. A large number of the settings can be parameterized. By having multiple configurations, it allows us to set up things such as `Dev/Test/UAT/Production` without having to reconfigure every artifact.
Deployment Packages	Packages are compiled dataflows, along with their associated artifacts, that will be executed by the integration engine—either scheduled or on demand.
Operator Templates	Within a dataflow, we can configure `Read`, `Write`, and `Transformation` operators. Once configured, we can save that operator as a template to be reused.
External Files	These are basically any type of file that might be used by data scripts.
Library References	When we add a reference to a library, all that library's artifacts will become available within the project as if they were part of the project.

Configuring connections

Before we can read or write data with QlikView Expressor, we need to configure a connection. We have a choice of three different connections. To add a connection, we can either right-click on the `Connections` folder under the project or we can click on the **Connection** button in the ribbon bar:

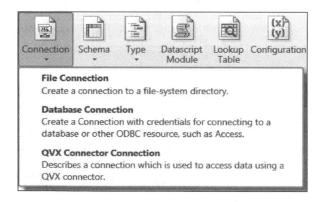

Here is a description of the different connection types:

Connection	Description
File	The **File** connection allows us to connect to a folder on the filesystem—either a local folder or a server share. We can use this folder to both read and write data. Typically though, read will be from one connection and write will be to another.
Database	The **Database** connection allows us to connect to different databases using an ODBC driver. Drivers are supplied for some of the more common databases and you can use an existing DSN for others. The connection can be read and/or write. As with the **File** connection, the typical implementation will have different connections for read and for write, or you will read from a database connection and write to a file connection.
QVX Connector	The **QVX** connection allows us to use the installed QlikView Expressor connector—the same one that you can use from within QlikView—to execute an existing package and read the QVX data. This is a read-only connection.

Configuring a File connection

Configuring a **File** connection is quite straightforward. We just need to know the path to the folder:

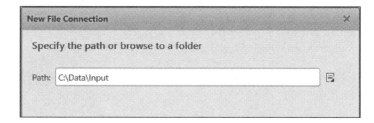

After clicking on the **Next** button, we can enter a name (remember, no spaces) for the connection and a description:

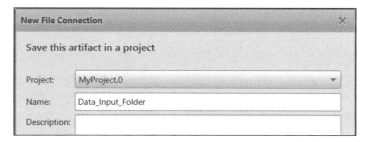

We continue adding **File** connections for every folder that we are going to read from or write to.

If we are going to have many projects reading from or writing to the same set of folders, the connections should be configured in a library.

Connecting to a database

The connection to a database is fairly straightforward. Expressor comes with drivers installed for the following:

- Apache Hive
- Cloudera Impala
- IMB DB2
- Microsoft SQL Server
- MySQL Enterprise Edition
- Oracle Database
- PostgreSQL
- Sybase ASE
- Teradata

In addition, Expressor will natively support (can use its own property dialogs to configure the connection) the following drivers if they are installed from the vendor websites:

- Informix
- MySQL Community Edition
- Netezza

Finally, Expressor will also support other ODBC drivers, but a DSN will need to be configured outside of Expressor.

To add the database connection, we first need to select the correct driver to use:

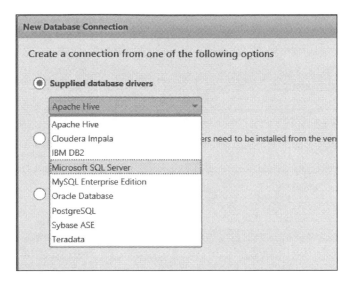

We then fill in the database specific connection information (Expressor will test the connection before allowing you to continue) and then give the connection a name.

Creating a QVX Connector Connection

The **QVX Connector Connection** uses the same connector that we would use in QlikView to connect to an on-demand package. The only packages that can be used are those that will generate a QVX output.

There is a slightly different approach here in that we name the connection before we enter the connection details:

When we click on the **Create** button, Expressor will go ahead and save the connection and open the properties for us to edit.

We select the **QlikViewExpressorConnector.exe** option as the connector to use (you may also see the governance connector in the list, if you have the Governance Dashboard installed on the same machine). Click on the **Actions** button and select **Build Connection String**:

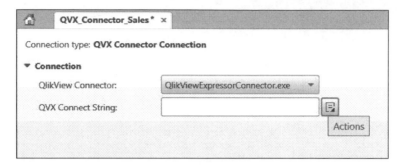

The following instructions are seen in the dialog box:

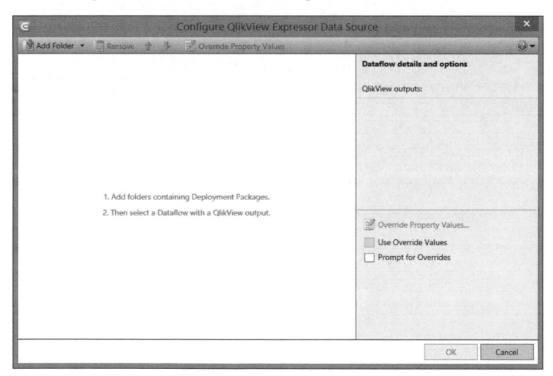

The instructions are as follows:

1. **Add folders containing Deployment Packages**: Click on the **Add Folder** button and browse for a folder that contains a workspace (the default folder for workspaces is `c:\users\username\documents\expressor\Workspaces`) and select a `Project` folder that contains a package (the dialog won't let you select a folder unless there is a package in it).

2. Then select a Dataflow with a QlikView output:

Configuring types and schemas

As we just mentioned, we have two kinds of types, **Atomic** and **Composite**.

Adding additional Atomic types

At its simplest, an **Atomic** type is simply a basic type such as string, date, number, and so forth. We can extend these basic types by adding constraints, such as length or value, to those basic types—implementing business rules.

We add a new **Atomic** type by right-clicking on the `Types` folder under the project and/or by clicking on **Type** in the ribbon bar:

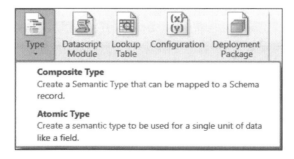

We can now give a name to our **Atomic** type and Expressor will open the properties page for us to enter basic type and constraint information:

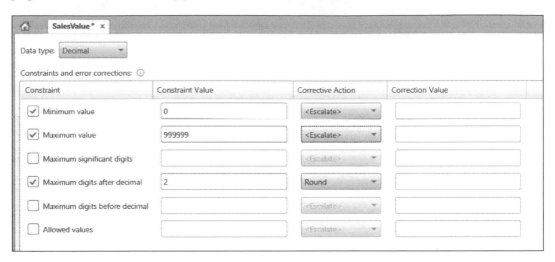

Depending on the base datatype, we can set different levels of constraint. If the constraint rule fails, we can set different corrective actions to be performed. The default is that the type should **Escalate** the breach of the constraint, which would normally throw an error in the dataflow.

Once we have set our constraints, we can save the **Atomic** type.

Creating Composite types

A **Composite** type is a collection of types that we can map our data onto. So, for example, we can create an order **Composite** type that represents exactly how we think an order should look. When we import external data, we can map that external data to our Composite type. By mapping everything to a **Composite** type, which can also encapsulate data constraints, we ensure consistency.

We create a **Composite** type by right-clicking on the Types folder under the project or by clicking on **Type** on the ribbon bar, as with the **Atomic** type. We name the artifact as usual and Expressor will open the properties window:

We can click on the **Add** button to add a new **Atomic** type to our **Composite** type:

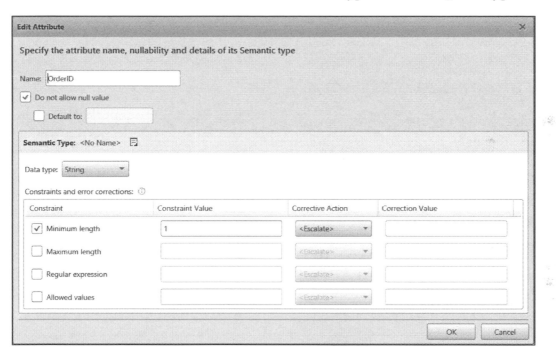

For each attribute, we can assign a datatype and any constraints. We can also assign a **Semantic Type** (**Atomic** type) that we have previously configured (**Shared**) or create a new **Atomic** type (**New (local)** that will be added to the current project):

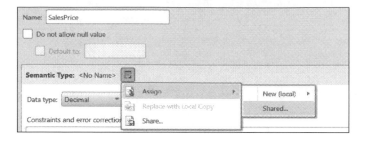

If we do assign a **Semantic Type** to the field, the constraint options will become grayed out because the constraints will be inherited from the **Atomic** type.

Configuring a schema

A schema represents the data that is being read or being written. We can have different types of schema for different types of data. For example, text data is handled differently than database data, which is handled differently from QlikView data. A schema can be configured from either the data itself—which is the usual way—or from a **Composite** type that we have already configured.

To configure a schema, we can either right-click the schemas folder under the project or click on the **Schema** button in the ribbon bar:

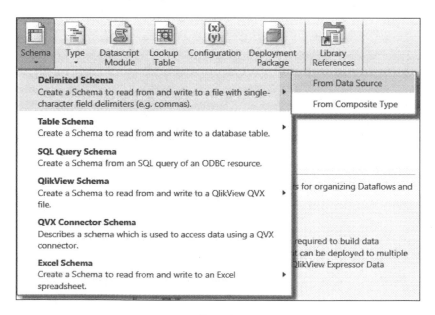

A wizard will open that will allow us to configure the schema from the data. For file sources, we can either browse to the file or we can just paste some sample rows (browsing for the file will just load the first 10 rows):

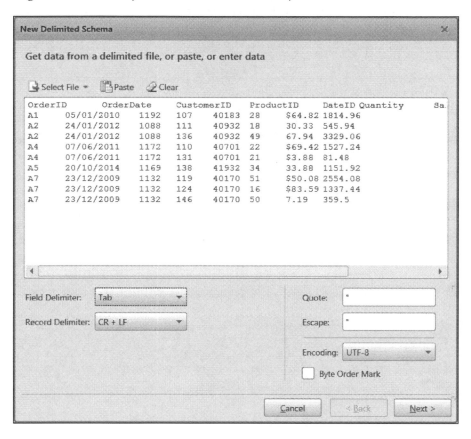

We then specify the **Field Delimiter** value and the **Record Delimiter** value, any quote information, and the **Encoding** type. When we click on **Next**, the dialog will preview the data and show us the column headings. We can use the first row of the data for column headings by clicking on the **Set All Names from Selected Row** button:

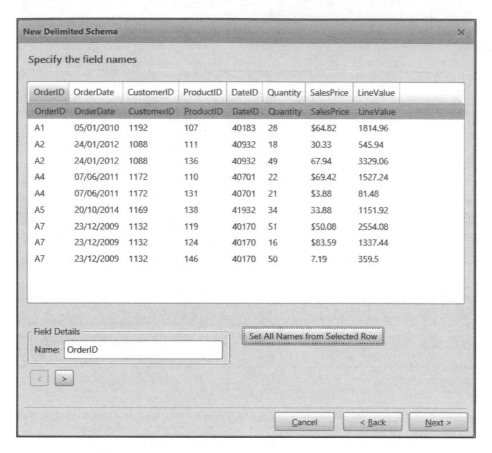

After clicking on **Next** again, we can give a name to the schema (usual artifact name rules apply) and click on **Finish** to save the schema. Once we have saved the schema, we need to edit the details—we right-click on it and select **Open**:

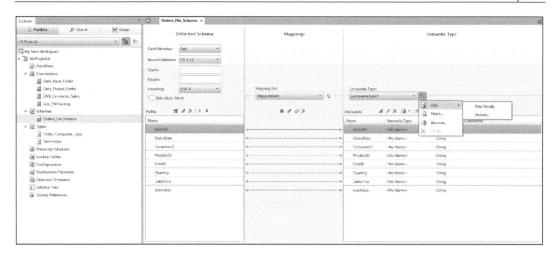

We note that the schema has been assigned a generated **Composite** type (**CompositeType1**) and that the input fields are mapped to it. However, we want to assign our **Composite** type that we have already configured.

On clicking the **Actions** button to the right-hand side of **CompositeType1**, we can select to add a **Shared** type. When we select our **Composite** type, we will be prompted to generate a new mapping:

We would normally choose **Yes** to allow the system to make the mappings for us:

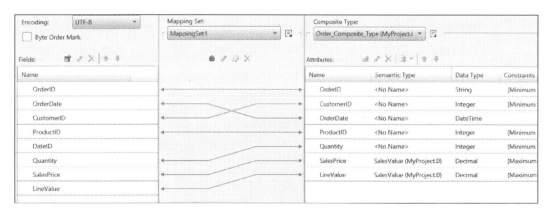

We do need to tweak a couple of the mappings. If you click on the link from **OrderDate to OrderDate** and then click on the pencil icon above it (or just double-click on the link), we can enter the correct format string for Expressor to interpret the text:

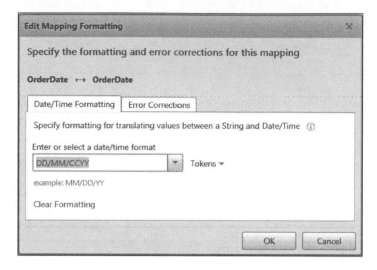

In this case, the data is in UK date format, so we need to specify **DD/MM/CCYY**, where **D** represents day, **M** represents month, **C** represents century, and **Y** represents year.

We should also edit the mapping for the sales price field because there is a dollar symbol. Expressor allows us to take care of that:

We can now select the **CompositeType1** type from the drop-down menu and use the **Actions** button to delete it. Hit the **Save** button to save the schema.

This schema that we have just created can be used to either read or write text files. In fact, it is a good idea to design your schemas based on the required output rather than the inputs.

Creating and packaging a basic dataflow

Now that we have configured connections, types, and schemas, we can create a simple dataflow to move data from a text object into a QVX file for consumption by QlikView.

Understanding the dataflow toolbox

When creating a dataflow, we have a toolbox available of different operators that we can use within the dataflow. There are four categories:

- Inputs
- Outputs
- Transformers
- Utility

Inputs

The **Inputs** toolbox contains eight options (depending on what extensions you have turned on), each used to read data:

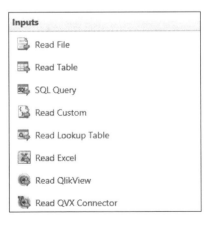

This table describes each of the read operators:

Operator	Description
Read File	The **Read File** operator will connect to a file using one of the file connections and one of the schemas that we have built
Read Table	The **Read Table** operator will connect to a table using a database connection and read the data
SQL Query	The **SQL Query** operator will execute a query that has been defined in a schema against a database connection
Read Custom	**Read Custom** allows you to run a data script to read and generate data that can be passed to another operator — this is an extremely powerful option
Read Lookup Table	This operator reads a lookup table that has been populated by another dataflow step
Read Excel	This is part of the Excel extension that allow us to read data from Excel files
Read QlikView	This QlikView operator is part of the QlikView extension and can read from QVW, QVD, and QVX
Read QVX Connector	The **Read QVX Connector** operator can read data from a QVX connector

Outputs

The **Outputs** toolbox contains nine operators (depending on what extensions you have turned on), each used to write data in different ways:

This table describes each of the write operators:

Operator	Description
Write File	The **Write File** operator will write data to a text file in a folder specified by a file connection.
Write Table	**Write Table** uses a database connection to write a database table. We can specify that a table should be created in the database if it does not exist.
Write Teradata PT	This allows you to write data to Teradata using **Parallel Transporter**. Note that you will need to download additional client libraries—TTU v13.10 or later.
Write Custom	**Write Custom** allows you to write data out using a data script. This is a powerful feature.
Write Lookup Table	This is used to populate an Expressor lookup table—not unlike a QlikView mapping table.
Write Parameters	This allows us to generate a `parameters` file that can be used to pass parameters to other options in the dataflow.
Trash	This is an interesting option—**Trash** takes an input and does nothing with it, it is as if you had thrown it away. It can be useful during development and troubleshooting.
Write Excel	This uses the Excel extension to create Excel output.
Write QlikView	This uses the QlikView extension to generate QVX output.

Transformers

Transformers are operators that allow us to transform data. As such, they will form a central part of almost any dataflow. There are six operators available:

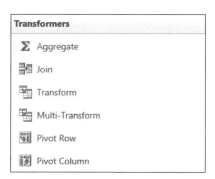

This table describes each of the transformer operators:

Operator	Description
Aggregate	This operator allows you to perform grouping and aggregation on data
Join	The **Join** operator allows us to join—inner, left, right, and outer—data tables together
Transform	This is the core transformation operator, where we perform many of the applications of business rules
Multi-Transform	The multi operator will allow multiple transformations to be performed and up to nine different output streams
Pivot Row	This is similar to the `CrossTable` function in QlikView that takes data in columns and generates a new row for each column
Pivot Column	The **Pivot Column** operator is the opposite of **Pivot Row**—it takes multiple rows and creates one row with multiple columns

Utility

The **Utility** operators contain several operators that operate on data in ways that are not transformative, but are useful in an ETL system. There are six operators available:

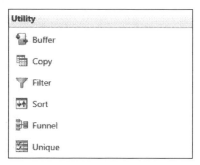

This table describes each of the utility operators:

Operator	Description
Buffer	This is a useful operator where there may be issues with the timing of arrival of records to a multi-input operator (such as a **Join**). It will temporarily buffer data to disk until the next operator is ready to process it.
Copy	The **Copy** operator will take one input stream and allow us to split that into up to 10 output streams, each containing the same data.

Operator	Description
Filter	The **Filter** operator allows us to create rules to filter data into multiple different output streams.
Sort	The **Sort** operator does what we expect: it sorts the data. We can assign a certain amount of memory for the operator to use as well as disk storage if it needs it.
Funnel	**Funnel** is similar to QlikView's **Concatenate** but more like **SQL Union**—it accepts multiple input streams and returns the union in one output stream.
Unique	The **Unique** operator will return one row for multiple values of a key field.

Creating the dataflow

We add a new dataflow in a similar manner to other artifacts—right-click or use the ribbon. When the dataflow is first added, a blank workspace appears:

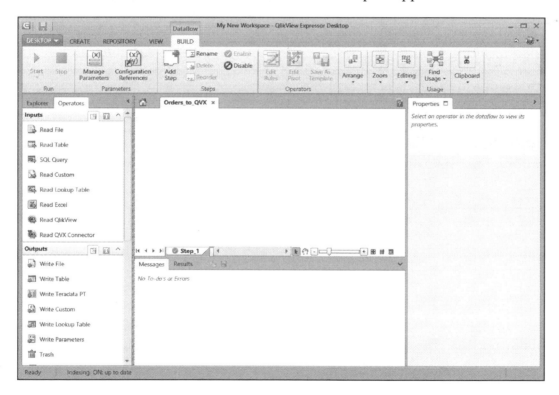

To the left-hand side, we have the operator panel. We can click-and-drag any operator from the panel onto the dataflow workspace:

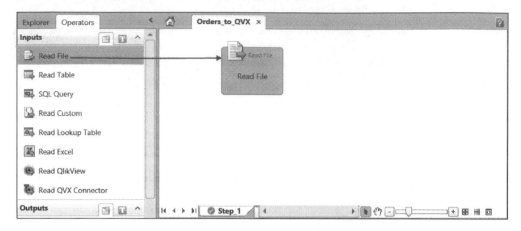

On the right-hand side is a properties panel that allows us to set the properties for the currently selected object.

Configuring a Read File operator

After we have dragged an operator such as **Read File** onto the dataflow, we need to modify its properties:

The properties that you need to fill out are as follows:

Property	Description
Name	Free text name that we want to apply to the operator.
Connection	The file connection from which you want to read the file. All available connections will be in the dropdown.
Schema	The name of the schema that you will use.
Type	The **Composite** type that the schema will map to.
Mapping	The mapping set that will be used.
File name	The name of the file.
Quotes	Choose **May have quotes** or **No quotes** – depending on whether the file will have quotes or not.
Skip rows	If your text file has a header row, you will want to set this to 1.
Error handling	Either abort the dataflow, skip the record, reject the record, skip remaining records, or reject the remaining. Rejected records are put out the rejected records stream.
Show errors	Set whether the errors are shown or not.

Adding a Transformation operation

If we drag a **Transformation** operator from the **Transformation** panel onto the dataflow, we can then click on the output of the **Read File** operator and drag the mouse to the input of the **Transformation** operator:

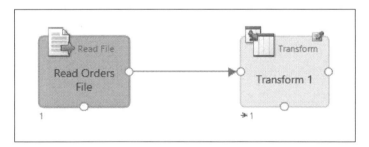

The **Read File** operator should now change to green because it is complete and doesn't need us to do anything else. If it doesn't, we need to look at the messages panel to find out what we have forgotten!

If we click on the **Edit Rules** button on the **Transformation** operator's properties panel (or double-click on the **Transformation** operator), then the edit rules dialog opens:

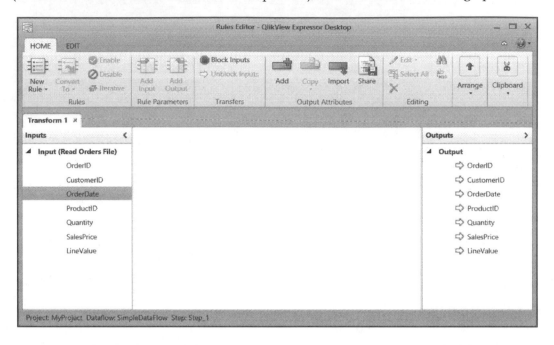

The list of fields on the left-hand side is the list from the incoming stream. The list on the right-hand side is the list of fields that will be output. With nothing else changed, we see that the lists match. Every input field will be output. The white arrow to the left of each output field indicates that they are being output because they are input fields.

We can block an input field from being output by selecting that field in the left-hand side list and clicking on the **Block Inputs** button on the ribbon bar. If we do that for the **LineValue** field, the lists will look like this:

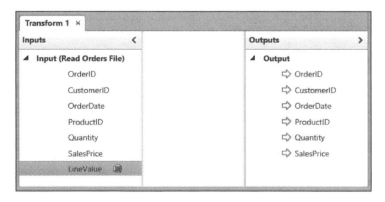

If we want to actually output a field that contains the line value, we can calculate it from the **Quantity** and **SalesPrice** fields. We need to first click on the **Add** button on the ribbon bar to add a new attribute to the **Outputs** list—for example, **LineSalesAmount**.

We then click on the **New Rule** button on the ribbon bar and select **Expression Rule**. We drag **Quantity** and **SalesPrice** onto the **Add Input** side of the rule and we drag our new **LineSalesAmount** field onto the **Add Output** side of the rule. In the expression area, we can replace `nil` with `Input.Quantity*Input.SalesPrice`:

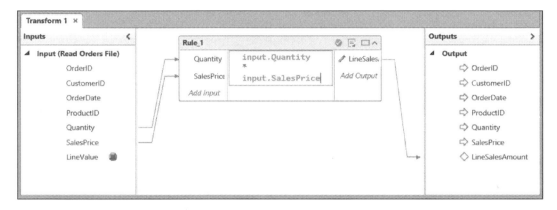

Creating a QVX output

Once we have configured the **Transformation** operator, we can now drag a **Write** QlikView operator from the **Outputs** panel to dataflow and connect the output of the **Transformation** operator to the input of the **Write** QlikView operator.

 QVX is an open format to allow any developer to extract data into a file or data stream that QlikView and Qlik Sense can read. Like QVD files, QVX files only contain one table of data. At time of writing, the only Qlik format that Expressor can write is QVX.

We then set the properties of the output. Now, we haven't defined a schema for the output file, but Expressor has a nice facility where it can generate a new schema from the output of the previous operator. Clicking on the **Actions** button to the right-hand side of the **Schema** dropdown gives us a menu where we can select this option.

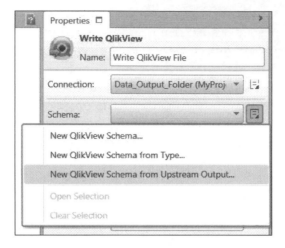

Once all the operators have been configured, they should all turn green. Now we can save it and test it. If all goes well, we should have a QVX file in the output folder.

Packaging the dataflow

Now that we have a working dataflow, we can package it up.

We simply add a new deployment package to the project and we can drag our dataflow into the **Compiled Dataflows** section.

That's it! The package can now be used in Expressor connectors and also with the integration engine on a schedule.

Summary

This chapter has been a very important one from a data loading point of view. As a QlikView developer, you should now have a great understanding of QVDs and why and how we should use them to implement an ETL approach. The folder structure model here will support an implementation from small business to enterprise.

We also looked at implementing really important techniques such as incremental load and partial load.

Finally, we had an introduction to Qlik's ETL tool, QlikView Expressor, and understand why it might be implemented instead of the QVD approach. There is a lot more to learn about Expressor and hopefully this introduction will spur you on to learn more about the product.

In the next chapter, we will learn about best practices around data governance in QlikView. We will also see more about Expressor's technology when we look in detail at the Governance Dashboard.

4
Data Governance

"The most valuable commodity I know of is information."

— *Gordon Gekko, Wall Street*

Do you know how many QlikView applications are being used in your organization? Do you know who is using these applications? Do you know where all the data comes from for those applications? How are people calculating different metrics?

The answer to all of these questions might actually be, "Yes, yes I do." If so, it may be that you already have a data governance strategy in place or you just might not need one. If everything is tightly controlled within a small group of QlikView developers, perhaps a QlikView Center of Excellence, then you probably have a good grip on this. However, if your organization is less structured than that and you have many QlikView developers spread around, all creating their own applications, then you will need to think about answering these questions.

Data governance starts at the top of the organization. Without serious management buy-in to the process, most efforts at data governance will inevitably fail. Whatever team is assigned to the task of creating a data governance plan will have to take many facets into consideration, and the implementation of Qlik is just one of these.

The first part of establishing a good data governance plan for Qlik is to develop a good ETL process (see *Chapter 3, Best Practices for Loading Data*) to ensure that developers have a set of well-formed dimensional models (see *Chapter 2, QlikView Data Modeling*) to use. You should ensure that you understand these concepts. Of course, another part of establishing good data governance is to ensure that developers are using such data sources, and this is something that we will look at in this chapter.

After reviewing some basic concepts that you should be aware of, we will look at how developers can establish metadata in their QlikView applications that can help users to know which fields they are using when they create their own charts.

We will go on to discuss the concept of data lineage and how this applies in QlikView, especially in the Governance Dashboard. This is QlikView's free tool that utilizes the Expressor technology to scan your applications and source files to tell you where the information comes from. The Dashboard also scans the QlikView server logs to tell us exactly what users are doing with our applications.

 We should be aware that in some countries, the monitoring of employee behavior might be subject to legal restriction or subject to industrial relation agreements.

The following are the topics we'll cover in this chapter:

- Reviewing basic concepts of data governance
- Establishing descriptive metadata
- Understanding lineage information in QlikView
- Deploying the QlikView Governance Dashboard

Reviewing basic concepts of data governance

We already should know enough, technically, to handle all of the QlikView elements in this chapter. Therefore, the only element that I want to review is the whole concept of metadata.

Understanding what metadata is

So, what exactly is metadata and how does it apply to QlikView?

The prefix **meta** means several things, depending on how it is used. In the area of Epistemology, the study of knowledge, meta simply means *about*. So, metadata is information about data: where the data has come from, who owns the data, who produced the data, when the data was produced, what format the data is in, and so forth.

One piece of data can have quite a lot of metadata. Traditionally, metadata has been broken down into two types: **structural** and **descriptive**. A third type, **administrative**, is critical for correct data governance.

Each of these types can be broken down into many more subtypes, but we really need to be careful about how far we go with the process. We want to create some metadata, but we don't want to spend 2 years creating it. QlikView does a lot to help us here, but we will have to do some work.

Structural metadata

Structural metadata gives us information about how the data hangs together. At a simple level, the table viewer in QlikView is structural metadata. We can get additional information from the **Tables** tab in **Document Properties**, and we can export this information to tab delimited text files:

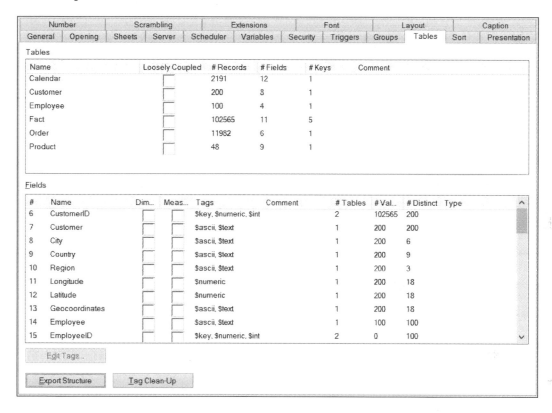

As QlikView developers and designers, this information is very important to us. We need to know how the data model is built and how everything hangs together to be able to build the most effective QlikView applications.

Other important structural information is where the data comes from and what are the data sources, files, and so forth that make up the data. Knowing this data lineage information allows us to make decisions on the impact any changes to these sources might have. We can also analyze to see where data sources are shared among multiple applications so that we can make decisions about the reuse of data via QVD. Knowing which files are in use also allows us to work out which files are not in use and either clean up the file structure or ask questions about why these files aren't in use.

Descriptive metadata

Descriptive metadata is any additional data that we add to our applications to give more information and context about the application and the individual elements of the data.

This information is very useful to application designers and business users who need to know more about what they are using. It is also useful to add commentary about what we are doing so that we can review and recall at a later date.

This information can be added in multiple places in QlikView, and we will review this in the *Establishing descriptive metadata* section.

Administrative metadata

Administrative metadata is, as it sounds, information of interest to system administrators and managers—information about where applications reside, who can access an application, who is actually using them, and what they are being used for. All of this data is available from QlikView logs and system information, but it is not always easy to collate. Obviously, a QlikView application that can collate this information for us will be very useful.

Establishing descriptive metadata

Structural and administrative metadata can all be derived from the system. The only area where we can add value, and it can be a lot of value, is with descriptive metadata. In this section, we are going to look at the following areas:

- Adding document-level information
- Renaming fields
- Tagging fields
- Adding field comments
- Renaming, tagging, and commenting fields in script
- Commenting in charts
- Extracting metadata

Adding document-level information

Document-level information gives users information about the application, for example, what its purpose is, who created it, and anything that would be useful for users to know about.

We can add this information in two places: **Document Properties** and via **Qlik Management Console**.

Documents without any additional metadata

If a document has no metadata added, a user will see this in AccessPoint:

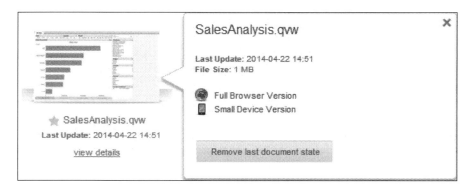

When a user opens that application, the tab that they see in their browser will just have the name of the QVW file:

Later, we will see that adding some descriptive metadata will give more information to the users.

Document Properties

Within the **General** tab in the **Document Properties** window, there are two information boxes that can be populated:

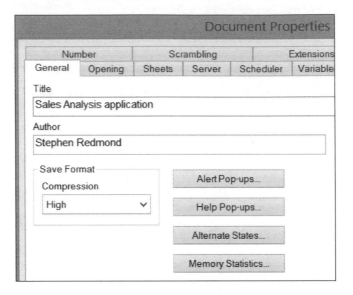

If you populate the **Title** box, then this will immediately replace the full path that is displayed in the QlikView desktop window caption. It will also be displayed in the browser tab, which is friendlier for users:

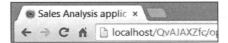

The author's name will not be displayed to users, but does give information to developers who might have to maintain this application later.

Management Console

Within the QMC, we can add additional information for users via the **User Documents** tab under **Documents**:

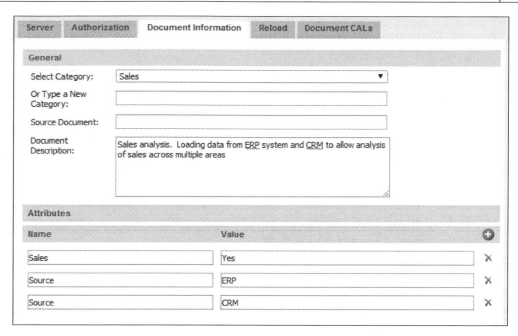

You can also specify this data using a QlikView Publisher task that will update it on the server.

Once we have specified this information, it will appear in AccessPoint:

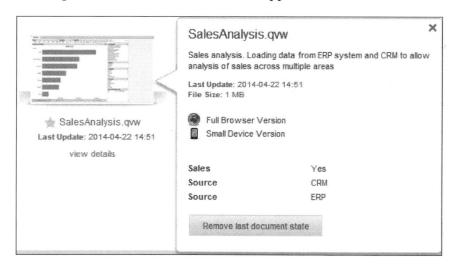

Users can now also choose to search applications in AccessPoint using the attributes that have been specified:

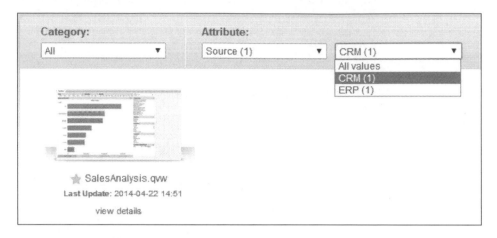

Naming and renaming fields

Naming and renaming fields may seem a very simple thing to do, but it is the easiest way to help users understand the content of any field in a dataset and is the easiest and most straightforward descriptive metadata used to enable the fields to describe themselves.

As an example, consider the SAP ERP system. In SAP, many of the field names are 5-letter abbreviations of German words. For example, the customer number field is called KUNNR. Even in German, this is not easy for business users to understand the content just by looking at the field name.

We know that we should rename this field to make it more understandable, but what name should we call it? `Cust_No.`, `Customer#`? These are common names that developers might use but again, they are abbreviations that are not so easy for business users to understand easily. In QlikView, there is no reason why this field should not be renamed `Customer Number`.

We should always rename our fields to make them understandable. Abbreviations should be avoided, unless they are so well known that there is no question of anything being misunderstood. Renaming fields can be handled in several ways, so we need to pick the way that is the easiest to implement for us as developers and most maintainable for the business.

Guidelines to rename fields

We don't need to be too prescriptive here but it is important to have some kind of naming guidelines for fields that all developers in an organization will use. By being consistent, we make it easier for our users to find what they are looking for and understand what they are looking at. Of course, it can be useful for developers too.

We have the following three types of fields that we need to consider for naming:

- Dimensions
- Key fields
- Measures

Dimensions

Probably the most common field type in our dataset, dimensions, shouldn't need to be specially identified to users but they should be named using descriptive language, including spaces and punctuation where appropriate.

Key fields

We should pick a character, or a set of characters, to prefix all of our key fields. This is a good discipline to have for the following reasons:

- It identifies the fields as key fields very quickly
- It differentiates them from dimension fields
- Fields are grouped together alphabetically
- A field that we have tagged as a key field but is not used as a key field can be spotted quickly
- A field that we have not tagged as a key field but is used as a key field can also be spotted
- Such fields can be automatically hidden from users

A good choice for this purpose is often the % character. QlikView allows it as the first character of a field name and it will not be commonly used for any other fields.

Typically, as these fields are not meant to be quickly identifiable to business users, key fields will not include spaces and appropriate punctuation. Instead, proper case might be used where there are multiple words.

We can hide fields that have a common first set of characters from users by setting the `HidePrefix` variable, for example, to `%`. We can also tag fields with the `$hidden` tag, and they will also be hidden from users.

Measures

Many of the reasons to prefix key field names will also apply for measures.

A good choice for this purpose is the `#` character because it is not commonly used for other fields and it often symbolizes numbers to people.

Although not critical, it can often be a good idea to use underscores instead of spaces and not use punctuation in measure field names. This further differentiates them from dimensions and can make them a little easier to handle in expressions (because we won't need to use square brackets).

Renaming fields using As

Renaming fields using `As` is something that we should already know about; it is something that we will probably have used in every script that we have written. We know that we can simply rename a field in the load script by adding the `As` keyword followed by the new field name:

```
Load
    Field1 As %NewFieldName1,
    Field2 As #New_Field_Name_2,
    Field3 As [New Field Name 3],
    Field4 As "New Field Name 4",
```

We know that if we want to add spaces into the new field name, we must enclose the new name in either square brackets or double quotes. Square brackets are often preferred as they do not confuse with text qualifiers.

Using Qualify

`Qualify` is used to automatically rename all of the fields in a table by prefixing the fields with the name of the table and a period (`.`).This can help a lot where there are very many similarly named fields in several tables that cause invalid associations and synthetic keys.

For example, suppose that we have a table like the following:

```
TABLE1:
Load
    KeyField,
    DimField1,
    DimField2,
    DimField3,
    Measure1,
    Measure2
From DataTable.qvd (qvd);
```

We can add a Qualify statement at any time before the load statement in the following manner:

```
QUALIFY *;

TABLE1:
Load
    KeyField,
    DimField1,
    DimField2,
    DimField3,
    Measure1,
    Measure2
From DataTable.qvd (qvd);
```

This will result in an in-memory table like the following:

The * symbol here is interesting because this is actually a field list, but is using a wildcard. Instead of the * symbol, we can issue a Qualify statement in the following manner:

```
QUALIFY DimField1, DimField2, DimField3;
```

This will result in a table like the following:

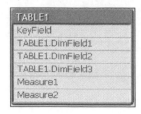

We can see that only the fields in this list are now qualified.

Normally, the list of fields that we want to qualify, which contains most of the fields in a table, is much longer than the list of fields that we might not want qualified, which has just the key fields. So, instead of identifying these fields that we want to have qualified in the list (which would be very long), we will issue the full query `Qualify *` but then add another statement with an `UnQualify` statement to tell QlikView which fields to not add the table name to. This works something like the following:

```
QUALIFY *;
UNQUALIFY KeyField;

TABLE1:
Load
    KeyField,
    DimField1,
    DimField2,
    DimField3,
    Measure1,
    Measure2
From DataTable.qvd (qvd);
```

The preceding code will result in a table like the following:

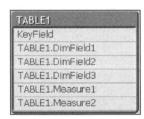

Of course, in normal practice, we will rename our fields and prefix key fields with %. This means that we can issue an UnQualify statement with a wildcard so as to stop qualifying key fields automatically. This is shown in the following example:

```
QUALIFY *;
UNQUALIFY [%*];

TABLE1:
Load
   KeyField as %Table1Key,
   DimField1 as [Dim Field 1],
   DimField2 as [Dim Field 2],
   DimField3 as [Dim Field 3],
   Measure1 as #Measure1,
   Measure2 as #Measure2
From DataTable.qvd (qvd);
```

Another thing that we should consider is that it is not just field names that should be changed when we use Qualify; we should also consider whether table names should be renamed to be friendlier to business users.

As a final note on Qualify, many developers will avoid it because they do not like the field names that are created, which can cause other problems in the script. One place that even these developers will like to use it is where there are several well-known fields that recur in every table that you have in your dataset. By adding a Qualify statement with just these fields, we can avoid the invalid associations that might be caused when loading these tables, for example:

```
QUALIFY CreateUser, CreateDate, ModifyUser, ModifyDate, Version;
```

Renaming fields using Rename

Instead of renaming fields while being loaded using the As keyword, we can also rename fields after they have been loaded using the Rename function.

The statement takes the following form:

```
Rename OldFieldName to NewFieldName;
```

So, if we take the example of the simple table previously discussed, we can rename the fields in the following manner:

```
TABLE1:
Load
   KeyField,
```

```
    DimField1,
    DimField2,
    DimField3,
    Measure1,
    Measure2
From DataTable.qvd (qvd);
RENAME Field KeyField to %KeyField;
RENAME Field Measure1 to #Measure1;
RENAME Field DimField1 to [Dim Field 1];
```

We can also rename a table using the following statement:

```
RENAME Table TABLE1 to Table1;
```

Using a mapping table to rename fields

One of the features that was added a couple of versions ago was the ability to rename fields using a mapping table along with the Rename function.

We know that a mapping table, usually used with ApplyMap, is a table that has the following features:

- It has only two fields, a lookup field and a return field
- The names of the fields are not important, only the order is
- It is loaded with the Mapping keyword

The typical use of a mapping table is that the first field will be some kind of numeric ID and the second field is a text value that will be returned by the mapping. In the case of a mapping table to be used with Rename, the first column will have the old field name and the second column will have the new field name. The syntax is as follows:

```
Rename Fields Using MappingTableName;
```

So again, let's use the previous table:

```
TABLE1:
Load
    KeyField,
    DimField1,
    DimField2,
    DimField3,
    Measure1,
    Measure2
From DataTable.qvd (qvd);
```

```
Rename_Map:
Mapping
Load * Inline [
old_name, new_name
KeyField, %KeyField
DimField1, Dim Field 1
DimField2, Dim Field 2
DimField3, Dim Field 3
Measure1, #Measure1
Measure2, #Measure2
];

RENAME Fields using Rename_Map;
```

The advantage of this method is that we, as developers, can load field names in whatever way we want but then create a data source, perhaps in Excel, to allow a business user to name the fields as they want.

Tagging fields

Another way of delivering information to users about fields is with the use of tags. Tags are textual information, usually of a single word, that can help users discover further information about a particular field. In fact, QlikView will already tag fields with additional metadata when these fields are loaded.

Users can see these tags in the **Fields** tab of the sheet properties by hovering over a field name:

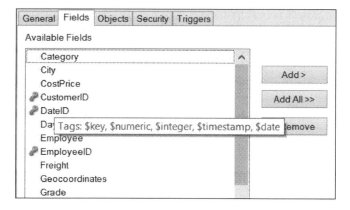

Tags can also be seen in the **Table Viewer** window as well as in the **Tables** tab of **Document Properties**:

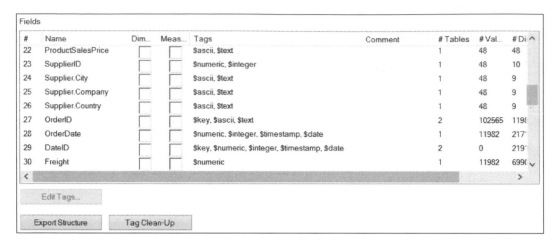

There are a number of tags that will be added by the system that we can't change. Others are added that we can change. We can also add our own tags that are not system tags. System tags are identified by a $ symbol at the beginning of the tag name.

The system tags that you can't change are as follows:

Tag	Description
$system	This indicates a system field such as $Field, $Table, and $Info
$key	This identifies that the field is an associative key field
$keypart	This indicates that the field is part of a synthetic key
$synthetic	This identifies that the field is a synthetic key

The other system fields that might be added automatically, but can be modified in the script, are listed in the following table:

Tag	Description
$hidden	This indicates that the field is hidden by default
$numeric	This indicates that all field values (excluding nulls) are numbers
$integer	All of the non-null field values are integers; obviously, if a field has this tag then it will have $numeric tag too

Tag	Description
$text	This identifies that none of the field values are numbers
$ascii	All of the field values will contain only the standard ASCII characters; they are not Unicode
$date	All of the values are dates or can be interpreted as dates (as with an integer that might be a date)
$timestamp	All of the values are timestamps or numeric values that could be a timestamp

There are additional two system tags that we can either add via the script or checkboxes in the **Tables** tab of **Document Properties**:

Tag	Description
$dimension	This identifies the field as a dimension. This means that the field will automatically sort to the top in dimension lists in the client.
$measure	This indicates that the field is a measure field. The field will be sorted to the top in the **Expression Editor** field dropdown.

We can also add our own tags to a field. This metadata will both be available to a user and can also be extracted into a tool such as the Governance Dashboard.

Using the Tag statement to tag a field

We can add either system tags or our own tags to a field using the Tag statement. There are many reasons to add our own tags, not the least of which is to add additional information to help users understand where the field has come from. For example, we might rename a field for ease of use, but some users might like to see the original database field name. By adding the original field name as a tag, these users can see the information if they wish.

The syntax is very similar to the Rename statement (mentioned previously):

```
Tag FieldName with 'tagname';
```

Consider the following example:

```
Tag Year With '$dimension';
Tag Year With 'MyTag';
Tag LineValue With '$measure';
```

In this case, the hover-over on the **Year** field would look like the following:

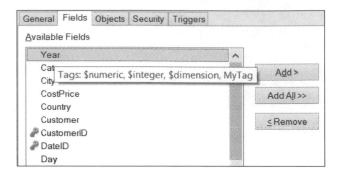

There is also an `Untag` statement, with the same syntax, that will remove a tag from a field.

Tagging fields using a mapping table

In a way similar to how we renamed fields using a mapping table, we can tag fields using a mapping table.

We have to be aware that as with a typical mapping table, which will only map to the first value found in the first field, if one field is listed multiple times in the tag mapping table, then only the first of those entries will be added to the field's tags from that mapping table. If we want to add multiple tags to a field, we will need to use multiple mapping tables. Consider the following example:

```
TABLE1:
Load
    KeyField,
    DimField1,
    DimField2,
    DimField3,
    Measure1,
    Measure2
From DataTable.qvd (qvd);

Tag_Map:
Mapping
Load * Inline [
field_name, tag
DimField1, $dimension
DimField2, $dimension
Measure1, $measure
```

```
Measure2, $measure
];

Tag_Map2:
Mapping
Load * Inline [
field_name, tag
KeyField, My Key Field
DimField1, Primary Dimension
DimField2, Secondary Dimension
Measure1, Primary Measure
Measure2, Secondary Measure
];

TAG Fields using Tag_Map;
TAG Fields using Tag_Map2;
```

When we hover over one of the fields, we can see that the tags have been added.

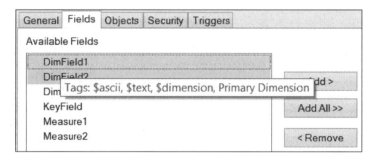

Hiding fields

Hiding fields is a common operation in QlikView. It is useful to have some fields automatically hidden from users. Fields such as association key fields are not usually necessary for users to want to use as dimensions or measures. Also, we can mark a field as hidden, and if it is in a listbox or other sheet object and a selection is made on that field, the selection does not appear in **Current Selections**. This is useful for some fields that we use for navigation rather than information.

Hiding fields automatically based on prefix or suffix

QlikView has two system variables that define a string of characters that will be compared to fields' beginning characters or end characters. If there is a match, the field will be tagged as hidden. These variables are `HidePrefix` and `HideSuffix`.

We set these variables in the script. For example, we might set one in the following manner:

```
set HidePrefix='%' ;
```

Now, all fields that begin with this character (such as key fields) will now be hidden.

Using tagging to hide fields

Not all fields that we want to hide will always match to a particular name and we might not want to name them to match, as that might cause confusion as to their purpose. For example, if we have a field that is used in navigation, we don't want to prefix it with % because it might be confused as a key field. Instead, we can simply tag these fields with $hidden:

```
TAG Field NavigationField with '$hidden';
```

Adding field comments

Another way that QlikView allows us to communicate information about the contents of a field to users is by adding text commentary to the field's metadata. As with renaming and tagging, we have two methods of adding this information— one field at a time, or via a mapping table:

```
COMMENT Field DimField1 With 'This field is the primary dimension of
the TABLE1 table.';


Comment_Map:
Mapping
Load * Inline [
field_name, comment
DimField2, This field is a secondary dimension in TABLE1
Measure1, This is the primary measure for TABLE1
Measure2, This is a secondary measure in TABLE1
];


COMMENT Fields Using Comment_Map;
```

The commentary appears to the user when they hover over the field, appearing above the tags:

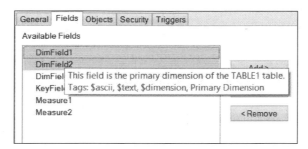

Commentary and tag information is also visible when we hover over a field in **Table Viewer**:

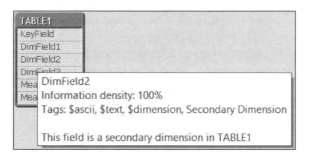

Renaming and commenting on tables

All of the tagging, commenting, and renaming commands that we have been applying to fields can also be applied to tables. For example:

```
COMMENT Table TABLE1 With 'This is our main fact table.';
```

This comment is visible in the **Tables** tab of **Document Properties** as well as in **Table Viewer**:

Commenting in charts

As well as adding metadata into fields and tables, we can also add commentary to our dimensions and expressions in charts. There are two main reasons to add commentary to what we are doing in QlikView:

- If someone else is supporting our work, they will be able to understand what we were doing

- If we are supporting our own work, several months later, we will be able to understand what we were doing

Commenting dimensions

Under most circumstances, commenting a dimension might not seem necessary, especially if that dimension is well named. However, there are cases where it is useful to add a comment, such as when we have a calculated dimension or if the dimension label is calculated (such as with multilingual applications). The **Comment** entry appears below the dimension label:

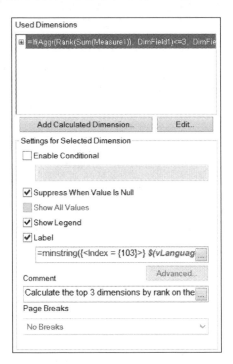

The **Comment** entry does have an ellipses button, so it opens **Expression Editor**. However, we should use this only for access to more text lines rather than trying to calculate anything as this calculation won't be seen anywhere.

Entering an expression comment

Similar to a dimension, we can add an appropriate comment to each expression. We should consider commenting almost every expression that we add, especially if it is anything beyond a simple sum or count.

The **Comment** entry is shown below the **Definition** expression:

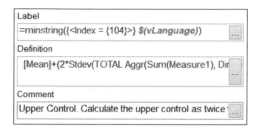

Automatically renaming qualified fields

If we adopt a `Qualify` approach to loading, especially when loading dimension tables, we can still rename the fields afterwards (but before creating sheet objects!) to make them friendlier.

We know that we can create a mapping table to rename our fields. This is something that we will often ask the business users to create. We will provide a table (for example, in Excel) with a list of qualified field names and then ask the business users to create the friendly names. However, the users might not be as careful to not create duplicates, or they might think that this is correct, but this can cause a problem for us.

What we need is a handy script that will handle several scenarios. First, we are going to define a data table format to fill in the rename details:

Field	Description
SOURCE QVD	This is the name of the QVD that this field comes from (the dimension table)
SOURCE TABLE	This is the name of the table in the original source (lineage)
SOURCE FIELD	This is the name of the field in the original source (lineage)
QLIKVIEW TABLE	This is the name of the table in the current data structure
NEW TABLE NAME	This gives a new name for the table (if we want to rename the table)
QLIKVIEW FIELD	This is the name of the field in the current data structure
NEW FIELD NAME	This is the new name for the field
COMMENTS	This helps add any comments to the field

Field	Description
DIMENSION	This is set to 1 to tag the field as a dimension
MEASURE	This is set to 1 to tag the field as a measure

Our rename script will generally be the very last tab in the main script. First, we will need to make sure that any qualification is turned off:

```
UNQUALIFY *;
```

Now, we load the main table:

```
Full_Map:
LOAD [SOURCE QVD],
     [SOURCE TABLE],
     [SOURCE FIELD],
     [QLIKVIEW TABLE],
     [NEW TABLE NAME],
     [QLIKVIEW FIELD],
     // If the new name already exists, qualify it
   trim(if(exists([NEW FIELD NAME]),[NEW TABLE NAME]&'.'&[NEW FIELD
NAME], [NEW FIELD NAME])) as [NEW FIELD NAME],
     COMMENTS,
     DIMENSION,
     MEASURE
FROM
RenameFields.xlsx
(ooxml, embedded labels, table is Mapping);
```

Now, load the field rename map from the main table:

```
FieldMap:
Mapping
Load distinct
    [QLIKVIEW FIELD],
    [NEW FIELD NAME]
Resident Full_Map;
```

Load the table rename map:

```
TableMap:
Mapping
Load Distinct
    [QLIKVIEW TABLE],
    [NEW TABLE NAME]
Resident Full_Map
Where Len([NEW TABLE NAME])>0;
```

We load our first tag map, that is, the original table name:

```
tagmap:
Mapping
Load
    [NEW FIELD NAME] as TagFrom,
    'Original Table: ' & [SOURCE TABLE] as Tag
Resident Full_Map;
```

Our second tag map applies the original field name tagging:

```
tagmap2:
Mapping
Load
    [NEW FIELD NAME],
    'Original Field: ' & [SOURCE FIELD]
Resident Full_Map;
```

Then, a tag map for the QVD name:

```
tagmap3:
Mapping
Load
    [NEW FIELD NAME],
    'QVD file: ' & [SOURCE QVD]
Resident Full_Map;
```

Our next tag maps are for the dimension and measure tags:

```
DimMap:
Mapping
Load
    [NEW FIELD NAME], '$dimension'
Resident Full_Map
Where DIMENSION=1;

MeasureMap:
Mapping
Load
    [NEW FIELD NAME], '$measure'
Resident Full_Map
Where MEASURE=1;
```

The final tag map is for the comments:

```
commentmap:
Mapping
Load
    [NEW FIELD NAME],
    COMMENTS
Resident Full_Map
Where Len(COMMENTS)>0;
```

Now, apply all the maps:

```
Rename fields using FieldMap;
Tag fields using tagmap;
Tag fields using tagmap2;
Tag fields using tagmap3;
Comment fields using commentmap;
Tag Field Using DimMap;
Tag Field Using MeasureMap;
Rename Tables using TableMap;
```

Extracting metadata

There are a number of ways of extracting metadata from our QlikView applications, and some are easier than others.

> The Governance Dashboard (as explained later) extracts metadata and imports log information into a good application to manage your data. However, another tool that I really recommend to use to look at metadata and the details of the document is Rob Wunderlich's **Document Analyzer** (`http://robwunderlich.com/downloads/`).

Exporting the structure

Structure exporting is a facility that has existed in QlikView for many versions — we can export the data structure information into tab-delimited text files.

In the **Tables** tab of **Document Properties**, there is an **Export Structure** button.

This will export three files — table information, a mapping table from tables to fields, and field information:

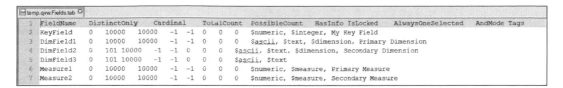

These tables can be read into another QlikView file for analysis.

Extracting from QVD files

A QVD has an XML header that we can easily read into a QlikView document. In the table wizard, if we change the selector from **QVD** to **Xml**, we can get access to all of the QVD metadata:

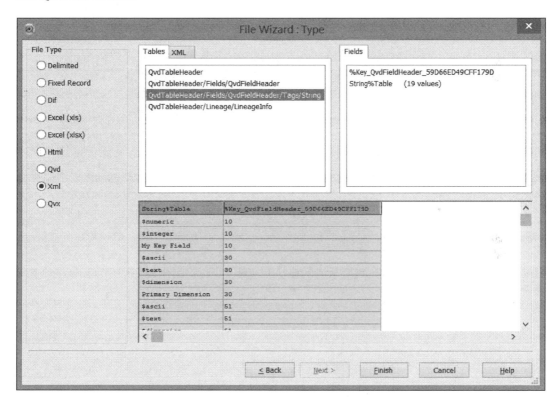

This information includes all of the field information, tags that have been added to fields, and data lineage information.

Extracting from QVW files

Many developers do not realize that a QlikView document has an XML metadata store embedded in it that we can actually read into QlikView. Again, it is picked up by the table wizard:

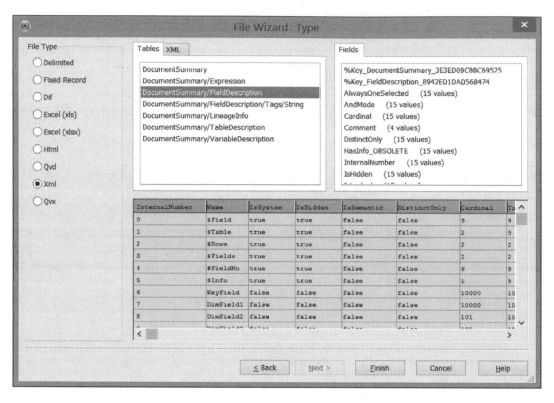

This data includes all the document fields and table information with tags and groups, expressions, variables, and lineage information.

Here is an example of loading this information for analysis; the vDocument variable contains the path to a QVW file.

First, load the sheets and sheet object information:

```
GroupDescription:
LOAD Trim(Name) As GroupName,
    if(IsCyclic='false', 'Drill-down', 'Cyclic') As GroupType,
    %Key_GroupDescription_CB92F98E8506AF37 as %GroupId  // Key for
this table: DocumentSummary/GroupDescription
FROM [$(vDocument)] (XmlSimple, Table is [DocumentSummary/
GroupDescription]);
```

```
Group_Map:
Mapping
Load
   GroupName,
   %GroupId
Resident GroupDescription;

GroupFields:
LOAD Name as GroupField,
   Type as GroupFieldType,
   %Key_GroupDescription_CB92F98E8506AF37 as %GroupId  // Key to
parent table: DocumentSummary/GroupDescription
FROM [$(vDocument)] (XmlSimple, Table is [DocumentSummary/
GroupDescription/FieldDefs/FieldDefEx]);

Sheet:
LOAD SheetId,
   Title,
   %Key_Sheet_A4D568A6CD8BD40A as %SheetID  // Key for this table:
DocumentSummary/Sheet
FROM [$(vDocument)] (XmlSimple, Table is [DocumentSummary/Sheet]);

SheetChildObjects:
LOAD ObjectId%Table as ObjectId,
   %Key_Sheet_A4D568A6CD8BD40A as %SheetID  // Key to parent table:
DocumentSummary/Sheet
FROM [$(vDocument)] (XmlSimple, Table is [DocumentSummary/Sheet/
ChildObjects/ObjectId]);

SheetObject:
LOAD ObjectId,
   SubField(ObjectId, '\', 2) As SimpleObjectId,
   Caption,
   Type,
   Field,
   Text
FROM [$(vDocument)] (XmlSimple, Table is [DocumentSummary/
SheetObject]);

Expression:
LOAD ObjectId as SimpleObjectId,
   Definition as Expression
FROM [$(vDocument)] (XmlSimple, Table is [DocumentSummary/
Expression]);
```

```
Dimension:
LOAD ObjectId as SimpleObjectId,
    PseudoDef as Dimension,
    ApplyMap('Group_Map', Trim(PseudoDef), Null()) As %GroupId
FROM [$(vDocument)] (XmlSimple, Table is [DocumentSummary/Dimension]);

// Variables
VariableDescription:
LOAD Name as VariableName,
    IsConfig,
    IsReserved,
    RawValue
FROM [$(vDocument)] (XmlSimple, Table is [DocumentSummary/
VariableDescription]);
```

Now, load the table and field information:

```
GroupDescription:
LOAD Trim(Name) As GroupName,
    if(IsCyclic='false', 'Drill-down', 'Cyclic') As GroupType,
    %Key_GroupDescription_CB92F98E8506AF37 as %GroupId  // Key for
this table: DocumentSummary/GroupDescription
FROM [$(vDocument)] (XmlSimple, Table is [DocumentSummary/
GroupDescription]);

Group_Map:
Mapping
Load
    GroupName,
    %GroupId
Resident GroupDescription;

GroupFields:
LOAD Name as GroupField,
    Type as GroupFieldType,
    %Key_GroupDescription_CB92F98E8506AF37 as %GroupId  // Key to
parent table: DocumentSummary/GroupDescription
FROM [$(vDocument)] (XmlSimple, Table is [DocumentSummary/
GroupDescription/FieldDefs/FieldDefEx]);

Sheet:
LOAD SheetId,
    Title,
    %Key_Sheet_A4D568A6CD8BD40A as %SheetID  // Key for this table:
DocumentSummary/Sheet
FROM [$(vDocument)] (XmlSimple, Table is [DocumentSummary/Sheet]);
```

```
SheetChildObjects:
LOAD ObjectId%Table as ObjectId,
    %Key_Sheet_A4D568A6CD8BD40A as %SheetID  // Key to parent table:
DocumentSummary/Sheet
FROM [$(vDocument)] (XmlSimple, Table is [DocumentSummary/Sheet/
ChildObjects/ObjectId]);

SheetObject:
LOAD ObjectId,
    SubField(ObjectId, '\', 2) As SimpleObjectId,
    Caption,
    Type,
    Field,
    Text
FROM [$(vDocument)] (XmlSimple, Table is [DocumentSummary/
SheetObject]);

Expression:
LOAD ObjectId as SimpleObjectId,
    Definition as Expression
FROM [$(vDocument)] (XmlSimple, Table is [DocumentSummary/
Expression]);

Dimension:
LOAD ObjectId as SimpleObjectId,
    PseudoDef as Dimension,
    ApplyMap('Group_Map', Trim(PseudoDef), Null()) As %GroupId
FROM [$(vDocument)] (XmlSimple, Table is [DocumentSummary/Dimension]);

// Variables
VariableDescription:
LOAD Name as VariableName,
    IsConfig,
    IsReserved,
    RawValue
FROM [$(vDocument)] (XmlSimple, Table is [DocumentSummary/
VariableDescription]);

///$tab Tables and Fields
// Tables
TableDescription:
LOAD InternalNumber as Table.InternalNumber,
    Name as TableName,
    $(YesNoFlag(IsSystem)) As Table.IsSystem,
```

```
    $(YesNoFlag(IsSemantic)) As Table.IsSemantic,
    $(YesNoFlag(IsLoose)) As IsLoose,
    NoOfRows,
    NoOfFields,
    NoOfKeyFields,
    $(YesNoFlag(IsLinked)) As IsLinked
FROM [$(vDocument)] (XmlSimple, Table is [DocumentSummary/
TableDescription]);


TableFields:
LOAD String%Table as TableName,
    %Key_FieldDescription_8942ED1DAD568474 as %FieldId  // Key to
parent table: DocumentSummary/FieldDescription
FROM [$(vDocument)] (XmlSimple, Table is [DocumentSummary/
FieldDescription/SrcTables/String]);


FieldAssociationCount_Map:
Mapping Load
    %FieldId,
    Count(TableName) as FieldCount
Resident
    TableFields
Group by %FieldId;


FieldDescription:
LOAD InternalNumber as Field.InternalNumber,
    Name as FieldName,
    $(YesNoFlag(IsSystem)) as Field.IsSystem,
    $(YesNoFlag(IsHidden)) As IsHidden,
    $(YesNoFlag(IsSemantic)) as Field.IsSemantic,
    $(YesNoFlag(DistinctOnly)) As DistinctOnly,
    Cardinal,
    TotalCount,
    PossibleCount_OBSOLETE,
    HasInfo_OBSOLETE,
    $(YesNoFlag(IsLocked)) As IsLocked,
    $(YesNoFlag(AlwaysOneSelected)) As AlwaysOneSelected,
    $(YesNoFlag(AndMode)) As AndMode,
    $(YesNoFlag(IsNumeric)) As IsNumeric,
    ApplyMap('FieldAssociationCount_Map', %Key_FieldDescription_8942ED
1DAD568474, 0) As Field.AssociationCount,
    If(ApplyMap('FieldAssociationCount_Map', %Key_FieldDescriptio
n_8942ED1DAD568474, 0)>1, Dual('Yes',-1), Dual('No',0)) As Field.
IsKeyField,
```

```
    %Key_FieldDescription_8942ED1DAD568474 as %FieldId  // Key for
this table: DocumentSummary/FieldDescription
FROM [$(vDocument)] (XmlSimple, Table is [DocumentSummary/
FieldDescription]);

tmp_Tags:
LOAD String%Table,
    %Key_FieldDescription_8942ED1DAD568474 as %FieldId  // Key to
parent table: DocumentSummary/FieldDescription
FROM [$(vDocument)] (XmlSimple, Table is [DocumentSummary/
FieldDescription/Tags/String]);


Left Join (FieldDescription)
LOAD
    %FieldId,
    Concat(String%Table, ', ') As Field.Tags
Resident tmp_Tags
Group by %FieldId;

Drop table tmp_Tags;
```

Finally, use the data loaded previously to establish whether a field is actually being used in the document:

```
// Establish a list of field usage in different objects

// First, Group fields used in charts.
// Note that we don't just grab them from the GroupFields
// table because there may be groups that are not used.
FieldsUsedInObjects:
Load
    Distinct %GroupId
Resident
    Dimension;

Left Join
Load
    %GroupId,
    GroupField as UsedField
Resident
    GroupFields;

Drop Field %GroupId from FieldsUsedInObjects;
```

```
// Now add dimensions used in charts
Concatenate (FieldsUsedInObjects)
Load
    Dimension as UsedField
Resident
    Dimension
Where Len(%GroupId)=0
AND Left(Trim(Dimension),1) <> '=';

// Now, dimensions used in listboxes
Concatenate (FieldsUsedInObjects)
Load
    Field as UsedField
Resident
    SheetObject
Where Len(Field) > 0;

// We will use this Field Map to try and locate field names in
expressions.
// Is is simply the field name and then a string that we can easily
find.
FieldMap:
Mapping
Load
    FieldName,
    '|%%%FIELD.MAP%%%|' & FieldName & '|'
Resident
    FieldDescription;

// Create a table of all the Expressions
// Begin with the Expression table
ExpressionLocations:
Load
    Expression
Resident
    Expression;

// Now add the Text value from SheetObjects, but only if it starts
with '='
Concatenate (ExpressionLocations)
Load
    Text As Expression
Resident
    SheetObject
Where Len(Trim(Text))>0 and Left(Trim(Text), 1) = '=';
```

```
// Same rule for Captions
Concatenate (ExpressionLocations)
Load
    Caption As Expression
Resident
    SheetObject
Where Len(Trim(Caption))>0 and Left(Trim(Caption), 1) = '=';

// Add calculated dimensions - again, start with '='
Concatenate (ExpressionLocations)
Load
    Dimension as Expression
Resident
    Dimension
Where Len(%GroupId)=0
AND Left(Trim(Dimension),1) = '=';



// Add in variables. We don't exclude based on '=' here because
// a variable without '=' might still hold a field name
Concatenate (ExpressionLocations)
Load
    RawValue as Expression
Resident
    VariableDescription;



// Now, we will parse out any CRLF and LF in expressions
// (SubField with only 2 parameters will create multiple rows)
// and then we can use MapSubString to try and map our field
// list against each expression row. If it maps, we can parse
// out the field name using SubField (again!)
// This list is concatenated onto the table that we started
// creating earlier.
Concatenate (FieldsUsedInObjects)
Load
    SubField(Mid(TempExpr, Index(TempExpr, '|%%%FIELD.MAP%%%|')),'|',3)
As UsedField;
Load
    MapSubString('FieldMap', Expression) as TempExpr;
Load
    SubField(Expression, chr(10)) As Expression;
Load
```

```
    SubField(Expression, chr(13) & chr(10)) as Expression
Resident
    ExpressionLocations;

Drop Table ExpressionLocations;

// Add in Key fields to the IsUsed list
Concatenate (FieldsUsedInObjects)
Load
    FieldName as UsedField
Resident
    FieldDescription
Where Field.IsKeyField=-1;


// Create a temp table:
tmp_Used:
Load Distinct
    UsedField,
    $(YesNoFlag(1)) As Field.IsUsed
Resident
    FieldsUsedInObjects;

Concatenate (tmp_Used)
Load Distinct
    FieldName as UsedField,
    $(YesNoFlag(0)) as Field.IsUsed
Resident
    FieldDescription
Where Not Exists(UsedField, FieldName);

Let vRowCount=NoOfRows('FieldDescription');

// Now, join this into the field table
Left Join (FieldDescription)
Load UsedField as FieldName,
    Field.IsUsed
Resident
    tmp_Used;

Drop Table tmp_Used;

Let vRowCount=NoOfRows('FieldDescription');
```

[Note that Rob Wunderlich's Document Analyzer does a more
in-depth job of analyzing whether a field is being used or not.]

Deploying the QlikView Governance Dashboard

The QlikView Governance Dashboard is a tool provided by Qlik that allows you to import multiple data sources from your QlikView implementation and view all information in one place:

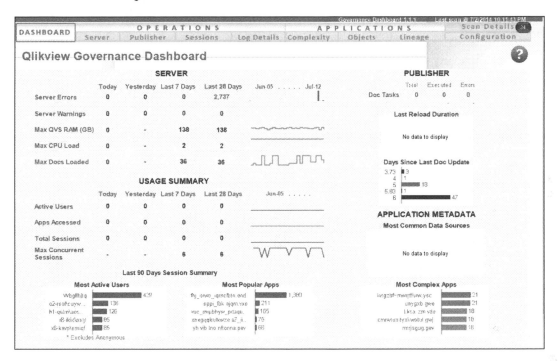

Managing profiles

The Governance Dashboard is a QlikView application, and therefore, we can have different copies of this application for different purposes, for example:

- Complete access to all information (default)
- Access to just operational information
- Access to just document metadata
- Access to just a subset of documents

The install sets things up so that we can quickly create new profiles with different settings.

The installation will, by default, install to `C:\ProgramData\QlikTech\Governance_1.1`. It will create a subfolder here called `profiles` and within that there will be three further subfolders:

Folder	Description
`default`	This contains the default dashboard that will be most people's first (and only!) use of it
`template`	A blank template containing all the files and subfolders that we will need to create a new profile
`template_MultiClusterProfileFolder`	A template to use when we are performing analysis in a multicluster environment

To create a new profile, we simply copy the entire `template` folder and rename the new folder to whatever name we want to call it. Now, we can open the `Governance Dashboard.qvw` file in this folder and configure the settings.

Configuring the Dashboard options

Before we run the Governance Dashboard reload, we need to configure the settings in the **Configuration** tab:

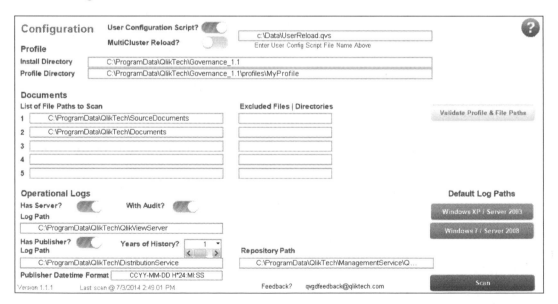

The main configuration areas are as follows:

Area	Description
User Configuration Script?	This allows us to specify a text file that contains script that will be included in the reload. This script is usually to modify variables, but you can add any valid QlikView script into it.
Multi-cluster Reload?	If this is on, all the other options are disabled and the reload will use the `MultiCluster_UserConfig_Template.txt` file for its settings.
Profile	This allows us to specify the install directory for the Governance Dashboard and the folder for our profile settings.
Documents	Here, we will list a set of folders that will contain QVW, QVD, or QVX files that we want to be scanned.
Operational Logs	Here, we can turn settings around what operational logs should be included in the dashboard on or off.
Repository Path	The repository stores all the server, publisher, and similar settings in XML files.

Once the configuration has been entered, you can click on the **Validate Profile & File Paths** button to verify that all is valid. If a path is incorrect, an alert will be shown:

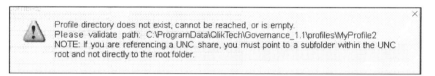

Once the configuration is entered and tested, we can click on the **Scan** button to begin the reload.

You might get an error from the reload, and unfortunately, it is very difficult to know exactly what that error is because the entire script has been put into a hidden script and error messages are not displayed from within the hidden script:

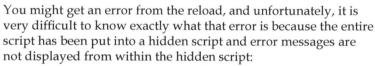

The only thing that you can immediately do is double-check all your configurations and see whether you have made a mistake somewhere. If you still have difficulties, get onto the Qlik Community and ask questions there.

Reviewing operational information

Once the reload is complete, you can use operational dashboards to review information about applications that users use and when they use them:

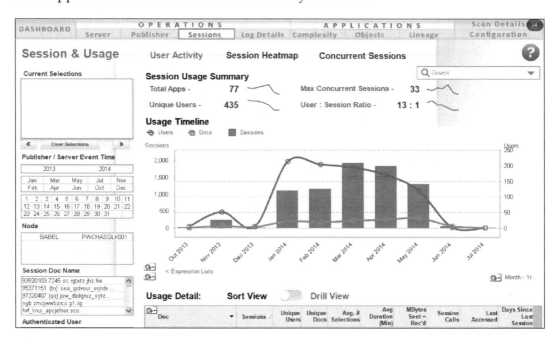

The tabs under **OPERATIONS** provide you with the following information:

Tab	Description
Server	This gives server memory usage statistics and is useful when analyzing for memory-related issues
Publisher	This gives reload and other task statuses and times
Sessions	This provides information on the number of sessions, users, and documents
Log Details	This provides detailed log information, which is very good for error hunting

Analyzing application information

The other side of the Governance Dashboard is the information on your applications such as complexity and data lineage. This is useful from many aspects of application maintenance, for example, being able to look at expressions and look for instances where an expression is actually used across multiple applications:

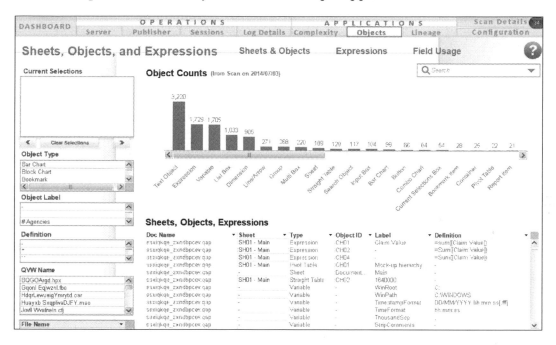

 In his blog post on the QlikView cache, Henric Cronström explains that the text of an expression is part of the cache key and so differences in case will make a difference! (http://community.qlik.com/blogs/ qlikviewdesignblog/2014/04/14/the-qlikview-cache) Sum([Claim Value]) is not the same as sum([Claim Value])!

The tabs in the **APPLICATIONS** area are as follows:

Tab	Description
Complexity	This will assign a score to each application based on a number of metrics, such as number of objects, rows, and expressions. The more complex an application, the lower its performance is likely to be.

Tab	Description
Objects	This allows you to drill into the actual objects in each document to analyze which ones might be causing you problems, which ones have incorrect expressions, and so forth.
Lineage	This will list all the data sources for an application and also allow you to discover which sources are shared across multiple applications.

Summary

This chapter has given us a lot of information on an area that many QlikView developers might rather avoid—metadata. However, we should realize now that metadata is important, and more importantly, is straightforward to add to our QlikView applications.

We now have a range of tools to help us manage our metadata, including the QlikView Governance Dashboard.

In the next chapter, we will get into the, fun for many, subject of advanced expressions. This will include plenty of work around the subjects of Set Analysis and AGGR, which are very powerful tools that will really propel our mastery of QlikView.

5
Advanced Expressions

"The general who wins a battle makes many calculations in his temple before the battle is fought. The general who loses a battle makes but few calculations beforehand. Thus do many calculations lead to victory, and few calculations to defeat: how much more no calculation at all! It is by attention to this point that I can foresee who is likely to win or lose."

— Sun Tzu, The Art of War

There is a great skill in creating the right expression to calculate the right answer. Being able to do this in all circumstances relies on having a good knowledge of creating advanced expressions. This is what this chapter aims to teach you. Of course, the best path to mastery in this subject is actually getting out and doing it, but there is a great argument here for regularly practicing with dummy or test datasets.

When presented with a problem that needs to be solved, all the QlikView masters will not necessarily know immediately how to answer it. What they will have though is a very good idea of where to start, that is, what to try and what not to try. This is what I hope to impart to you here. Knowing how to create many advanced expressions will arm you to know where to apply them—and where not to apply them.

This is one area of QlikView that is alien to many people. For some reason, they fear the whole idea of concepts such as Set Analysis and `Aggr`. However, the reality is that these concepts are actually very simple and supremely logical. Once you get your head around them, you will wonder what all the fuss was about.

The following are the topics we'll cover in this chapter:

- Reviewing basic concepts
- Using range functions
- Understanding Dollar-sign Expansion

- Using advanced Set Analysis
- Calculating vertically

Reviewing basic concepts

Before we set off on the journey of advanced expressions, it is a good idea to step back and look at some of the simpler methods of doing things. Set Analysis only arrived in Version 8.5 of QlikView, so those of us who worked with the versions before that will have done things in a few different ways.

Searching in QlikView

Field searching in QlikView is one of the most powerful features. It is a feature that has been added and enhanced over the years. Many users will be familiar with the search icon on a listbox:

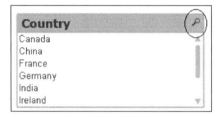

Clicking on this icon will open the search box for that field:

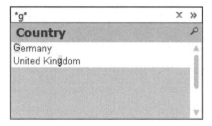

When we enter search text, the results are highlighted in the listbox. We can choose to click on any of the results to make a selection, press the *Enter* key to select all of the matching results, or press *Ctrl + Enter* to add the matching results to the existing selections.

There are some other ways that we can call up the search box for a listbox. The easiest way is to actually just click on the listbox's caption and just start typing, and the default search type for that listbox will get activated. The other way that you can activate a search is by right-clicking on the listbox and selecting the required search from the menu:

Field searches can also be activated in other sheet objects. Search will be on by default in the multibox but can also be enabled in the table box, current selections box, straight table, and pivot table (using the **Dropdown Select** option in the **Presentation** tab). They can be identified from the small black down arrow alongside the field caption:

Clicking on this down arrow will show a captionless listbox. You can select in this listbox just as with a normal listbox. If you start typing, the search box will appear, just as when you click on the caption of a normal listbox. If you right-click on this pop-up listbox, you will get the same options as if you right-click on a normal listbox.

There are several search types that we need to understand; they are discussed in the upcoming sections.

Searching for text

Text-based searches are the most frequently used. There are two main options for text-based search: **normal** and **wildcard**. The default setting for the search mode is specified in the **Presentation** tab under **Document Properties**:

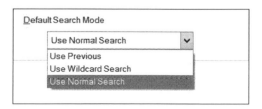

There is a third option in these properties: **Use Previous**. What this means is that whatever the user has done last will be the default. The user can override the search type that is presented, so this setting remembers whatever they have done.

Wildcard search

A wildcard search uses one of the two wildcard characters, in whatever combination we desire, to search for text. The characters are as follows:

Character	Description
*	This wildcard replaces zero or more characters
?	This wildcard replaces exactly one character

Some example searches are shown in the following table:

Example search	Example results in country
g	Germany, Gabon, British Guiana, United Kingdom, Argentina
g*	Germany, Gabon
*on	Lebanon, Gabon
*o?	Gabon, United Kingdom, Lebanon
f*e	France

Wildcards are extremely flexible, but can be very expensive if used to search a lot of data.

If the default search is not a wildcard, you can start typing the * or ? character and QlikView will automatically switch to a wildcard search.

> We should consider that the search will start working immediately when we start typing. There can be a delay with fields that have many values, so we need to be careful about the default search options.

Normal search

A normal search doesn't use wildcards at all. Instead, it tries to match the beginning of words in the data to what the user is typing. This is actually a more natural type of search for users because they will often type the start of what they are looking for and might be confused by wildcard options. If the user types multiple words, separated by a space, all of the words are used to attempt a match.

The following are some example searches:

Example search	Example results in country
g	Germany, Gabon, British Guiana
ger	Germany
k	Kenya, United Kingdom
un kin	United Kingdom
blah king	United Kingdom

If the default search is wildcard, you can switch to the normal search by simply deleting the wildcard characters and then typing. QlikView will automatically switch to the normal search.

Fuzzy search

Fuzzy search isn't a text comparison. Instead, it applies a phonetic algorithm to the search term and the data and then sorts the listbox based on the search score. Words that are a better phonetic match will be sorted to the top and those that are not a good match will be at the bottom.

Associative search

The associative search option will search for a value across other fields, not including the field that you are searching in. When you select the value in the associative search, it then selects the values in the field that you are searching in that are associated with the value that you have selected. Ok, that sounds like a bit of a mouthful, so I will give an example. When I click on the search button, say, the **Country** field, I can see a double chevron (**>>**) button. Clicking on this button activates the associative search, as follows:

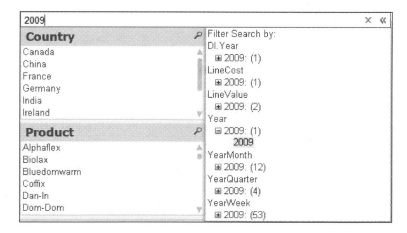

If I type 2009 into this search box now, it doesn't search in **Country**; it searches every other field except **Country**. I can see that it has found a value under **Year**; if I select this and then press *Enter*, it will select all of the countries that are associated with the value 2009 in **Year**.

Let's put this functionality in a little more perspective; to achieve the same result without an associative search, we would need to select **2009** in the **Year** field, select the possible values from the **Country** field (there is a right-click option to select possible values), and then clear the **Year** field. It is a pretty cool search function!

Of course, it is not always logical that an associative search should look in every single field. For example, in the preceding screenshot, we see that the field **DI.Year** is searched. This is a field in a data island table (for more information on data islands, refer to the *Data islands* section) and so will not be associated. Also, there are many fields in the dataset, for example, keys and numeric values, that should not be searched. It is possible, in the listbox properties, to select those fields that should be included rather than looking at all fields.

In the **General** tab of the listbox properties, there is a button called **More Search Settings** that will open a dialog box to allow us to configure this:

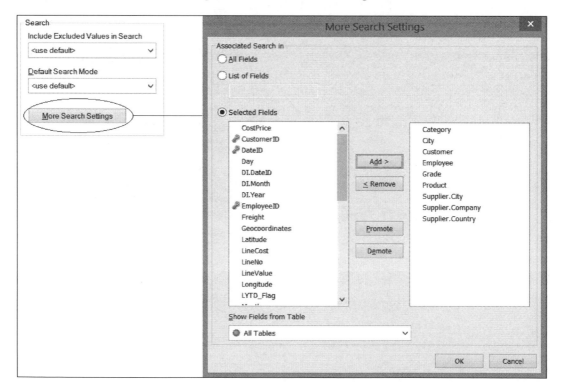

Advanced search

The advanced search feature in QlikView is actually incredibly powerful. It allows us to search for values in a field based on the comparison of an expression. It is as if we create a simple straight table with the searched field as the dimension and the expression that we want to calculate, then select those dimensions in the chart that meet whatever criteria we choose.

To open the advanced search dialog, we can right-click on a listbox and select **Advanced Search** from the menu:

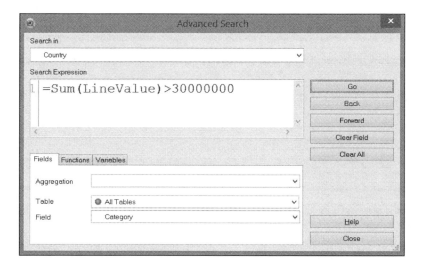

We enter the = sign, which indicates that this is an advanced search, and then the expression that we want to calculate. When we click on the **Go** button, this expression is evaluated against all the values in the field (in this case, **Country**), and where it is true, these values are selected.

The really powerful thing about this is that this expression can be as complex as we need it to be. As long as it is valid QlikView syntax, it can be used in an advanced search. All that is needed is that the expression will return a Boolean response: true or false.

Searching numeric fields

All of the text searching options mentioned previously — wildcard, normal, fuzzy, associative, and advanced — also work with numeric fields. Additionally, we can also use a numeric search with numeric fields.

Numeric search

The numeric search option allows us to use combinations of >, <, and = to perform numeric searches. The following are some example combinations:

Example search	Description
>99	This searches for all values that are greater than 99
<99	This searches for all values that are less than 99
>=99	This searches for all values that are greater than or equal to 99
<=99	This searches for all values that are less than or equal to 99
>99<199	This searches for all values that are greater than 99 but less than 199
>=99<=199	This search for all values that are greater than or equal to 99 but less than or equal to 199

When we type the search expression into the numeric listbox, it will react in a way similar to that of a text-based search:

Automatic interpretation of searches

This is quite clever. When we use a search box, we can do any of the standard searches—normal, wildcard, numeric, fuzzy, and advanced—and QlikView will automatically interpret what type of search it is based on what we type. Consider the following scenarios:

- If we just type text, without any special characters, QlikView will perform a normal search

- If we use wildcards, *or ?, then QlikView will perform a wildcard search

- If we start the search with a ~ sign, then QlikView will perform a fuzzy search

- If we start the search with an = sign, then QlikView will perform an advanced search

- If we use a < or > sign, then QlikView will perform a numeric search

- If we enclose in parentheses and use a pipe symbol, QlikView will expect multiple values

Multiple values search

We can pass multiple values to a search by enclosing them in parentheses and separating the multiple values using a pipe symbol, for example:

```
(Germany|China)
(*ge*|*ch*)
(>=2009<=2011|>=2013<=2014)
(>=2009<=2011|*14)
```

Any valid search syntax will be acceptable within the different values. QlikView will automatically interpret the search based on the rules mentioned.

 It is worth noting that this syntax can also be used to pass multiple values when using a **Select in Field** action.

Searching in multiple listboxes

If we select multiple listboxes either by dragging across them or by clicking on them while holding down the *Shift* key and then start typing, the subsequent search will be performed across all of the selected listboxes:

 Note that you cannot use the *Enter* key here to make a selection. You can only now make a selection by clicking the mouse in one of the listboxes.

Understanding bookmarks

We should know that a bookmark is a saved set of selections. When we save a bookmark, all of the current selections will be stored. It is important to note that this will include any advanced searches, so bookmarks can be used to store advanced logic.

A bookmark can be recalled by the user, but they can also be used to set the parameters for reports and alerts and can be used in Set Analysis.

Saving a bookmark

We can save a bookmark using the menu options or if there is a bookmark object added to the user interface, we can use that to create it. Either way, the **Add Bookmark** dialog will appear:

The options for the bookmark are as follows:

Option	Description
Make this bookmark a document (server) bookmark	This tells QlikView to store the bookmark in the document for use by all users (or on the server if using a server document, where we also have the option to share with other users).
Share Bookmark with Other Users	This option is for server bookmarks only; we can choose to share them with other server users.
Include Selections in Bookmark	This will normally be a default option—you usually want your selections to be stored in the bookmark! Of course, there are use cases where you might not, such as only storing the layout state or input field values.
Make bookmark apply on top of current selection	By default, this is off and the bookmark's store selections will completely replace whatever current selections we have when the bookmark is recalled. If this option is on, only the fields that have stored values in the bookmark will have their values changed and all other selections will be retained.
Include Layout State	This will retain information about which tab is open and which charts are currently active. When recalled, the same tab and charts should be opened.
Include Scroll Position	If your chart is a tabular chart, the bookmark will retain information about how far you have scrolled down the chart. Worth noting is the fact that this will always be a "best guess" effort as the data will probably change in the meantime.
Include Input Field Values	This will cause any input field values to be stored in the bookmark. This is actually the only way to share input field values between different users.
Info Text	This could be just information that we want to store to remind ourselves about what this bookmark contains. It will be the text displayed if the pop-up option is selected.
Pop-Up Message	If this is selected (and I strongly recommend that it should not be!), every time the bookmark is recalled, **Info Text** will be displayed in a message box. It becomes very annoying after a while.

Managing bookmarks

The **More** option from the **Bookmarks** menu (*Ctrl* + *Shift* + *B*) allows us to manage our bookmarks:

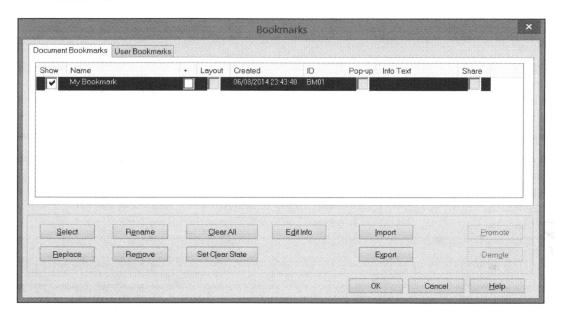

Possibly, the most interesting option here is the **Export** and **Import** buttons. These allow us to export bookmarks to an XML file and then import them into different documents later.

Using variables in QlikView

Many calculations will rely on a variable. This can be a simple value, such as an exchange rate entered into an input box, a percentage entered using a slider, or a more complex calculation.

SET versus LET

We are probably aware that variables can be entered either in the QlikView script via the **Variables** tab under **Document Properties** or using the **Variable Overview** dialog.

When creating a variable in the script, we do this using either the SET or LET keywords. For example, to create the v1 and v2 variables, use:

```
SET v1=1+1;
LET v2=1+1;
```

The SET keyword will assign the text on the right-hand side of the equals sign to the variable. The LET keyword will instead evaluate the text on the right-hand side of the equals sign and then assign the result to the variable. If we load this script in the QlikView debugger, we will see the following result:

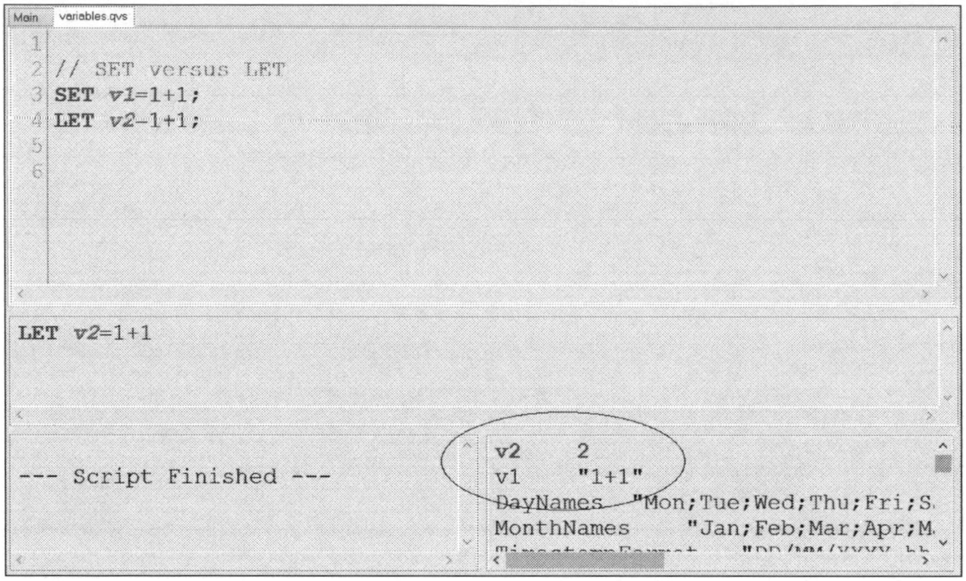

We can see that v1 has been assigned the text "1+1", whereas for v2, the text has been evaluated and the value of 2 has been assigned to the variable.

We can achieve a similar result when using the **Variables** tab under **Document Properties** or using the **Variable Overview** dialog, to create a variable. When we add a variable, we can either just enter text in the **Definition** box, in which case just the text is assigned to the variable, or we can begin the definition with an = sign that causes the expression to be evaluated and the result of the calculation gets assigned to the variable, for example, using the **Variable Overview** to create v3 and v4, you get the following:

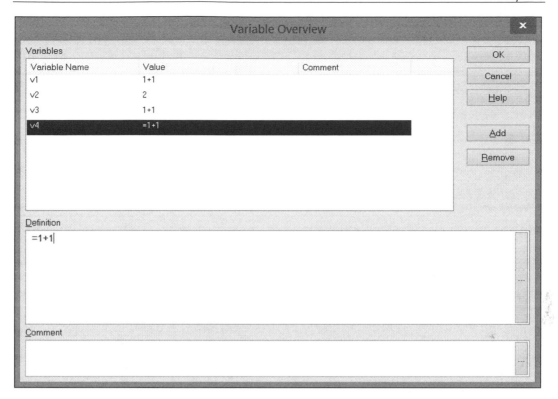

As with v1 and v2, v3 will have the text "1+1" while v4 will evaluate to 2.

There is no difference between using SET in the script and assigning text to a variable in the **Variable Overview** window. There is, however, a difference between using LET in the script and using = at the start of the variable definition. In the script, the result is calculated once during the script execution and the variable will then have a static value. If we use the = sign at the start of the definition, the variable's value will be recalculated every time there is a new selection made by users.

Using variables to hold common expressions

We will quite often use variables to hold commonly used expressions. That way, if the expression needs to change, then we don't need to hunt down every use of the expression; we can just change the variable.

The best practice here is to define these variables in the script with a SET statement. Quite often, these SET statements are stored in a separate QVS that might be shared with several documents, especially if the expressions in question are for color values that will be used throughout the organization. For example, we can have an external variables file with the following lines:

```
// Color expressions
SET cCompanyGreen=ARGB(255,20,228,68);
SET cCompanyBlue=ARGB(200,0,32,200);
SET cCompanyAlert=ARGB(255,255,0,0);
SET cCompanyWarning=ARGB(200,255,126,0);
```

Then, we can load them into our main script using the following:

```
$(Must_Include=..\scripts\variables.qvs);
```

If one of the colors needs to change, we can simply update the file and the change will be updated in every document that uses it on the next reload.

Using variables with Dollar-sign Expansion

We probably have seen variables being used in scripts and expressions and might have come across the concept of **Dollar-sign Expansion**. This function, which we will delve into in much more detail, allows us to access variable values in a way that is not quite intuitive for those who are used to common programming languages. To add to the confusion, we don't always need to use Dollar-sign Expansion with variables; we can use them sometimes just like other programming languages!

With Dollar-sign Expansion, we will wrap the variable name in parentheses preceded by a dollar sign, for example:

```
LET vx=$(vy)*2;
```

When this is processed, what happens is that the value inside the parentheses is evaluated and placed into the expression to replace the dollar sign. Once all the Dollar-sign Expansions have been completed, the whole expression is evaluated with the expanded values. We can think of it as a two-step process, for example, if vy has a value of 2, LET vx=$(vy)*2; becomes LET vx=2*2;.

This is now evaluated and the result, 4, is placed in vx. If we were looking at this script in the debugger window, we would actually see this two-step process in action. The central bar of the debugger will display the line that is about to be executed. If there are Dollar-sign Expansions, then the line that is displayed is with the values already expanded:

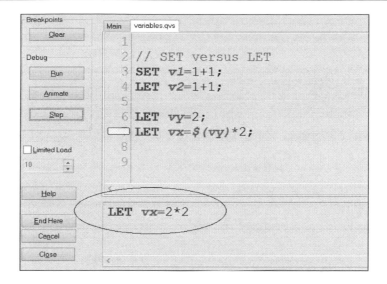

In fact, this is one of the situations where we don't have to use Dollar-sign Expansion. If a variable contains just a numeric value, then it is allowable to just call:

```
LET vx=vy*2;
```

Limiting calculations

There are quite a few ways of restricting a calculation to something other than the current selections. Before we had Set Analysis, we had to do things differently. It is useful to know about these because there are still circumstances in which they are still good to use.

Sum of If

A **Sum of If** means that we are performing an aggregation, such as `Sum`, on the results of an `If` statement. Consider the following example:

```
Sum(If(Country='Germany', Sales, 0))
```

In this case, the `Sales` value will only be summed if `Country` is equal to `Germany`.

On a smaller dataset, you will not see much of an issue with this calculation. However, as the dataset increases in size, we will find that this way of performing calculations is relatively inefficient, not least because the comparison is text-based. Also, we need to consider that if a user selects a set of countries, or any other selection that excludes Germany, then the result will be zero, which might not be what you want to happen.

It isn't a QlikView issue, but just a computer issue; however, any comparison that is done using text values is always going to be more expensive than a comparison using numbers.

Flag arithmetic

One of the ways that we can improve performance of a comparison calculation is to create a numeric flag field in the script. For example, we can do the following in the script:

```
Load
   ...
   If(Country='Germany',1,0) As Germany_Flag,
   ...
```

This will create a (quite efficiently stored) field that contains just 1 or 0. We can use this in an expression like the following:

```
Sum(If(Germany_Flag=1, Sales, 0))
```

This expression will perform an order of magnitude better than the equivalent text comparison. However, the following calculation will be even better:

```
Sum(Germany_Flag * Sales)
```

As there is no comparison happening here, it is a fairly straightforward mathematical calculation for the system to calculate, and it will be performed even faster than the Sum of If.

> As noted in the *Creating flags for well-known conditions* section of *Chapter 1, Performance Tuning and Scalability*, the flag arithmetic works better if there are relatively fewer rows in the dimension table than in the fact table. Where there are a large number of rows in the dimension table, Set Analysis with the flag field will perform better.

This type of flag arithmetic is very common, and we will always look to create flags like these in the script to improve the efficiency of calculations in chart expressions. Here are a couple of examples of flags that we will often create in fact or calendar tables:

```
Load
   ...
   -YearToDate(DateField)        As YTD_Flag,
    -YearToDate(DateField,-1)    As LYTD_Flag,
   ...
```

In this case, we are using a QlikView function (`YearToDate`) that returns a Boolean result. In QlikView, Boolean `false` is always represented by `0`. Any non-zero value is Boolean `true`; however, QlikView functions will always return `-1` for `true`. Hence, the minus sign prefixed to the function will change the `-1` result to a `1`.

Calculations using variables

On occasions where we might want some flexibility around what we calculate from what the users select, we might ask those users to change variables, usually using the slider or calendar controls, and then use those variables in the expressions.

For example, if we had two variables called `vMinDate` and `vMaxDate`, we can add calendar controls to allow the user to modify them:

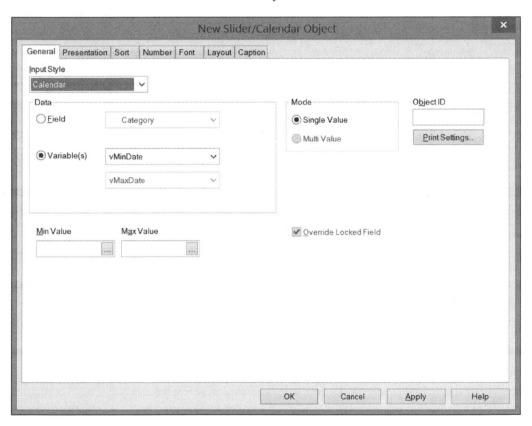

We can now add an expression to calculate the sales between those two values in the following manner:

```
Sum(if(DateID>=$(vMinDate) and DateID<=$(vMaxDate), LineValue, 0))
```

We can also grab the to-date calculation (for example, to calculate a balance) in the following manner:

```
Sum(if(DateID<=$(vMaxDate), LineValue, 0))
```

Data islands

Using a variable or set of variables can be quite flexible but sometimes we might want to give users even more options for selections, while still keeping those selections separate from the main data model. In these circumstances, we can create a completely separate data model, which has full QlikView selectability, and then derive the values from this data model that should be used in the calculations for the main data model. When we create separate data models like this, the non-main data model is called a **data island**. For example, we can load a calendar table in the following manner:

```
// Load the Date Island
Let vMinDate=Floor(MakeDate(2009,1,1));
Let vMaxDate=Floor(MakeDate(2014,12,31));
Let vDiff=vMaxDate-vMinDate+1;

Qualify *;
DI:
Load
    TempDate as DateID,
    Year(TempDate) As Year,
    Month(TempDate) As Month;
Load
    $(vMinDate)+RecNo()-1 As TempDate
AutoGenerate($(vDiff));
Unqualify *;
Set vMinDate="=Min(DI.DateID)";
Set vMaxDate="=Max(DI.DateID)";
```

The `Qualify` statement prefixes the name of the table (`DI`) to each field so that these fields should not be associated to the rest of the data model.

We use the `SET` statements at the end to add the calculation of minimum and maximum dates to the variables. We can then use those variables in expressions as shown:

```
Sum(if(DateID>=$(vMinDate) and DateID<=$(vMaxDate), LineValue, 0))
```

Otherwise, we can use those variables as shown in the following expression:

```
Sum(if(DateID<=$(vMaxDate), LineValue, 0))
```

This data island does not need to be just a single table. If it makes sense, it can be a small data model in itself and perhaps two separate calendar tables connected via a link table.

We do have to be careful that a data island does not become a separate data model, with its own facts and dimensions, as this can be against the license agreement when using **document licenses**.

Set Analysis

After having done any basic QlikView training, we will have had some sort of introduction to Set Analysis. This is one of the most powerful features of QlikView and allows us to create some great solutions. Of course, like any powerful feature, there is room for misuse and abuse.

In this segment, we will revisit some of the basics of Set Analysis and will explore more advanced topics later on in this chapter.

Explaining what we mean by a set

Understanding a little about sets is the key to understanding how QlikView works. We already know about the symbol tables and the logical inference engine. A simple Venn Diagram can help us understand how they hang together.

As I am writing this, it happens to be the 180th birthday of John Venn (Google has a doodle!). John Venn was a mathematician, fellow of the Royal Society, and President of Gonville and Caius College, Cambridge. He also formalized and generalized the use of what he called Eulerian Circles, but what we know today as Venn Diagrams.

When we load data into a QlikView document and we have no selections made, we will have access to all the data points for the purpose of performing calculations, as you can see:

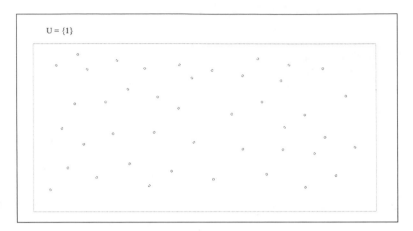

In mathematical terms, this is our universe. It contains all of the entities that we might want to consider. If we perform a simple Sum calculation across a field, we will get the total value of all the values in that field.

Now, let's consider what happens when we make a selection in QlikView. For example, if we were to select the value 2013 in the **Year** field, QlikView would immediately apply the logical inference engine to establish all of the values that are still available, as follows:

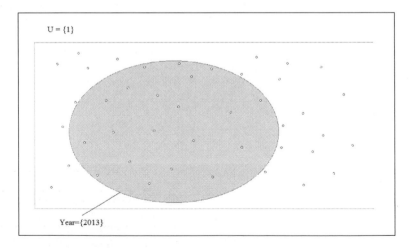

Now, when we perform the same Sum calculation, we only get a result based on the values contained within the shaded area.

If we were to make a further selection, for example, if we select both **China** and **Germany** in **Country**, then QlikView will further reduce the dataset upon which calculations are performed, as follows:

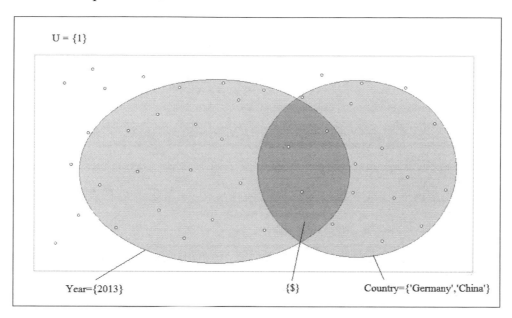

Now, the calculation of the Sum expression is only performed on the shaded area where the two ellipses overlap.

That, in a nutshell, is how QlikView works. It is beautifully simple and a great way of working with data from a data discovery point of view. However, we often want to think about other considerations. For example, if the user has selected **Germany**, what might be the value of everything else that isn't Germany? In the preceding model, we no longer have access to the data about "not Germany" because it has been excluded by selection.

Set identifiers

There are two main SET identifiers in every QlikView document:

Identifier	Description
{1}	This is the universe—the set of all possible values in the document, regardless of any selections
{$}	This represents the set of values based on current selections

Note that the $ sign here is completely unrelated to the $ sign used for Dollar-sign Expansion!

With no selections made in the document, {1} and {$} are identical. As selections are made, {1} will not change while {$} will get smaller.

Other identifiers are possible in a QlikView document. All bookmarks will be a set of the values based on the selections contained in the bookmark. Each Alternate State will also be a set of its current selections.

We write a SET identifier into an expression inside the function to which the set will apply, for example:

```
Sum({1} LineValue)
Sum({$} LineValue)
Sum({BM01} LineValue)
Sum({[My Bookmark]} LineValue)
```

If the SET identifier is not specified (as with most expressions), then the {$} set is used.

Set modifiers

The real power of Set Analysis comes when we can modify a set using modifiers. Any set, such as {1}, {$}, bookmark, and so on, can be modified. We modify a set by specifying an alternate set of values for a field. The values we specify will override the values selected in this field in this set.

Set modifiers are written inside the SET identifier's curly braces using angle brackets. The syntax will look like the following:

```
Function({Set_ID<Field1=NewSet1, Field2=NewSet2>} FieldValue)
```

What can sometimes confuse new users is that NewSet1 in the preceding syntax is often a set of specified values that are written, again, inside curly braces. For example, a set of values for **Year** can be written as follows:

```
{2009,2010,2011}
```

When this is included in a function, it looks like the following:

```
Sum({$<Year={2009,2010,2011}>} LineValue)
```

Otherwise, we can have multiple fields as shown:

```
Sum({$<Year={2011}, Country={'Germany','China'}>} LineValue)
```

There are a lot of different brackets here (not to mention that if the field name has a space, then you will need to use square brackets!) and this can lead to confusion.

There is an old developer's trick that can help you when writing out a set expression: always open and close a pair of brackets before entering the content inside them. This way, you always know that you will have a correctly matching pair. I might write one of the previous expressions in the following steps:

```
Sum()
Sum({})
Sum({$<>})
Sum({$<Year={}>})
Sum({$<Year={2009,2010,2011}>} LineValue)
```

Now, of course, these set modifiers do not have to be static values. We can introduce Dollar-sign Expansion into the expression to provide more dynamic calculations:

```
Sum({$<Year={$(vThisYear)}>} LineValue)
Sum({$<Year={$(vLastYear)}>} LineValue)
```

Understanding Dollar-sign Expansion

Dollar-sign Expansion is a process that allows us to replace text in an expression, or line of script, with either the value of a variable or some other calculation.

Suppose that we have a variable with a value of 10 and we write an expression like the following:

```
Sum(If(Field1=$(vValue), 1, 0))
```

The Dollar-sign expression, `$(vValue)`, will get expanded to its value (10) and the expression that gets executed will be as follows:

```
Sum(If(Field1=10, 1, 0))
```

We can also have a calculation inside the Dollar-sign expression like the following:

```
If(Year=$(=Year(Today())), LightGreen())
```

In this case, the function `Year(Today())` will be calculated and its value replaced into the main expression in the following manner:

```
If(Year=2014, LightGreen())
```

We do have to be aware that it is the exact value of the Dollar-sign expression that is replaced into the main expression, and it becomes as if we have typed that value there. Therefore, if it is a string value rather than a numeric value, then we need to make sure that we include the single quotes around the value.

For example, suppose that we have a variable called vCountry with a value of Germany and we have a color expression in a bar chart like the following:

```
If(Country=$(vCountry), LightGreen())
```

We might be surprised to find that the Germany bar is not highlighted. This is not such a surprise if we consider that the Dollar-sign Expansion will result in the following expression:

```
If(Country=Germany, LightGreen())
```

To QlikView, this looks like you are trying to compare the **Country** field to another field called **Germany**. Instead, we should have our original expression as shown:

```
If(Country='$(vCountry)', LightGreen())
```

This will expand out to the following:

```
If(Country='Germany', LightGreen())
```

 Of course, it can be interesting to use Dollar-sign Expansion to put different field names into an expression!

This issue is equally critical with dates. The problem is that sometimes all looks OK, but we need to consider that, without quotes, the value 8/9/2014 will actually be evaluated to 4.413549597263599e-4 (8 divided by 9 and then divided by 2014).

With dates, you can use quotes and then they will be evaluated correctly—as long as the text of the date matches the field's date format. However, it can often be a better practice to use a function like Floor or Num to transform your dates into numbers instead of relying on the text format being correct.

Following the two-step process

As was mentioned in the *Reviewing basic concepts* section, whenever Dollar-expansion is used, there is always a two-step process followed:

1. The expression or variable inside the Dollar-sign Expansion's parentheses is calculated and its value is placed into the expression, or script line, to replace the dollar-sign.

2. The newly formed expression or script line is executed.

Following the steps in the script debugger

We can use the script debugger to follow the two steps of the Dollar-sign Expansion process. For example, suppose that we had a piece of script as shown:

```
Let vMinDate=Floor(MakeDate(2009,1,1));
Let vMaxDate=Floor(MakeDate(2014,12,31));
Let vDiff=vMaxDate-vMinDate+1;

DI:
Load
    TempDate as DateID,
    Year(TempDate) As Year,
    Month(TempDate) As Month;
Load
    $(vMinDate)+RecNo()-1 As TempDate
AutoGenerate($(vDiff));
```

If we run the script debugger and put a breakpoint on the second load statement, we can observe what is happening when the Dollar-sign Expansion happens:

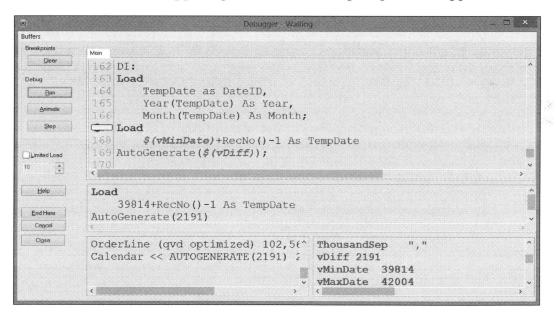

If we look at the central panel, we can see that the Dollar-sign Expansion has replaced $(vMinDate) with 39814 and $(vDiff) with 2191. The original expression is as follows:

```
Load
    $(vMinDate)+RecNo()-1 As TempDate
AutoGenerate($(vDiff));
```

This preceding code is now changed to the following:

```
Load
    39814+RecNo()-1 As TempDate
AutoGenerate(2191);
```

This debugger process is an excellent way of testing our Dollar-sign Expansion in the script.

 We can also use the Trace statement to echo variable values to the **Script Execution Dialog** box and to the document log file.

Following the steps in a chart expression

The best way to follow the steps in a chart expression, and hence to debug the Dollar-sign Expansion, is to use a Straight Table. One of the features of all charts is that if you don't specify a label for an expression, then the expression itself is used as the label, but not just the expression as entered — it is the expression after the first step with the Dollar-sign Expansion complete. This label is the easiest seen in a Straight Table.

For example, I add a Straight Table to my document, with no dimension, and have set the expression to the following:

```
Sum(If(Country='$(vCountry)', 1, 0))
```

Then, I can see the expanded expression by hovering over the label of the expression:

We can also right-click on the label and choose **Copy to Clipboard | Cell Value**, which allows us to paste the expression into a text editor (or another chart or text object). This can be useful if the expression is very long.

Understanding when the steps happen in chart expressions

One thing that might become apparent here is that because the first step, the actual expansion, happens before the expression is calculated; this means that the first step is not calculated in reference to the dimensions of the chart. The first step is calculated outside of the chart.

This can be a slight downside because it means that we can't successfully use a chart's dimension value in a Dollar-sign Expansion expression used inside that chart.

Just to illustrate this, suppose that I add a Straight Table with Country as a dimension, and then, I add the following expression:

```
'$(=MaxString(Country))'
```

I might expect that this should just calculate out the same value as the dimension on each row. However, this is not what happens:

Country	'United Kingdom'
Canada	United Kingdom
China	United Kingdom
France	United Kingdom
Germany	United Kingdom
India	United Kingdom
Ireland	United Kingdom
Russia	United Kingdom
United Kingdom	United Kingdom
USA	United Kingdom

Because the Dollar-sign Expansion has been calculated outside of the chart, it will just calculate MaxString based on the current selections in the document.

Using parameters with variables and Dollar-sign Expansion

We can use parameters in variables and then pass those parameters when we use the Dollar-sign Expansion. This creates a type of macro that can be used in script or in expressions.

A variable parameter is identified with a Dollar-sign and a number. The first parameter will be $1, the second will be $2, and so on.

For example, if I have fields that contain a code and a description separated by a period, I can define a couple of variables in the script in the following manner:

```
// Macros
SET mLefty=Left($1, index($1, '.')-1);
SET mRighty=Mid($1, index($1, '.')+1);
```

Then, I can load my data in the following manner:

```
Test:
Load
    $(mLefty(Field1)) as Field1.Code,
    $(mRighty(Field1)) as Field1.Desc
Inline [
Field1
001.Value one
002.Value two
003.Value three
];
```

I can also call it in an expression, for example:

```
=$(mLefty('004.Field Four'))
```

Of course, this might not work so well in a chart, because of the step order, but it would work well in a text object, caption, and so on.

Using variables in expressions

In many cases, we can just use a variable in an expression as we would in any other programming language:

```
If(Country=vCountry, Sum(LineValue), 0)
```

However, if the variable does not contain a simple value, but instead contains an expression, then it will not work like this and we need to use Dollar-sign Expansion instead.

For example, if we have a variable called `cCompanyWarning` that has a value of `ARGB(200,255,126,0)`, then we cannot simply use this in a color expression because, as far as QlikView is concerned, this is not a color, it is just text. However, suppose that we put it into an expression like the following:

```
=$(cCompanyWarning)
```

We can see that it is no longer just text. The text will get replaced into the expression and then QlikView will evaluate the `ARGB` function as if we had typed it there in the first place.

Using advanced Set Analysis

Basic Set Analysis should be in even the most junior QlikView developer's arsenal of tools. The ability to add modifiers, most frequently to the `$` set, allows us to perform some very useful calculations that we either couldn't perform at all without Set Analysis, or that would have required us to do a lot more work.

Identifying the identifiers

We should already know about at least two of the identifiers that we can use in a Set Analysis expression: `1` and `$`. We also should know that the `$` set is the default so that if there is no set identifier specified, then QlikView will use the `$` set, which is just for current selections.

The following table shows a list of all the identifiers that you may come across:

Identifier	Description
1	This is the universe—it represents all of the values within the document, ignoring any selections.
$	This is the set that represents the values in the dataset as they are based on current selections. This is the default set.
$n	This set represents the nth last set of current selections that you might navigate by clicking on the **Back** button on the navigation toolbar. $1 is the set of selections before you made the most recent selection, $2 is the second last set, and so on. This is rarely used.

Identifier	Description
$_n	This is similar to $n except that it gives access to the *n*th forward set of selections that you might navigate by clicking on the Forward button on the navigation toolbar. Therefore, it is only available if a user has clicked on the **Back** button. This is even more rarely used than $n.
Bookmark (ID or name)	We can use a bookmark as a set identifier, representing the set of values that would be if the bookmark were applied. The identifier can be used as either the bookmark name or bookmark identifier (for example, BM01).
State name	When we use Alternate States in an application, each state name becomes an identifier that represents the current selections in that state. In this case, the $ identifier will still represent the current selections set in the default state, but the default set in an expression will depend on the state of the object containing the expression.

Understanding that modifiers are sets

We know that the true power of Set Analysis comes not just with the ability to specify different identifiers in an expression (although having just that could be quite powerful) but with the ability to modify those sets with our own set of selections.

At this stage, we should be familiar with using a Set Analysis expression with modifiers as shown:

```
Sum({$<Year={2012,2013}>} SalesValue)
```

Here, we appear to have a field called Year compared to an element value list of {2012,2013}.

It makes some kind of sense that Year is equal to either 2012 or 2013 but actually the = sign here does not actually mean "equals". It can't really because Year can't be "equal" to both values.

What we have to understand is that the values on both sides of the = sign are both sets. Year is a data field but that is actually a set of values. The {2012,2013} list is also a set. Therefore, the = sign becomes not a direct comparison, but like a union operation between the set of all Year values and the set of values in the braces.

We have to be careful about this because I have seen confusion around it. For example, it is valid to have another field instead of an element list (the list of values enclosed in {}) as shown:

```
Sum({$<OrderDate=DeliveryDate>} OrderValue)
```

I have seen this described as being where `OrderDate` is equal to `DeliveryDate`. This is incorrect! This set will give you all values where the `OrderDate` values are in the range of the `DeliveryDate` values. For example, suppose that we have the following dataset:

```
Orders:
Load * Inline [
OrderID, OrderDate, DeliveryDate, OrderValue
1, 2014-08-10, 2014-08-10, 100
2, 2014-08-10, 2014-08-11, 100
3, 2014-08-11, 2014-08-12, 100
4, 2014-08-13, 2014-08-14, 100
] ;
```

We might expect that the preceding expression would only match for the first order. However, it could match for the first three orders! The union of the values in the `OrderDate` field with the values in `DeliveryDate` will actually only exclude the last order. The order dates in orders 1 and 2 match to the delivery date from order 1, while the order date from order 3 matches to the delivery date from order 2.

 Note that when using a field instead of an element value list, the comparison set of values becomes the selected values in the field, not the possible values. If you want the possible values, you should use a `P ()` set (as discussed later).

Set arithmetic

We can use mathematical set arithmetic with any set such as identifier, field, or element list. The operators only work on sets and return a set result. The operators are listed in the following table:

Operator	Description	Venn diagram
+ (Union)	The result is a set that represents the union of the sets.	

Operator	Description	Venn diagram
- (Exclusion)	The result will be all of the values in the first set that are not included in the second set. - can also be used as a unary operator (just with one set) where it will return the complement set, for example: `Sum({$<OrderDa te=-{'2014-08-10'}>} OrderValue)`	
* (Intersection)	The result will be a set of all the values that are common to both sets.	
/ (Symmetric difference)	The result will be a set of all the values that are in either set but not the values that are common to both.	

As stated previously, these sets can be applied to identifiers, fields, and element lists. So we can create a set in the following manner:

```
Sum({$*BM01} SalesValue)
```

This will give us the intersection of current selections and the bookmark `BM01`.

We can also have a set as follows:

```
Sum({$<OrderDate=DeliveryDate-{'2014-08-13','2014-08-11'}>}
OrderValue)
```

We can get quite sophisticated with this set arithmetic. If we do need to have more than one set operators, we should remember to use parentheses because `($*BM01)-BM02` is different from `$*(BM01-BM02)`.

Where there is a set comparison that includes the field that we are modifying, we can make use of some shorthand; this will be familiar to C/C#/Java programmers. For example, if we want every year except for one particular year, we can perform the following:

```
Sum({$<Year=Year-{2013}>} SalesValue)
```

We can shorten the expression in the following manner:

```
Sum({$<Year-={2013}>} SalesValue)
```

We can equally perform similar shorthand with the other operators:

```
+=
*=
/=
```

Using searches in Set Analysis

When we first learned to use Set Analysis, we might have learned that we can use wildcard search within a modifier. This is quite a powerful feature. However, we can really enhance what we can do with Set Analysis when we learn that we can also use advanced search within our modifiers.

Essentially, any exact match, wildcard, or advanced search that we can use in a search dialog in a listbox can be used in a modifier.

For example, if we want to see the sales for Germany, we can use an exact match:

```
Sum({<Country={'Germany'}>} LineValue)
```

If we are looking for sales for years in the 2010s, we might do this:

```
Sum({<Year={"201*"}>} LineValue)
```

If we want sales since 2011, we can do this:

```
Sum({<Year={">=2011"}>} LineValue)
```

How about we check for all sales for those countries that sold more than 5, 000, 000 in 2013:

```
Sum({<Country={"=Sum({<Year={2013}>} LineValue)>5000000"}>} LineValue)
```

We know that if we want to get the sales for a list of countries, we can simply list them in an element value list like this:

```
Sum({<Country={'Germany','China'}>} LineValue)
```

However, we also have the option to use search syntax like this:

```
Sum({<Country={"(Germany|China)"}>} LineValue)
```

And, as we saw in the earlier part of this chapter, that syntax allows us to include multiple search options:

```
Sum({<Year={"(2010|2013|200*)"}>} LineValue)
```

This can also be expressed as follows:

```
Sum({<Year={2010,2013,"200*"}>} LineValue)
```

 There is a convention that we should use single quotes with literal values and use double quotes with wildcard and other searches. However, they are actually interchangeable. This is useful to know if you need to use one or the other in the text of the search.

Using Dollar-sign Expansion with Set Analysis

So far, we have used mostly static values in our example modifiers. However, the most power will come when we combine modifiers and Dollar-sign Expansion.

There is no great magic here. Wherever we might use a static value, we just replace it with a Dollar-sign Expansion. For example, we can use the following:

```
Sum({<Year={$(vMaxYear)}>} LineValue)
```

We can also use the following:

```
Sum({<Year={$(=Max(Year))}>} LineValue)
```

The only thing that we need to really consider here is that when performing an exact match with dates, we need to make sure that the value returned from the Dollar-sign Expansion matches the text of the date's dual value. It isn't such an issue if you are doing a greater-than or less-than comparison, because then you can use either the dual text or numeric format. For example, if we have a Month field that is Dual('Jan',1), Dual('Feb',2), and so on, then we can't do the following:

```
Sum({<Month={3}>} LineValue)
```

Instead, we need to do this:

```
Sum({<Month={'Mar'}>} LineValue)
```

Although the following is also fine:

```
Sum({<Month={">=3<5"}>} LineValue)
```

Comparing to other fields

Quite often, in a set modifier, we will want to compare the field to be modified to the values in a different field. There are a number of different options, and they are discussed in the upcoming sections.

Direct field comparison

We have seen this already, but it is acceptable for the set comparison to be directly against another field. For example:

```
Sum({<Year=DI.Year>} LineValue)
```

We can use set arithmetic on these like this:

```
Sum({<Year=Year+DI.Year>} LineValue)
```

 We must recall that the set of values in the comparison field (in this case, `DI.Year`) is only the selected values—not possible values.

Using Concat with Dollar-sign Expansion

One way that we can get over the limitation of only seeing selected values in the other field is to use the `Concat` function along with Dollar-sign Expansion to derive an element value list, for example:

```
Sum({<Year={$(=Concat(Distinct DI.Year,','))}>} LineValue)
```

This might expand to something like this:

```
Sum({<Year={2011,2012,2013}>} LineValue)
```

With text values, we might need to make use of the `Chr(39)` function, which returns a single quote, to derive the correct list:

```
Sum({<Country={'$(=Concat(Distinct DI.Cntr,Chr(39)&','&Chr(39)))'}>}
LineValue)
```

This might expand to something like the following:

```
Sum({<Country={'France','Germany','Ireland','USA'}>} LineValue)
```

Using the P and E element functions

The `P` and `E` functions, which can only be used in a set modifier expression, will return a set of either the possible or excluded values. As they are functions, they can themselves accept a set identifier and modifier. We can also specify which field we want to return the set of values for. If left out, the field that we are modifying will be returned.

Let's look at some examples. First, if we perhaps want to modify the `Year` field with the years that are selected in a particular bookmark, use:

```
Sum({<Year=P({BM01} Year)>} LineValue)
```

What if we want to modify the `Year` field with all of the values in the `DI.Year` field:

```
Sum({<Year=P({$} DI.Year)>} LineValue)
```

Otherwise, to get all of the values in the `DI.Year` field that are not selected:

```
Sum({<Year=E({$} DI.Year)>} LineValue)
```

Set Analysis with Alternate States

When using Alternate States in a QlikView document, we can now add additional complexity to calculations. The syntax is quite straightforward though.

Using Alternate States as identifiers

When we want to access the values in an Alternate State, we can simply add the Alternate State name as the set identifier:

```
Sum({State1} LineValue)
```

Of course, all of the usual set arithmetic is applicable:

```
Sum({$*State1} LineValue)
```

Comparing fields between states

We can also modify a field in a set expression using the set of values from a field in another state. The syntax uses the state name, a double-colon (::), and the name of the field. For example:

```
Sum({State1<Year=$::Year, Month=$::Month} LineValue)
```

Calculating vertically

One of the most powerful features in QlikView is the ability to create vertical calculations in charts. We normally calculate values horizontally, where all values are in reference to the dimensions in the chart. It is a very important feature for us to also make vertical calculations across those horizontal numbers. For example, we might want to know what the total of all our calculations is so that we can calculate a ratio.

We might want to know the average, or the standard deviation, to draw a line in a chart. We might want to accumulate just the last four results to calculate a rolling average.

Using inter-record and range functions

There are several functions that allow us to compare between different records in a chart. Some work in all charts, but others are specific to a particular chart type, such as a pivot table. In the graphical charts (Bar, Pie, and so on), we should imagine their Straight Table equivalent to understand how these functions will work.

The main functions that we can use here are listed in the following table:

Function	Description
Above	This allows us to access the values in the chart above the current row
Below	Like Above, we get only access to the values below the current row
Before	This is used in a pivot table to access the values before the current column
After	Again, this is used in a pivot table to get access to the values after the current column
Top	This gives us access to the value in the first row of the chart
Bottom	This gives us access to the value in the last row of the chart
First	In a pivot table, this gives us access to the value in the first column of the chart
Last	This gives us the value in the last column in a pivot table
RowNo	This tells us the number of the current row in the chart
ColumnNo	In a pivot table, this tells us the number of the current column
NoOfRows	This tells us how many rows there are in the chart
NoOfColumns	In a pivot table, this tells us the number of columns

The default for the Above, Below, Before, After, Top, Bottom, First, and Last functions are to just return one value that will be, as you would expect, the value in the direction stated in the name of the function. Consider the following example:

```
Above(Sum(LineValue))
```

This will give us the value of Sum(LineValue) in the row directly above it.

These functions also take additional, optional parameters. The second parameter will accept an offset value, defaulting to 1, indicating how many rows above we want to take the value. So, consider the following example:

```
Above(Sum(LineValue),2)
```

This will give us the value two rows above. In fact, we can actually specify 0 as the offset and this will just give us the current row.

The third optional parameter, which defaults to 1, will specify how many row values we want to return. Consider the following example:

```
Above(Sum(LineValue),0,4)
```

This will give us four values, starting with the current row. Now, QlikView cannot handle multiple values like this, and if we try to use this in a chart, it will return null. This is where we need to use the range functions, which will handle a range of values like this. There are several range functions, such as RangeSum, RangeCount, and RangeAvg, that are designed for this purpose. So, if we want the average of the four values above, we would do the following:

```
RangeAvg(Above(Sum(LineValue),0,4))
```

This will give us, if the dimension in this chart were in months, a four-month moving average:

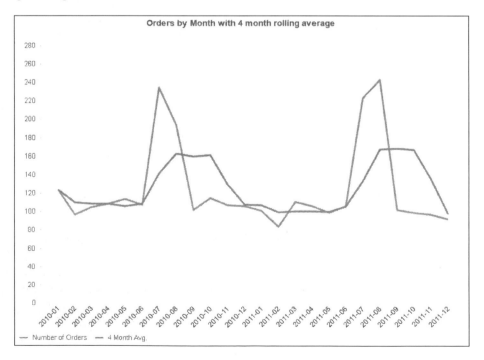

If we include the RowNo function to tell us what row we are on, we can calculate a cumulative value:

```
RangeAvg(Above(Sum(LineValue),0,RowNo()))
```

This might be used in, say, a Pareto analysis:

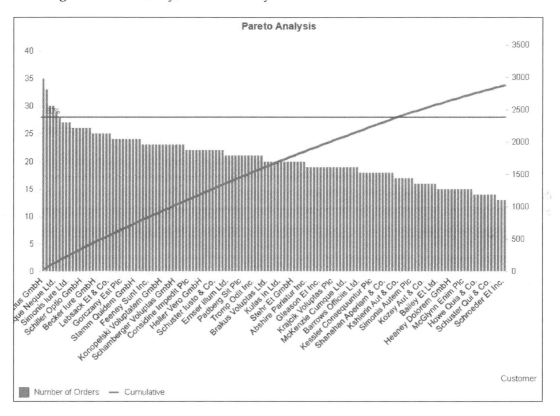

Applying the Total qualifier

By default, of course, expressions in charts will be calculated with respect to the dimensions in the chart. The Sum calculation on the USA row will only calculate for values that are associated with the USA. This is exactly what we will expect.

Sometimes, we will want to override this behavior so that we can create a calculation that ignores the dimensions in the chart. For example, we might want to calculate the percentage of the current value versus the total. When we add the Total qualifier into our expression, then the dimensions will be ignored and the expression will be calculated for the whole chart.

For example, suppose that we have a chart that has the following expression:

```
Sum(LineValue)
```

Now, we add a second expression with the `Total` qualifier:

```
Sum(Total LineValue)
```

We can see the effect of the `Total` qualifier:

Country	Sum(LineValue)	Sum(Total LineValue)
	288,715,597	**288,715,597**
Canada	26,305,874	288,715,597
China	18,349,460	288,715,597
France	18,601,651	288,715,597
Germany	38,453,709	288,715,597
India	7,081,852	288,715,597
Ireland	18,243,189	288,715,597
Russia	19,982,932	288,715,597
United Kingdom	60,134,504	288,715,597
USA	81,562,425	288,715,597

We can see that the dimensions in the chart have been ignored and the same total value has been calculated on each row. We can then change this to divide one by the other:

```
Sum(LineValue)/Sum(Total LineValue)
```

We will get a percentage calculated:

Country	Sum(LineValue)	Sum(LineValue)/Sum (Total LineValue)
	288,715,597	**100.00%**
Canada	26,305,874	9.11%
China	18,349,460	6.36%
France	18,601,651	6.44%
Germany	38,453,709	13.32%
India	7,081,852	2.45%
Ireland	18,243,189	6.32%
Russia	19,982,932	6.92%
United Kingdom	60,134,504	20.83%
USA	81,562,425	28.25%

Now, if we were to add a second dimension to this chart, we would get the percentage of each row in reference to the total as before. However, what if we wanted to see the percentage of the second dimension in reference to the first dimension's total? In this case, we can add a modifier to the `Total` qualifier to indicate that it should not ignore some dimensions:

```
Sum(LineValue)/Sum(Total<Region>LineValue)
```

Now, only the second dimension is ignored:

Region	Country	Sum(LineValue)	Sum(LineValue)/Sum (Total LineValue)	Sum(LineValue)/Sum (Total<Region> LineValue)
Americas	⊟ Canada	26,305,874	9.11%	24.39%
	USA	81,562,425	28.25%	75.61%
	Total	**107,868,300**	**37.36%**	**100.00%**
Asia/Pac	⊟ China	18,349,460	6.36%	72.15%
	India	7,081,852	2.45%	27.85%
	Total	**25,431,312**	**8.81%**	**100.00%**
Europe	⊟ France	18,601,651	6.44%	11.97%
	Germany	38,453,709	13.32%	24.74%
	Ireland	18,243,189	6.32%	11.74%
	Russia	19,982,932	6.92%	12.86%
	United Kingdom	60,134,504	20.83%	38.69%
	Total	**155,415,986**	**53.83%**	**100.00%**
Total		**288,715,597**	**100.00%**	**100.00%**

Creating advanced aggregations with Aggr

QlikView has a fantastic chart engine. It is no surprise that we can get additional access to this chart engine, inside or outside of a chart, so as to create more advanced calculations. The `Aggr` function allows us to create a virtual chart—we can imagine it like a Straight Table—and then, we can do something with the set of values that are returned, that is, the expression column in our imaginary Straight Table.

Like a chart, the `Aggr` function takes an expression as a parameter. It also takes one or more dimensions. It then calculates the expression against the dimensions and returns a set of the results that we generally use in another aggregation function such as `Sum`, `Avg`, `Max`, `Stdev`, and so on. For example, suppose we were to perform the following `Aggr` function:

```
Aggr(Sum(OrderCounter), Country)
```

Then, we can imagine the virtual Straight Table that this will create:

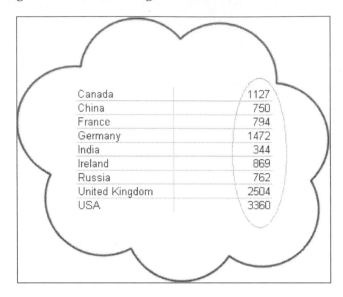

Canada	1127
China	750
France	794
Germany	1472
India	344
Ireland	869
Russia	762
United Kingdom	2504
USA	3360

We might then want to calculate the average of these values:

```
Avg(Aggr(Sum(OrderCounter), Country))
```

When an `Aggr` function is used within a chart, its context is set by the dimensions of the chart. This means that on each row of the chart, the `Aggr` function will only have access to the values that are related to the dimension values for that row. For example, if we want to use the `Aggr` above in a chart that contains the `Country` dimension, we will need to add the `Total` qualifier:

```
Avg(Total Aggr(Sum(OrderCounter), Country))
```

If we didn't, the calculation will respect the dimensionality of the chart and just give us the sum of the `OrderCounter` field on each row:

Country	Sum(OrderCounter)	Avg(Aggr(Sum (OrderCounter), Country))	Avg(Total Aggr(Sum (OrderCounter), Country))
	11,982	**1,331.3**	**1,198.2**
Canada	1,127	1,127.0	1,198.2
China	750	750.0	1,198.2
France	794	794.0	1,198.2
Germany	1,472	1,472.0	1,198.2
India	344	344.0	1,198.2
Ireland	869	869.0	1,198.2
Russia	762	762.0	1,198.2
United Kingdom	2,504	2,504.0	1,198.2
USA	3,360	3,360.0	1,198.2

There is an interesting issue present in this table. The average of 1,198.2 does not appear to be correct! The average should be 1,331.3. However, if we turn off the `Supress Zero` option for the chart, we will find that there is another blank value, `Country`! If we include this in the average calculation, then we will get 1,198.2 and this is what `Aggr` is doing. We can exclude the blank value by using a bit of Set Analysis:

```
Avg(Total Aggr(Sum({<Country={*}>} OrderCounter),
Country))
```

Using Aggr to calculate a control chart

Statistical control charts were first proposed by Walter A. Shewhart, a statistician working for Bell Laboratories in the 1920s. They take into consideration that variation is normal in a process and that we should only be concerned with variation outside control limits.

A control chart will often use a combination and a mean of a range of values from a particular period to compare to another period. For example, we might say that we will treat 2012 as a sample for the deviation of our sales figures and then we want to see the trend of our sales figures in 2014.

To do this, we will have to have a calculation of the mean value that includes a Set Analysis statement to limit to the correct period:

```
Avg({$<Year={2012}>} Total Aggr(Sum({$<Year={2012}>} LineValue),
YearMonth))
```

Note that the Set Analysis expression needs to be contained in both the `Aggr` expressions and in the aggregation function that we use `Aggr` with.

We can add the upper control value for the control chart:

```
Avg({$<Year={2012}>} Total Aggr(Sum({$<Year={2012}>} LineValue),
YearMonth))
+
2*Stdev({$<Year={2012}>} Total Aggr(Sum({$<Year={2012}>} LineValue),
YearMonth))
```

We can add the lower control as well:

```
Avg({$<Year={2012}>} Total Aggr(Sum({$<Year={2012}>} LineValue),
YearMonth))
-
2*Stdev({$<Year={2012}>} Total Aggr(Sum({$<Year={2012}>} LineValue),
YearMonth))
```

Now we should have a chart that allows us to look at different year's performance versus the 2012 controls:

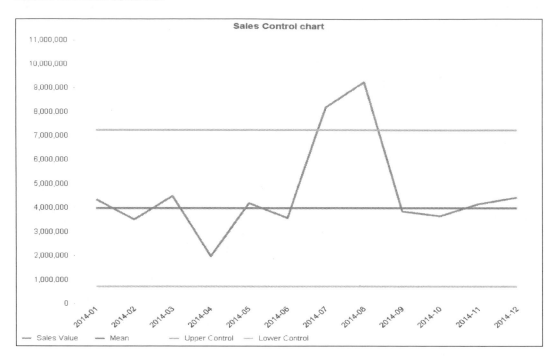

Calculated dimensions

Another use that we can put the `Aggr` function to is to create calculated dimension. Before we had dimension limitations in charts, this was the only way that we can limit some charts to, say, the top 5. In fact, we still need to turn to this to calculate the top x dimension values in pivot tables. For example, if we want to have the top 5 customers, we need to add a calculated dimension of the following:

```
=If(Aggr(Rank(Sum(LineValue)), Customer)<=5, Customer, Null())
```

We should also set the **Supress When Value is Null** option for this dimension. We can also add a second dimension such as `Year` to the chart:

Customer	Year	2012	2014	2013	2009	2011	2010	Total
Friesen Error Ltd.		222,947	93,059	1,025,501	305,584	233,207	553,275	2,433,572
McKenzie Cumque Ltd.		317,481	151,162	800,728	775,069	309,961	376,517	2,730,917
Nitzsche Et GmbH		133,538	260,544	426,261	654,781	412,128	443,324	2,330,576
Toy Sint GmbH		692,042	204,039	776,023	505,591	161,493	344,577	2,683,766
Parker In & Co.		196,973	209,892	858,076	341,792	308,938	404,377	2,320,048
Total		**1,562,981**	**918,696**	**3,886,589**	**2,582,816**	**1,425,726**	**2,122,070**	**12,498,879**

This is a really interesting thing because it is using the calculated virtual chart to provide the values for the dimension, but knows how the dimension values are associated to the data so that it can correctly calculate the totals.

No to nodistinct

The Aggr function has as an optional clause, that is, the possibility of stating that the aggregation will be either distinct or nodistinct.

The default option is distinct, and as such, is rarely ever stated. In this default operation, the aggregation will only produce distinct results for every combination of dimensions—just as you would expect from a normal chart or straight table.

The nodistinct option only makes sense within a chart, one that has more dimensions than are in the Aggr statement. In this case, the granularity of the chart is lower than the granularity of Aggr, and therefore, QlikView will only calculate that Aggr for the first occurrence of lower granularity dimensions and will return null for the other rows. If we specify nodistinct, the same result will be calculated across all of the lower granularity dimensions.

This can be difficult to understand without seeing an example, so let's look at a common use case for this option. We will start with a dataset:

```
ProductSales:
Load * Inline [
Product, Territory, Year, Sales
Product A, Territory A, 2013, 100
Product B, Territory A, 2013, 110
Product A, Territory B, 2013, 120
Product B, Territory B, 2013, 130
Product A, Territory A, 2014, 140
Product B, Territory A, 2014, 150
Product A, Territory B, 2014, 160
Product B, Territory B, 2014, 170
];
```

We will build a report from this data using a pivot table:

Sales Report					🖳 XL
Product	**Territory**	**Year**	2013	2014	**Total**
Product A	Territory A		100	140	**240**
	Territory B		120	160	**280**
Product B	Territory A		110	150	**260**
	Territory B		130	170	**300**

Now, we want to bring the value in the **Total** column into a new column under each year, perhaps to calculate a percentage for each year. We might think that, because the total is the sum for each `Product` and `Territory`, we might use an `Aggr` in the following manner:

```
Sum(Aggr(Sum(Sales), Product, Territory))
```

However, as stated previously, because the chart includes an additional dimension (`Year`) than `Aggr`, the expression will only be calculated for the first occurrence of each of the lower granularity dimensions (in this case, for `Year = 2013`):

Sales Report							XL
	Year		2013		2014		Total
Product	**Territory**	Sales $	Aggr Distinct	Sales $	Aggr Distinct	Sales $	Aggr Distinct
Product A	Territory A	100	240	140	0	240	240
	Territory B	120	280	160	0	280	280
Product B	Territory A	110	260	150	0	260	260
	Territory B	130	300	170	0	300	300

The commonly suggested fix for this is to use `Aggr` without `Sum` and with `nodistinct` as shown:

```
Aggr(NoDistinct Sum(Sales), Product, Territory)
```

This will allow the `Aggr` expression to be calculated across all the `Year` dimension values, and at first, it will appear to solve the problem:

Sales Report							XL
	Year		2013		2014		Total
Product	**Territory**	Sales $	Aggr Nodistinct	Sales $	Aggr Nodistinct	Sales $	Aggr Nodistinct
Product A	Territory A	100	240	140	240	240	240
	Territory B	120	280	160	280	280	280
Product B	Territory A	110	260	150	260	260	260
	Territory B	130	300	170	300	300	300

The problem occurs when we decide to have a total row on this chart:

Sales Report							XL
	Year		2013		2014		Total
Product	**Territory**	Sales $	Aggr Nodistinct	Sales $	Aggr Nodistinct	Sales $	Aggr Nodistinct
Product A	Territory A	100	240	140	240	240	240
	Territory B	120	280	160	280	280	280
	Total	220 -		300 -		520 -	
Product B	Territory A	110	260	150	260	260	260
	Territory B	130	300	170	300	300	300
	Total	240 -		320 -		560 -	
Total		460 -		620 -		1080 -	

As there is no aggregation function surrounding `Aggr`, it does not total correctly at the `Product` or `Territory` dimensions. We can't add an aggregation function, such as `Sum`, because it will break one of the other totals.

However, there is something different that we can do; something that doesn't involve `Aggr` at all! We can use our old friend `Total`:

```
Sum(Total<Product, Territory> Sales)
```

This will calculate correctly at all the levels:

Sales Report								XL
	Year		2013		2014			Total
Product	Territory	Sales $	Total	Sales $	Total	Sales $		Total
	Territory A	100	240	140	240	240		240
Product A	Territory B	120	280	160	280	280		280
	Total	**220**	**520**	**300**	**520**	**520**		**520**
	Territory A	110	260	150	260	260		260
Product B	Territory B	130	300	170	300	300		300
	Total	**240**	**560**	**320**	**560**	**560**		**560**
Total		**460**	**1080**	**620**	**1080**	**1080**		**1080**

There might be other use cases for using a `nodistinct` clause in `Aggr`, but they should be reviewed to see whether a simpler `Total` function will work instead.

Summary

This has been a really technical chapter and a very important one on the road to QlikView mastery.

We reviewed some very important concepts that we need to know before we can take on advanced expressions. We had an in-depth look at searching in QlikView, we reviewed bookmarks, we looked at how we use variables, and then discussed how we limit calculations.

Building on these basics, we delved into Dollar-sign Expansion. This feature is used in so many areas, especially Set Analysis, that we really need to have a good grasp of its use.

The *Using advanced Set Analysis* section showed how we can make use of one of QlikView's most powerful features. This is a feature that most QlikView developers will use in most applications.

Finally, we looked at the area of calculating vertically and discussed important functions such as the inter-record functions, the `Total` qualifier, and last but very much not least, the `Aggr` function. We now know that the `Aggr` function is extremely useful, but we don't need to apply it in all circumstances where we have vertical calculations.

In the next chapter, we'll deep dive into the QlikView script and will look at various advanced techniques needed to load data most effectively into QlikView.

6
Advanced Scripting

"In my opinion, the vast majority of scripts written ... are not very original, well-written, or interesting. It has always been that way, and I think it always will be."

— Viggo Mortensen

In anything more than the simplest of QlikView applications, the script is where we spend a very large percentage of our development time.

When we discussed the performance tuning of our applications (*Chapter 1, Performance Tuning and Scalability*), we discussed that almost all of the effort to make our applications more efficient and to consume less memory will be made in the script. Even when we tune expressions in the frontend, then this is more than likely going to be supported by script work.

All data modeling work is going to be in the script. Of course, implementing an ETL process is something that we do in the script. We can use the script to simplify advanced expressions.

Almost everything we discussed in this book so far is either directly script-related or directly influenced by what we do in the script. Therefore, to truly be a QlikView master, you need to master the QlikView script.

This chapter is all about learning great ways of manipulating data in the script. If you can master these methods, then you are well on your way to mastery of the whole product.

These are the topics we'll cover in this chapter:

- Counting records
- Loading data quickly

- Applying variables and the Dollar-sign Expansion in the script
- Using control structures
- Examining advanced Table File Wizard options
- Looking at data from different directions
- Reusing the code

Reviewing the basic concepts

We will have a quick look at some of the basic concepts that we should be aware of when first starting to load data. Anyone who has done basic QlikView training should be familiar with the concepts here, but it is worth reviewing them.

Using Table Files Wizard

We don't have to use Table Files Wizard to load data from file sources, but it is very useful to help us generate the necessary script to load the data correctly. We have some buttons in the script editor that give us access to Table Files Wizard:

These buttons are listed in the following table:

Button	Description
Table Files	This button opens a standard **File Open** dialog. Once a file is selected, the main Table Files Wizard will open with an appropriate file type, based on QlikView's interpretation of the file's content, already selected for us.
QlikView File	This won't actually open the wizard because it only allows a QlikView QVW file to be selected. It will insert a BINARY statement at the beginning of the active tab in the script. We need to be careful here because BINARY, if used, must be the very first statement in the script, so it should be on the very first tab in the script.
Web Files	This allows us to enter a web URI to point at a file source located on the Internet. This can be HTML, but can also be any of the other supported file types.

Button	Description
Field Data	This allows you to point at a field that you have already loaded into the script (therefore, you must have run the script at least once) and parse the contents of the field using a delimiter or fixed record rules.

Some of us might have (accidentally or on purpose) clicked on the **Back** button in the first screen that appears on Table Files Wizard and discovered the actual first page, which corresponds to three of the buttons:

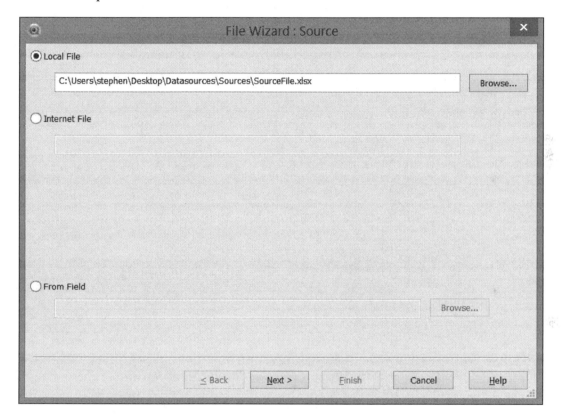

Using relative paths

When we load a file in QlikView, we can either use an absolute or a relative path.

When discussing file paths, an absolute path means the full path to a file starting with either a drive letter or a UNC path, for example, `C:\QVDocuments\Finance\Sources\Budget.xls` or `\\QVServer\QVDocuments\Finance\Sources\Budget.xls`.

A relative path means that the path is expressed relative to another path. The default start path is the location of the QlikView QVW file. So, if we have our QVW in:

```
C:\QVDocuments\Finance\Apps
```

Then, the relative path to the source file is:

```
..\Sources\Budget.xls
```

 The `.` and `..` are relative path indicators that have been around since the earliest Unix days. The `.` indicates the current folder and `..` indicates the parent folder. You can concatenate several of them, so `..\..` indicates the parent of the parent folder.

We can also specify an alternate start path using the `Directory` statement. So, if we issue this command:

Directory 'C:\QVDocuments\Finance';

Then, the relative path the source file becomes:

```
Sources\Budget.xls
```

Alternatively, you can also use:

```
.\Sources\Budget.xls
```

If we turn on the **Relative Paths** checkbox on the **Data** tab in the script editor, then Table Files Wizard will return the path as a relative path, relative to the document location. It will also automatically add a `Directory` statement like this:

```
Directory;
```

A `Directory` statement without specifying a path is actually superfluous, as it means to just use the default path—the location of the QVW file. Therefore, we can feel free to delete this statement if we don't want to use it.

The main reason why it is preferable to use relative paths instead of absolute paths is transportability—we can move a folder system from one server (for example, a development server) to another (for example, a preproduction system) and all of the paths should still work without having to make any edits to the script.

Delimited files

If the Wizard detects that the file content is just text, it usually guesses that we are dealing with a delimited file and will have a guess at what the delimiter is from the data:

It is often quite good at detecting some of these settings, especially the **Character Set** value, but we might need to tweak these sometimes. Usually, the tweak is just setting the **Labels** option from **None** to **Embedded Labels**.

 The usual options in the **Labels** section that we need to be concerned with are either **None** or **Embedded Labels**. The third option, **Explicit**, is only relevant for certain file types, specifically **Data Interchange Format** (**DIF**), which includes a header section that contains explicit labels.

If the first line of the file contains the labels, then we should choose the **Embedded Labels** option. If we choose **None**, then the fields will be named @1, @2, @3, and so forth. We can, of course, rename these fields like this:

```
LOAD
     @1 as SalesPerson,
     @2 as Company,
     @3 as [Sales Value],
     @4 as [Number of Orders]
FROM
[..\Sources\SalesReport.csv]
(txt, utf8, no labels, comment is #, delimiter is ',', msq);
```

To facilitate this, the wizard allows us to change the name in the data display grid, and then it will generate the As statement for us:

Besides changing the **Labels** options, we might also add an entry under **Comment**. Here, we can define a value that might appear at the beginning of a line in the text file (# or // are common), which indicates that this line is a comment and we don't need to load it. Rows beginning with this text will be ignored.

Fixed width files

When the data source has been outputted by a reporting system, it is quite common that the data is in a fixed width format. Every value in each report column takes up the same amount of space, with spaces added wherever necessary to pad the values out to fit. Consider the following example:

```
Country        Sales $  No. Orders
Germany        92,981.20        29
USA            26,265.16        16
France         25,002.56        15
```

To load this in QlikView, we just need to tell the wizard exactly the width each row takes up, and this can be done by a click of the mouse:

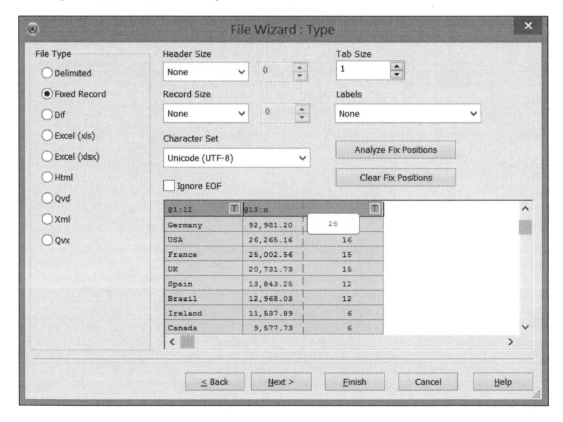

The field names that are generated by the wizard contain the position of the first character and the last character separated by a colon:

```
LOAD @1:12,
     @13:24,
     @25:n
FROM
[..\Sources\CountryReport.txt]
(fix, utf8);
```

The last field will usually have n specified as the ending character. This indicates the end of line position.

We are free to modify these manually, if we need to, as well as adding field aliases. We can even have fixed positions overlapping if it makes sense to do so:

```
LOAD [@1:20] As Field1,
     [@8:24] As Field2,
     [@16:n] As Field3
```

XML files

The wizard is very good at dealing with XML data, from simple tables to more complex relationships. For example, we can have an XML file with data like this:

```
<?xml version="1.0" encoding="utf-8" standalone="yes"?>
<CountryCity>
<Country name="USA">
  <City>New York</City>
  <City>Dallas</City>
  <City>Boston</City>
</Country>
<Country name="Austria">
  <City>Graz</City>
<City>Salzburg</City>
</Country>
<Country name="Belgium">
  <City>Bruxelles</City>
  <City>Charleroi</City>
</Country>
</CountryCity>
```

We can see that the previous data includes values in both tags and elements and also that there is a hierarchy of data between country and city.

When we load this data into Table Files Wizard, the tool automatically recognizes the hierarchies as different tables:

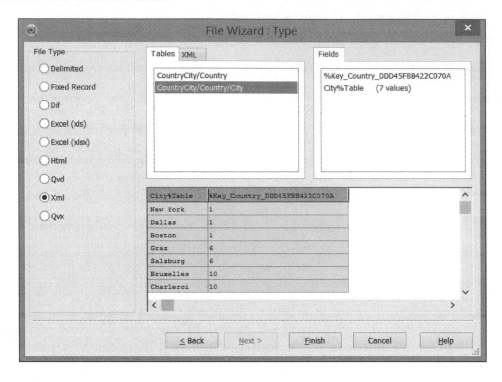

When we click on **Finish** in the wizard, it will generate the code to load each of the tables, with an automatically generated ID field to associate them:

```
// Start of [CountryCity.xml] LOAD statements
City:
LOAD City%Table,
    %Key_Country_DDD45FBB422C070A
// Key to parent table: CountryCity/Country
FROM [..\Sources\CountryCity.xml]
(XmlSimple, Table is [CountryCity/Country/City]);

Country:
LOAD name,
    %Key_Country_DDD45FBB422C070A
// Key for this table: CountryCity/Country
FROM [..\Sources\CountryCity.xml]
(XmlSimple, Table is [CountryCity/Country]);
// End of [CountryCity.xml] LOAD statements
```

Of course, we should probably think about joining these tables together and then dropping the key field.

HTML files

QlikView can handle most HTML files that have tables defined (sometimes, it has difficulty with XHTML). You can either connect to a file locally or a web URL.

For example, if you want to grab the currency conversion rates from the front page of `http://www.xe.com/`, enter the link as follows:

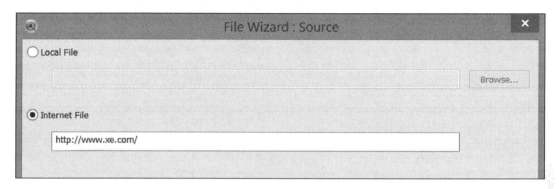

The wizard will connect to the website and retrieve information about all of the tables on the page. In this case, there is just one:

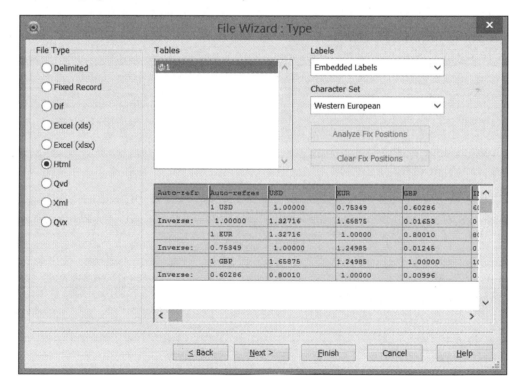

In other cases, you might need to click through the list of tables offered, **@1**, **@2**, **@3**, and so forth, and use the preview window to identify the correct one. The script might look like this:

```
LOAD [Auto-refresh  15x      0 : 59],
     [Auto-refresh  15x      0 : 591],
     USD,
     EUR,
     GBP,
     INR,
     AUD,
     CAD,
     ZAR,
     NZD,
     JPY
FROM
[http://www.xe.com/]
(html, codepage is 1252, embedded labels, table is @1);
```

It could be that the field name that is identified doesn't actually work when you try the reload (as in this case). You could try playing with the spacing—this works here:

```
LOAD [Auto-refresh15x0 : 59],
     [Auto-refresh15x0 : 591],
```

You can replace the fields with just a *:

```
LOAD *
FROM
[http://www.xe.com]
(html, codepage is 1252, embedded labels, table is @1);
```

QVD/QVX files

When it comes to QVD or QVX files, we don't get to modify any settings in the wizard to change the way the file is handled. Setting such as **Embedded Labels**, **Delimiter**, **Header Size**, and so forth, are meaningless when loading a QVD, as all of the information that is needed to interpret the file is already embedded in the file.

Connecting to databases

QlikView can connect to almost every on-premise database system in the world. In fact, the only ones that we might have trouble with are very archaic ones that do not have open drivers.

QlikView can use one of the three different driver types to connect to databases:

Driver type	Description
ODBC	An Open Database Connectivity driver allows us to connect to the majority of the world's database systems because most of the world's database vendors will either issue a driver for free, along with their client tools, or will have licenses for a third party to create a driver. ODBC drivers are configured at the operating system level and their settings are stored in the system registry. Therefore, if documents are moved from development to test/production systems, we need to ensure that the same driver is configured on all systems.
OLEDB	OLEDB is Microsoft's standard for connecting programmatically to databases. It is quite different in implementation from ODBC, but we don't really need to worry about that. Most of the larger database vendors will have an OLEDB driver available as well as the ODBC one. The OLEDB option tends to be faster, especially for Microsoft databases. The configuration information for an OLEDB connection is stored within the QlikView document's CONNECT statement, so it can be a little more portable; we just need to ensure that the drivers are installed on every server that needs them.
Custom	A custom driver can be written, using QlikView's APIs, to allow connections to many more systems. For example, Qlik has custom drivers available for both SAP and SalesForce.com—systems that we cannot otherwise connect directly to. They also have a custom driver that talks to their own server management service and can read information from that into QlikView. In theory, a custom connector can be built for almost any database system that we can think of.

Using the Connect button

When we look at the **Data** tab in the script editor, we see a dropdown that allows us to select the driver type that we want to use:

Once we have selected the driver type that we want to use, we click on the **Connect...** button, which will open a dialog that is appropriate to the selected driver. For ODBC, we don't need to provide any of the connection detail, just the username and password, and the dialog will look like this:

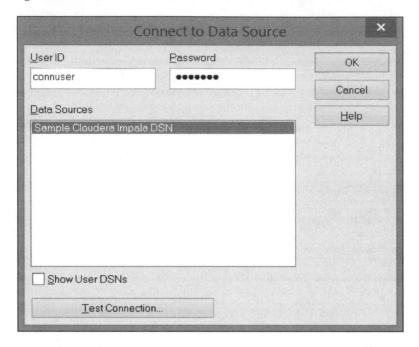

The connection dialog for OLEDB is different because we need to provide connection information. The OLEDB dialog is one that many developers will be familiar with because it comes from the operating system, not from QlikView. We first need to select the correct database driver, and then we can provide connection-specific information. For example, if we used a SQL Server connection, it might look like this:

Any custom connector will have its own dialog. Some have no dialogs at all!

Understanding the Connect To statement

The purpose of all of the dialogs is to generate a `Connect To` statement. This is the statement that tells QlikView how to connect to the driver that is being used.

The `Connect To` statement is usually preceded by an indication of the connection type: `ODBC`, `OLEDB`, or `CUSTOM`. If the connection type is omitted, then `ODBC` is assumed.

Here is an example `ODBC` `Connect To` statement:

```
ODBC CONNECT TO QVData_ODBC (XUserId is IMcKXZFMCC, XPassword is
GRdHfABOQDbKWZJFeE);
```

We can see that all we need is the ODBC name because the rest of the information necessary to make the connection is already configured within the ODBC connection. We have provided the username and password in the dialog box and QlikView will encrypt them so that casual viewers will not be able to see them.

Compare the ODBC Connect To statement to an OLEDB Connect To statement:

```
OLEDB CONNECT TO [Provider=SQLNCLI11.1;Integrated
Security=SSPI;Persist Security Info=False;User ID="";Initial
Catalog=QVData;Data Source=QVENTSQLWH;Use Procedure for
Prepare=1;Auto Translate=True;Packet Size=4096;Workstation
ID=SRVR1;Initial File Name="";Use Encryption for Data=False;Tag
with column collation when possible=False;MARS
Connection=False;DataTypeCompatibility=0;Trust Server
Certificate=False;Application Intent=READWRITE];
```

In this case, all of the information necessary to make the connection will be listed in the Connect string. This is similar to a Custom Connect To statement:

```
CUSTOM CONNECT TO
"Provider=QvsAdminDataProvider.dll;host=localhost;XUserId=HONSdKD;
XPassword=bfAXSUC;";
```

Explaining the Force 32 Bit option

Prior to QlikView Version 10, if your database vendor only supplied a 32-bit version of its driver, you can only connect to it with a 32-bit version of QlikView. This causes a lot of problems for QlikView customers running 64-bit server versions that could not perform automatic reloads without having to run a 32-bit QlikView desktop from the command line.

In QlikView Version 10.0, the **Force 32 Bit** option was introduced to overcome this problem. Now, along with specifying the connection string, we can also specify whether a 32- or 64-bit connection should be used in the Connect To statement:

```
ODBC CONNECT32 TO [QVData] (XUserId is WAKVcARMNLacWYB);
```

QlikView actually calls separate processes to open the connections and run queries. They are QVConnect32.exe and QVConnect64.exe, which are 32-bit and 64-bit applications, respectively. If we call a Connect To or Connect64 To statement using a 64-bit version of QlikView, QVConnect64.exe will be executed. If we call Connect32 To, then QVConnect32.exe will be executed. QlikView running on a 32-bit system can only execute QVConnect32.exe.

The **Force 32 Bit** option in the **Data** tab will mean that clicking on the **Connect** button will open 32-bit versions of the dialog that have access to 32-bit drivers. These dialogs will also generate a `Connect32 To` statement instead of just a `Connect To` statement.

The Select wizard

Once we have created a connection of any type, its details are cached in the document. This allows us to access the **Select** button and retrieve information about the tables and views in our database:

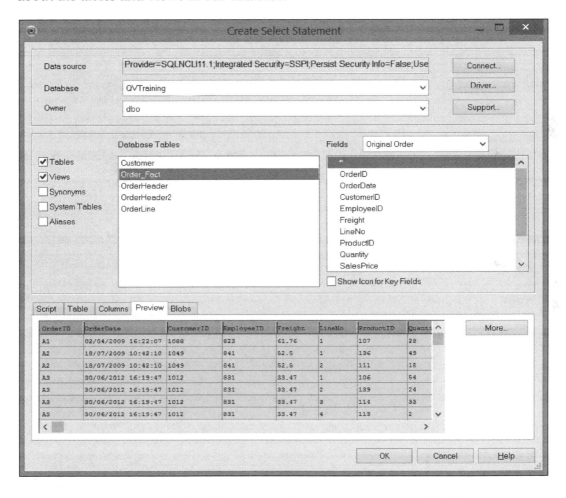

This wizard is a very useful tool because it allows us to interrogate the data structures in the database, preview the data that these tables and views contained, and generate appropriate SQL to retrieve the data.

The default option is for the wizard to generate a very simple `Select *` query to retrieve the data:

```
SQL SELECT *
FROM QVTraining.dbo."Order_Fact";
```

We can also select specific fields from the list of fields to create a more specific, yet still quite simple, query:

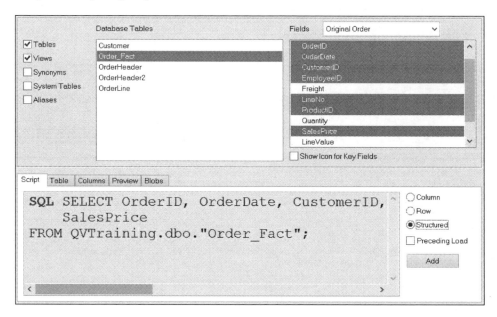

We can also turn on the (highly recommended) **Preceding Load** checkbox. This places a QlikView `Load` statement above the SQL statement. This preceding `Load` statement allows us to apply QlikView functions to the data as we are loading it from the database. A SQL statement with a preceding `Load` statement might look like this:

```
LOAD OrderID,
OrderDate,
CustomerID,
EmployeeID,
//Freight,
    "LineNo",
```

```
ProductID,
    Quantity,
SalesPrice,
LineValue,
LineCost;
SQL SELECT *
FROM QVTraining.dbo."Order_Fact";
```

We might note that even though the SQL query is a very simple `Select *`, we still get the full field list in the preceding `Load` statement.

Note the piece of script that the `Freight` field is commented out. Even though there will be a `Freight` field loaded from the database, if we do not load it in the preceding `Load` statement, then the field will not make it into the final data model.

Counting records

There are two main functions used to count records during load: `RecNo()` and `RowNo()`. After the data has been loaded, we can use another couple of interesting functions: `FieldValueCount()` and `NoOfRows()`. There is also a useful function, `NoOfFields()`, that tells us how many columns there are in a table.

RecNo

The `RecNo()` function gives us the number of the rows in the source table. While the output of the `RecNo` function will always be guaranteed to be ordered, there might be gaps in the sequence because rows may be excluded due to a where clause, for example, this `load` statement:

```
Table1:
Load *, RecNo() As RecNo1
Where Field1<>'C';
Load * Inline [
Field1
A
B
C
D
];
```

Only three rows will be loaded from the source because the row with C as a value is excluded by the Where clause. This results in this table:

Field1	RecNo1
A	1
B	2
D	4

The value 3 is missing in the sequence as the third row was not loaded.

It should also be noted that an additional load from a new source, even if it is concatenating to the same table, will have the numeric sequence restart at 1.

RowNo

The RowNo() function gives us the number of rows in the loaded in-memory table. There should be no gaps in the sequence because the next number is only assigned when the row is actually loaded. For example, if we replace the RecNo() function in the script in the previous example with RowNo(), we will get this result:

Field1	RowNo1
A	1
B	2
D	3

We have to watch out for one aspect of the RowNo() function when using the preceding loads. If we modified the preceding code like this:

```
Table1:
Load *, RowNo() As RowNo1
Where Field1<>'C';
Load *, RowNo() As RowNo2 Inline [
Field1
A
B
C
D
];
```

We will find that `RowNo1` will have values as expected; however, `RowNo2` will be all zeroes. This is because the `RowNo()` function only returns correctly in the top loader of a preceding load. It must be like this because each preceding load can have its own `Where` clause that can modify the number of rows loaded. Only at the topmost load do we actually know that a row is loaded.

`RowNo()` also differs from `RecNo()` because as it is the count of the number of rows actually loaded, additional concatenation of rows from different data sources does not reset the counter. So, if we had a couple of loads like this:

```
Table:
Load *, RecNo() As RecNo, RowNo() As RowNo
Inline [
Field
A
B
C
D
];

Load *, RecNo() As RecNo, RowNo() As RowNo
Where Field <> 'G';
Load *
Inline [
Field
E
F
G
H
];
```

The result would look like this:

Field	RecNo	RowNo
A	1	1
B	2	2
C	3	3
D	4	4
E	1	5
F	2	6
H	4	7

The `RecNo()` function as reset after the first load and skips the number for the excluded rows. The `RowNo()` sequence is unaffected by the fact of the second load.

FieldValueCount

The `FieldValueCount` function will return the number of values in a field. Be careful that it is not the number of rows in a table that contains the field, but it is the number of unique values in the field. The function takes the name of an existing field as a parameter; however, it needs to be passed as a string:

```
Let x=FieldValueCount('Field1');
```

NoOfRows

The `NoOfRows` function returns the actual number of rows that have been loaded in a table. As with the previous function, the table name is passed as a string value:

```
Let x=NoOfRows('Table1');
```

This function can actually be used inline during a table load. Logically, it will return `RowNo()-1`.

NoOfColumns

The `NoOfColumns` function is similar to the previous one except that it returns the number of columns. As before, we pass the table name as a string:

```
Let x=NoOfColumns('Table1');
```

A use case for both of these table functions is to check whether the expected number of rows and columns are in a table after `Join`.

Loading data quickly

In *Chapter 3, Best Practices for Loading Data*, we discussed fast loading using incremental load and binary load.

The fastest way of loading data into QlikView is to use the `Binary` statement. `Binary` will load the whole data table, symbol tables, and other data from one QVW file (Qlik Sense can binary load from either a QVW or QVF file).

The fastest way of getting a single table into QlikView is from an optimized load QVD because it contains a data table and symbol table.

In this section, we will explore some other options that we need to be aware of to load data quickly.

Understanding compression settings

This might not fit exactly into a chapter on script, but it is something that we need to be aware of and because the script defines the data size, the compression setting will define the on-disk size of the Qlik file. By default, QlikView will compress a QVW file when saving it using a high compression setting. We can change this so that medium compression is used, or we can turn off compression all together.

The main difference, obviously, is the on-disk size of the resultant file. We need to think about the algorithm that is being used to create the compression. It will require additional time for the file to be compressed. For smaller QVW files, this is not really a consideration. However, as the files begin to grow more than 1 GB or more, the compression takes longer and longer and this might become an issue for timings of reloads. For example, a 5 GB application might, depending on the hardware, take 5 minutes or so to compress and save. The same document, when saved without compression, might only take seconds. This is especially a consideration when saving to a network drive.

To change the settings for a particular QlikView document, navigate to **Settings** | **Document Properties** | **General** | **Save Format**:

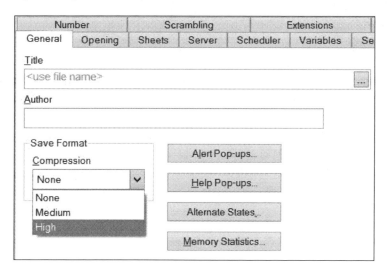

We can also specify this setting at a user level for the creation of new documents, in **Settings | User Preferences | Save**:

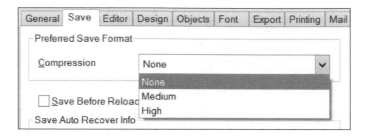

If disk space is not an issue, then there is probably no real benefit in allowing compression for larger applications. The applications will save quicker without it. For smaller applications, there is little difference in time.

Obviously, if we are binary loading the data from a QVW that has been compressed, then there will be that extra step of having to decompress the data. The fastest way of getting data into QlikView is by binary loading from an uncompressed QVW on very fast hardware—solid state disks are the best. We always need to balance the speed requirements with the disk space overhead.

Optimal loading from QVD

We have already discussed how the quickest way of loading a table of data is from a QVD file. This load will be listed in the script execution dialog box as **(qvd optimized)**:

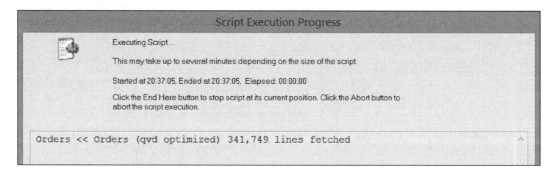

If we perform any additional calculations on this QVD data as it is being loaded— for example, adding additional fields based on QlikView functions, performing most `where` clauses, and so forth—then the optimized load will be lost and a normal, row-by-row, data load processing will be performed. Of course, if the QVD files are local to your reload engine (either the server or desktop), then that reload will still be quite fast.

There are a few things that we can do when loading QVDs that make sure that as optimal a load as possible will happen.

Using an Exists clause

The only things that we can do to a QVD load that will retain the optimization are:

- Rename fields with the As statement
- Use a Where Exists or Where Not Exists clause

The second option here is interesting because we know that a normal Where clause will cause a nonoptimized load. Therefore, if we can think of a way to use existing data, or perform a load of a temporary table that we can use with the Exists clause to keep the optimization.

For example, if we are loading some sales order detail lines into a data model in which we have already restricted the sales order headers, we can use an Exists clause on the ID field that associates them:

```
SalesOrderHeader:
Load *
From SalesOrderHeader.qvd (qvd)
Where Match(Year,2013,2014);

SalesOrderLine:
Load *
From SalesOrderLine.qvd (qvd)
Where Exists(OrderID);
```

In fact, we can replace the Where clause in the header table by preloading the years that we want in a temporary table:

```
TempYear:
Load
  2012+RowNo() As Year
AutoGenerate(2);

SalesOrderHeader:
Load *
From SalesOrderHeader.qvd (qvd)
Where Exists(Year);
//Where Match(Year,2013,2014);

SalesOrderLine:
Load *
```

```
From SalesOrderLine.qvd (qvd)
Where Exists(OrderID);

Drop Table TempYear;
```

If we look at the script execution dialog, we will see that the QVDs are optimized in loading:

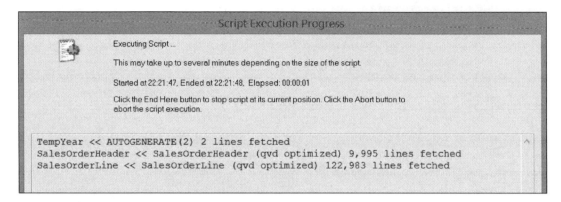

Preloading fields into QVDs

Let's imagine a scenario where we want to load sales information from `Sales.QVD` and then concatenate budget information from `Budget.QVD`. The script might look like this:

```
Fact:
Load
  DateID,
  SalesPersonID,
  CustomerID,
  ProductID,
  SalesQty,
  SalesValue
From
  Sales.QVD (QVD);

Concatenate (Fact)
Load
  DateID,
  SalesPersonID,
  CustomerID,
  ProductID,
  BudgetQty,
```

```
    BudgetValue
From
    Budget.QVD (QVD);
```

In this example, the `Sales.QVD` file will load optimized because we are not making any changes to it. The `Budget.QVD` file will not load optimized because it is being appended to the existing table and they do not have the same fields, so QlikView has some work to do.

What happens here is that QlikView will initially load a data table and symbol tables to accommodate the sales information. When we concatenate the budget information, there might be some additional entries into the symbol table but there will be a significant change to the data table, which will have to be widened to accommodate the index pointers for new fields. This change will be barely noticeable on a load of records measured in thousands, but if we have many millions of rows in one or both of the QVDs, then the delay will be significant.

If we were to take a step back and assuming an ETL approach is in place, when generating the QVDs, we should use the `null()` function to add the fields into the `Sales` table from the `Budget` table and add the fields into the `Budget` table into the `Sales` table, then both QVDs will load optimized. For example, in the transformation script, we might have code like this:

```
Sales:
Load
  DateID,
  SalesPersonID,
  CustomerID,
  ProductID,
  SalesQty,
  SalesValue,
  Null() As BudgetQty,
  Null() As BudgetValue
From
  SalesSource.QVD (QVD);

Store Sales into Sales.QVD;
Drop Table Sales;

Budget:
Load
  DateID,
  SalesPersonID,
  CustomerID,
```

```
     ProductID,
     BudgetQty,
     BudgetValue,
     Null() As SalesQty,
     Null() As SalesValue
From
     BudgetSource.QVD (QVD);

Store Budget into Budget.QVD;
Drop Table Budget;
```

Then, when loading into the final document we can do this:

```
Fact:
Load * From Sales.QVD;
Load * From Budget.QVD;
```

Both QVDs will load optimized.

Applying variables and the Dollar-sign Expansion in the script

We had a good discussion in *Chapter 5, Advanced Expressions*, on how to use variables with the Dollar-sign Expansion. Variables are so important to what we do in the script that it is worth just briefly reviewing the topic from a script point of view.

Variables can be assigned in the script using either a Set or Let statement.

A Set statement will assign the text on the right-hand side of the statement to the variable. A Let statement will try and evaluate the text on the right-hand side as an expression and will assign the result of that evaluation (which might be null!) to the variable. For example:

```
Set v1=1+1;
```

This will result in the v1 variable that contains the value 1+1. Consider the following example:

```
Let v2=1+1;
```

This will result in the v2 variable that contains the value 2.

A variable can be used simply in assignment to other variables. For example:

```
Let v3=v2+1;
```

The v3 variable will have the value 3 (2+1). Let's consider another example:

```
Let v4=v1+1;
```

This will not work! That is because v1 contains a string value, so a string plus a number does not make sense. However, we can do this:

```
Let v4=v1&'+1';
```

Now, v4 will have the value 1+1+1.

Generally, we use variables by using the Dollar-sign Expansion. In this case, the variables are wrapped in parentheses and preceded by the dollar sign. There is a two-step execution where the contents of the variable are first expanded and replace the dollar sign, and then, the expression is evaluated as if the value had been typed there in the first place. For example:

```
Let v5=$(v1)+1;
```

In the first step, the value of v1, that is 1+1, will be expanded and will replace the dollar sign:

```
Let v5=1+1+1;
```

In the second step, the expression is evaluated and the value of 3 is assigned to v5. We have seen previously that we can watch this two-step process in action using the central panel in the debug window:

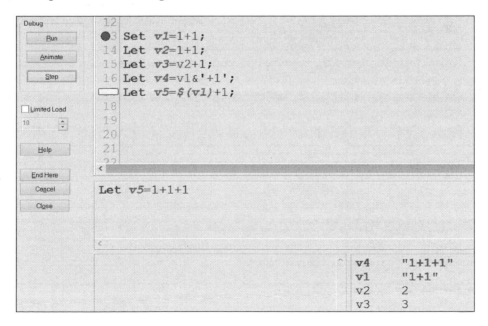

We need to be careful with this because there might be unintended consequences. For example:

```
Let vToday=Today();
Let vYesterday=$(vToday)-1;
```

We might wonder why the `vYesterday` variable has a value of `-0.9998411122145`! This makes sense if we think that the value of `vToday` is something like `8/25/2014` (August 25, 2014), so the second assignment will actually end up being:

```
Let vYesterday=8/25/2014-1;
```

A better way to assign this is:

```
Let vYesterday='$(vToday)'-1;
```

> Note that if you are using dates like this, it is much better to assign the numeric value of the date (for example, `41876` — the number of days since December 30, 1899) rather than the text representation because we have to always be sure that the text value will parse correctly whereas the numeric value is already parsed. `Floor` is a useful function for this as it also removes any time portion.

The following approach is better:

```
Let vToday=Floor(Today());
Let vYesterday=$(vToday)-1;
```

If a variable is assigned a `null` value (either from a failed expression or using the `Null()` function), then the variable will be removed (or not created!). This is useful to tidy up variables at the end of the script.

> Setting variables to null to remove them only applies to variables created within the script execution — variables that have been created in the document interfaces will not be removed by setting them to `null` in the script.

Examining common usage

There are some common use cases of using variables that come up in many applications, so it is worth examining them here.

Holding dates

It is very useful to know which day of the week it is. There is a simple function, `Today()`, that will return the date for today. However, does it really give today's date? It depends! The function can take a parameter:

Parameter value	Description
0	The date when the script was executed
1	The date at the time when the function is called
2	The date when the document was opened

It is interesting that many of us use this function without considering that the default value is 2 — the date when the document was opened. Depending on circumstances, this might not be what we want at all! This is where it can be useful to assign the result of the function to a variable:

```
Let vToday=Floor(Today(1));
```

By placing this call at the beginning of our script, we can then ensure that we are always using the same date throughout the script.

We might also be interested in a timestamp, and the `Now()` function will give us this. However, this function also has parameters that we need to be aware of.

Parameter value	Description
0	The date/time of the previously finished reload
1	The date/time at the time when the function is called
2	The date/time when the document was opened

These are slightly different from the `Today()` function, and the default is also different, which is 1, the time of the function call. We might need to be careful of this because if it is included in a long loop, it will be recalculated many times. It is a much better idea to calculate the value at the beginning of the script:

```
Let vNow=Num(Now(1));
```

As with the `Floor()` function for today, the `Num()` function will transform our timestamp into a numeric value. However, we might not always want the value in this format. We might want to have it in a particular format to use with database queries:

```
Let vCurrentExecution=Timestamp(vNow, 'YYYYMMDD hh:mm:ss');

Orders:
```

```
SQL SELECT OD.* FromvwOrderDetail OD
WHERE OD.TimeStamp>= '$(vPreviousExecution)'
AND OD.TimeStamp< '$(vCurrentExecution)';

Let vPreviousExecution=vCurrentExecution;
```

So, here, I use the `TimeStamp()` function to assign a format to the timestamp value. I can then use this in a SQL query.

In this example, we also have a second variable, which we fill with the current timestamp upon script completion. When the document is saved, we should expect that this variable should be saved with it so that on the next reload, the query should just get the delta change in the orders table. However, what about the very first execution? How can we populate this value if it hasn't been populated before?

A part of the problem is that if a variable hasn't been populated, then it won't exist, so we can't compare it to a value. What we can do, though, is Dollar-sign expand it. If it doesn't exist, the expansion just returns an empty string. We can check the length of this string to see whether it is blank:

```
If Len('$(vPreviousExecution)') = 0 Then
  // Set the variable to an arbitrary date in the past
  Let vPreviousExecution='19990101 00:00:00';
End If
```

Holding paths

We have discussed the uses of relative paths in loading and storing files. This is a generally good idea but there are circumstances where you might need to have absolute paths; for example, when using UNC paths for files, or if you might have changed paths for different purposes.

In these circumstances, rather than relative paths, we will specify the majority of the path using a variable. We might have this in our script:

```
Set vSourcePath='\\QVDataServer\SalesSource';
Set vQVDPath='\\QVServer\QVDPath';
```

Then, we will perform loads like this:

```
Sales:
LOAD *
FROM
[$(vSourcePath)\SalesReport.csv]
(txt, utf8, embedded labels, delimiter is ',', msq);
Store Sales into [$(vQVDPath)\Sales.qvd];
```

If the initial assignment of variables was kept in a separate file, it could be shared amongst several files using an include Dollar-sign Expansion:

```
$(Must_Include=PathVariables.qvs);
```

We use the `Must_Include` syntax here because the include must succeed for the script execution to run successfully.

Examining variable values during reloads

We have seen already that we can examine a variable value in the lower-right panel of the debug window. However, the debug window might not always be where we want it to be when executing a script, especially long running scripts. There is a better way.

The `Trace` statement will echo whatever is typed after it, up to its semicolon statement terminator, to both the script execution dialog and to the document log. As it is a standard statement, we can include variables with the Dollar-sign Expansion and expect their values to be echoed. For example:

```
Trace Previous Execution: $(vPreviousExecution);
Trace Current Execution: $(vCurrentExecution);
```

This will result in something similar to this **Script Execution Progress** dialog:

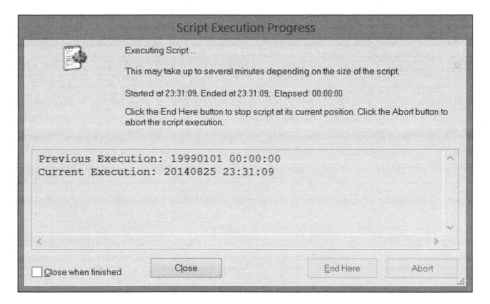

If the **Generate Logfile** option is selected in the **Document Properties**, then the Trace result will also be echoed in the logfile:

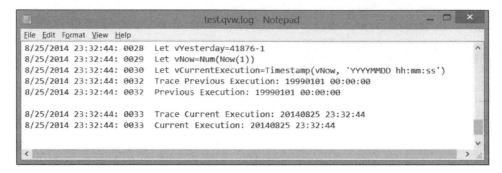

There is no real reason as to why we should not generate a logfile. It saves a load of time in troubleshooting reload issues, especially server executed reloads. If the option is turned on, a file called QVWName.qvw.log is created in the same folder as the QVW. If it is a server reload, the logfile is also copied into the Distribution Services log folder for that task.

Nesting Dollar-sign Expansions

It is possible to nest one or more Dollar-sign Expansions. This allows us to create some interesting functionality in scripts.

As an example, consider the variables used for path names. Imagine that we have a separate set of paths to be tested from production. We can do something like this:

```
Set vTestOrProd='Test';
Set vServerTest='\\DataServerTest\Test\Files';
Set vServerProd='\\DataServer1\Production';
Set vSourcePath='$(vServer$(vTestOrProd))\Sources';
Set vQVDPath='$(vServer$(vTestOrProd))\Sources';
```

We will see something like this in the **Debugger** window:

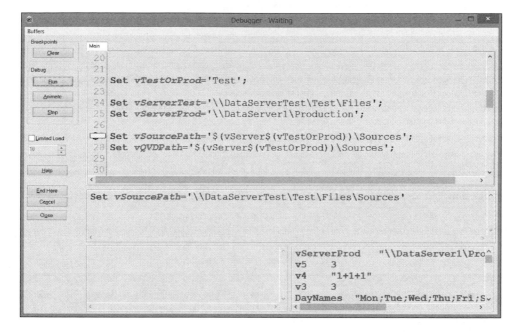

When we nest expansions like this, the inner expansions will be performed first. In this example, the inner expansion sets the name of the variable for the outer expansion.

This might look like a simplified test, but we can actually use something like this, using include files and windows security, to allow only certain people to update the script to start using production files!

Passing parameters to variables – macro functions

We can make a variable calculation a little more intelligent by actually passing parameters to it. This way, it can be like a pseudofunction.

When creating variables with parameters, we can only do so with the Set statement. The Let statement doesn't make any sense here because it tries to evaluate it at the time of assignment, so we can't pass a parameter.

We create parameters by using a dollar sign with a number. We can add multiple parameters; we just need to up the numeric sequence. For example:

```
Set vAdd=($1+$2);
Let vRes=$(vAdd(1,1));
Trace Result of add: $(vRes);
```

This will yield a result of 2. Not terribly complex.

As another example, how about if we wanted a function to format a 10-digit phone number in the (nnn) nnn-nnnn format. We can write a variable like this:

```
Set vPhone='(' &Left($1,3) & ') ' & Mid($1,4,3) & '-' & Right($1,4);

Load Phone, $(vPhone(Phone)) As Formatted Inline [
Phone
2025551234
2125554321
];
```

This is a relatively straightforward calculation but we can have this as complex as we like. Indeed, we can have several of such variables stored in an external file and then include them.

Subroutines

A subroutine is used where we have, generally, a more complex requirement, and we know that we are going to have to repeat it quite often.

A great example of using a subroutine that can be used in most implementations is the repetitive task of storing a table to QVD and then dropping the table that we will have in loader applications. We might implement it like this:

```
Sub StoreAndDrop(vTableName)

  Store [$(vTableName)] into [$(vQVDPath)\$(vTableName).qvd];
  Drop Table [$(vTableName)];

End Sub
```

Then, later in the script, we will call:

```
Call StoreAndDrop('TableName');
```

Note that the subroutine must be loaded in the script before it is called. We can also pass multiple parameters to the subroutine. The parameters become local variables in the subroutine. These are not available outside the subroutine, but variables defined outside the subroutine, global variables, are available.

Using control structures

Any basic development language will include some control structures to either repeat the execution of particular tasks or change what task will happen next based on conditions. QlikView is no different, so in this section we will examine the various options.

Branching with conditional statements

It can be enormously important to be able to execute different sets of statements based on different conditions. It gives us a lot of flexibility in implementing our solutions.

If ... Then ... ElseIf

`If ... Then ... ElseIf` is a fairly fundamental construct in many programming languages. We test a condition, and if it is true, we execute one set of statements. If it isn't true, then we can either execute a different set of statements or perform a new test and keep going.

As an example, if we wanted to test whether a file exists before trying to load it:

```
If Alt(FileSize('c:\temp\Data.qvd'),0)>0 Then

  Data:
  Load *
  From c:\temp\Data.qvd (qvd);

End if
```

 We use `Alt` here because the `FileSize` function returns `null` if the file doesn't exist.

If, instead of not doing anything, we want to load a different file, then we might do this:

```
If Alt(FileSize('c:\temp\Data1.qvd'),0)>0 Then

  Data:
```

```
    Load *
    From c:\temp\Data1.qvd (qvd);

ELSE

    Data:
    Load *
    From c:\temp\Data2.qvd (qvd);

End if
```

Of course, we should really check whether this second file exists:

```
If Alt(FileSize('c:\temp\Data1.qvd'),0)>0 Then

    Data:
    Load *
    From c:\temp\Data1.qvd (qvd);

ELSEIF Alt(FileSize('c:\temp\Data2.qvd'),0)>0 Then

    Data:
    Load *
    From c:\temp\Data2.qvd (qvd);

ELSE

    Trace We have no files to load!!!;

End if
```

A note about conditional functions

There are several functions in QlikView that return a Boolean result. For example, the YearToDate function accepts a date, and some other parameters and will return true or false if that date is in the year-to-date. Unlike other languages, QlikView does not actually have a Boolean type. Instead, Boolean functions will return an integer value—0 for false and -1 for true. In fact, as far as any condition in QlikView is concerned, 0 is always false and anything that is not 0 means true.

This means that there are several other functions that might not be considered to be strictly conditional and can be used as conditional functions. Any function that returns 0 as an indication of a failure to perform and a nonzero value when it succeeds can be used as a conditional function.

For example, the `Index` function returns the position of a substring in another string. If it fails to locate the substring, then it will return 0. We might think that we should use this in a condition like this:

```
Let vText='ABCDEFG';
Let vSearch='ABC';

If Index(vText, vSearch)>0 Then
  Trace Found $(vSearch) in $(vText);
End if
```

However, as the fail condition returns 0, we can just write the `If` statement like this:

```
If Index(vText, vSearch) Then
  Trace Found $(vSearch) in $(vText);
End if
```

There are a few other functions that return 0. If a function, such as `FileSize`, returns a `null` value for a fail, we can turn this into a zero by wrapping it in the `Alt` function as we did just now. In this case, we included the `>0` test, but we could have written the `If` statement without it:

```
If Alt(FileSize('c:\temp\Data.qvd'),0) Then

  Data:
  Load *
  From c:\temp\Data.qvd (qvd);

End if
```

Switch ... Case

`Switch ... Case` is a less frequently used construct than `If ... Then ... ElseIf`; this will be familiar to C/Java programmers. We test a value and then present several possible options for that value and execute script blocks if there is a match. We can also specify a default if there are no matches.

Here is a very simple example; note that we can pass several values to each `Case` statement:

```
Let vVal='Hello';
SWITCH vVal
CASE 'Hello','Hi'
  Trace Hello there!;
CASE 'Goodbye','Bye'
```

```
    Trace So long!;
DEFAULT
    Trace Glad you are staying;
END Switch
```

When and Unless

When and Unless are the equivalent of a single If ... Then statement. They usually appear as prefixes to a valid statement, but there are some control statements that can have them as suffixes. The statement is followed by a conditional test and then by the statement to execute if the condition is true or false. Consider this example:

```
When Alt(FileSize('c:\temp\Data2.qvd'),0) > 0
    Load * from c:\temp\Data2.qvd (qvd);
```

An example of Unless is:

```
Unless Alt(FileSize('c:\temp\Data1.qvd'),0)=0
  Load * from c:\temp\Data1.qvd (qvd);
```

Looping in the script

Repeating a step several times is something that we will have to do again and again. There are a number of ways of performing loops, depending on requirements.

AutoGenerate

AutoGenerate might not be called a loop by some people but it does actually perform a repeating task, the generation of multiple rows, for a set number of iterations. The statement takes one parameter: the number of rows to generate.

Generating empty rows is not very useful, so we need to combine this AutoGenerate with a function such as RecNo() or RowNo() and other calculations based on them. Often both functions are interchangeable because the number of rows generated as source will usually be the same as the number actually loaded. However, if we are going to use a preceding load, then we will need to use RecNo() as the RowNo() function will return zeroes.

Anywhere that we require to create a sequential list of values, we can think of perhaps using AutoGenerate. A great use case is the generation of a calendar table:

```
// Calendar starts on the 1st January 2010
Let vStartDate=Floor(MakeDate(2010,1,1));
```

```
// Calendar ends on the last day of last month
Let vEndDate=Floor(MonthStart(Today()))-1;
// How many rows do we need to generate?
Let vDiff=vEndDate-vStartDate+1;

// Generate the calendar table
Calendar:
Load
  TempDate as DateID,
  Year(TempDate) As Year,
  Month(TempDate) As Month,
  'Q' &Ceil(Month(TempDate)/3) As Quarter,
  Day(TempDate) As Day,
  Week(TempDate) As Week,
  Date(MonthStart(TempDate), 'YYYY-MM') As YearMonth,
  -YearToDate(TempDate, 0, 1, $(vEndDate)) As YTD_Flag,
  -YearToDate(TempDate, -1, 1, $(vEndDate)) As LYTD_Flag;
// Generate the number of rows required
Load
  RecNo()-1+$(vStartDate) As TempDate
AutoGenerate($(vDiff));
```

This script will generate the number of rows between two dates and use the start date as the first value and increment this by one for each subsequent row. The preceding load then transforms the `TempDate` field into various date values.

Creation of a calendar like this might be a piece of script that you store in a separate text file for inclusion in several QlikView applications.

For ... Next loops

The `For ... Next` type of loops are one of the most common in many programming languages. We assign an initial value to a variable, perform a sequence of statement, increment the variable by a fixed amount, then repeat until we have reached the end point.

Here is a very simple example:

```
For i = 1 to 10
  Trace The value of i is $(i);
Next
```

This will show in the script execution dialog like this:

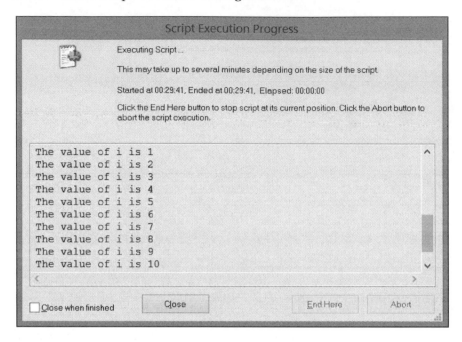

This loop started at 1, echoed the value to the screen, incremented by the default step of 1, and then repeated until it executed for the last value of 10.

If we want to use a step other than the default, we can add the Step to the For statement:

```
For i = 5 to 50 Step 5
  Trace The value of i is $(i);
Next
```

We can even go backwards:

```
For i = 10 to 1 Step -1
  Trace The value of i is $(i);
Next
```

The variable that is generated can be used anywhere that we might use a variable normally in QlikView. Consider this example:

```
For vYear=2010 to Year(Today())
  Data:
  SQL Select *
  From Data
```

```
    Where Year=$(vYear);

    Store Data into $(vQVDPath)\Data$(vYear).qvd;
    Drop Table Data;
  Next
```

This script will generate separate QVD files for each year from 2010 to the present year.

We can also nest loops inside each other:

```
For x = 1 to 10
  For y = 1 to 10
    Matrix:
    Load
      $(x) As X,
      $(y) As Y
    AutoGenerate(1);
  Next
Next
```

For Each ... Next loops

Not every loop that we want to make will be based on a sequence of number. The For Each syntax allows us to use a list of any values that we assign:

```
For Each vVar in 'A','B','C'
  Data:
  SQL Select * From Table$(vVar);

  Store Data into $(vQVDPath)\Table$(vVar).qvd;
  Drop Table Data;
Next
```

We can even derive the list of values from the data:

```
Temp:
Load
  Chr(39) &Concat(Field1,Chr(39)&','&Chr(39)) &Chr(39)
    As Temp_Field
Resident Table1;

Let vList=Peek('Temp_Field');

Drop Table Temp;
```

Note the use of Chr(39), which is the apostrophe character. We will also discuss the Peek function later in this chapter.

There are two filesystem-related functions that we can also use with For Each—FileList and DirList.

FileList

The FileList function takes a file mask using wildcards and will return a list containing the full file path of all files that match. We can then loop through that list with For Each and process them. Have a look at this example:

```
For Each vFile in FileList('c:\data\*.csv')
  Let vFileLen=FileSize('$(vFile)');
  Let vFileDate=FileTime('$(vFile)');
  Trace $(vFile) $(vFileLen) $(vFileDate);

  Data:
  LOAD *
  FROM
  [$(vFile)]
  (txt, utf8, embedded labels, delimiter is ',', msq);
Next
```

DirList

The DirList function is similar to FileList except that it returns a list of folders instead of files. This function is very often used with a nested FileList. The following is an example:

```
For Each vFolder in DirList('c:\data\*')
  For Each vFile in FileList('$(vFolder)\*.csv')
    Let vFileLen=FileSize('$(vFile)');
    Let vFileDate=FileTime('$(vFile)');
    Trace $(vFile) $(vFileLen) $(vFileDate);

    Data:
    LOAD *
    FROM
    [$(vFile)]
    (txt, utf8, embedded labels, delimiter is ',', msq);
  Next
Next
```

Do ... Loop

Another very common construction in programming is the Do ... Loop statements, which cause a block of script to be executed either while a condition is fulfilled or until a condition is fulfilled:

```
Let vLetters='ABCDEFGHIJKLMNOPQRSTUVWXYZ';

Do
  Load
    Left('$(vLetters)',1) As Letter,
    RowNo() As LetterIndex
  AutoGenerate(1);

  Let vLetters=Mid('$(vLetters)', 2);
Loop Until Len('$(vLetters)')=0
```

We can also write this by putting a clause at the beginning:

```
Do While vLetters<>''
  Load
    Left('$(vLetters)',1) As Letter,
    RowNo() As LetterIndex
  AutoGenerate(1);

  Let vLetters=Mid('$(vLetters)', 2);
Loop
```

The difference is that a clause at the beginning means that there is potential for the script block to never execute. A clause at the end means that the block will execute at least once.

Exiting

There are a few different circumstances in which we might want to break the execution of the script or a block of script.

Exiting the script

We can exit the entire script by calling the function:

```
Exit Script;
```

The script will terminate normally at this point, as if there were no additional script lines following it.

This can be an enormously useful thing for us to insert into our script to test and troubleshoot. By adding the function at any stage in our script, we can then find out what state our data is in.

We can enhance the troubleshooting functionality by adding a condition to the exit. We can use an If ... Then construct, but this is also a case where our conditional functions, When and Unless, can be appended. For example, if we want to stop our script unless some condition is true, the following code can be used:

```
EXIT Script when FieldValueCount('Letter')<>26;
```

This can also be written like this:

```
EXIT Script unless FieldValueCount('Letter')=26;
```

As another example, we might want the script to end at a certain point unless it is the first day of the month:

```
EXIT Script unless Day(Today())=1;
```

Exiting other constructs

We can also exit other script constructs such as For/For Each and Do loops and subroutines. The syntax is similar to the aforementioned, but we just need to use the correct keyword for the construct that we are in:

```
Exit For;
Exit Do;
Exit Sub;
```

We can also append conditional expressions:

```
Exit For when vFound=1;
```

Using variables for error handling

Rather than allowing QlikView to throw an error and stopping the execution of a script, there are a number of variables that we can use to handle error situations and allow the script to continue.

ErrorMode

There are three possible values for the ErrorMode variable:

ErrorMode	Description
0	QlikView will ignore any errors. The script execution will continue at the next line of script.
1	This is normal error handling. The script will halt and the user will be prompted for an action.
2	In this mode, the user will not be prompted and the script will fail as if the user clicked on **Cancel** on the prompt dialog.

To turn off error handling, we simply set the variable as follows:

```
Set ErrorMode=0;
```

To turn it back on, we set the variable again:

```
Set ErrorMode=1;
```

ScriptError

If we turn off error handling, we will need to do our own error handling by regularly querying the state of the ScriptError variable.

The ScriptError variable will contain a dual value with the error code as the number and the description as the text. If the error code is zero, then there is no error.

Some of the database errors will generate additional error messaging in the ScriptErrorDetails variable.

ScriptErrorCount and ScriptErrorList

If we are interested in the total number of errors and their details, we can query the ScriptErrorCount variable, which has the number, and ScriptErrorList will have the text of the errors, separated by carriage returns.

Examining advanced Table File Wizard options

The Table Files Wizard is used by many to load a file and generate the load script for it. However, there is a not-so-secret secret button with the word **Next** written on it that is often ignored:

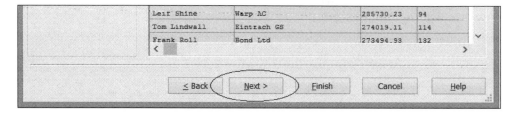

There are some great things in here that are worth looking at.

Enabling a transformation step

When we first hit that **Next** button on the wizard, we are presented with the interesting option, **Enable Transformation Step**:

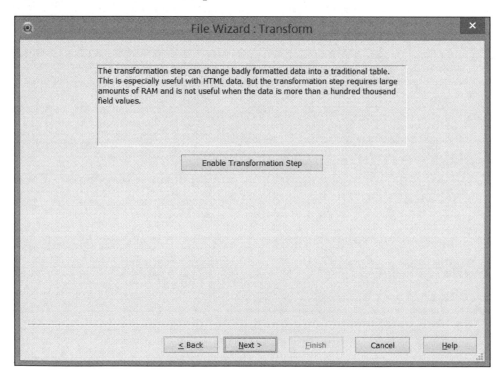

If we click on this button, it brings us to a new dialog with several tabs:

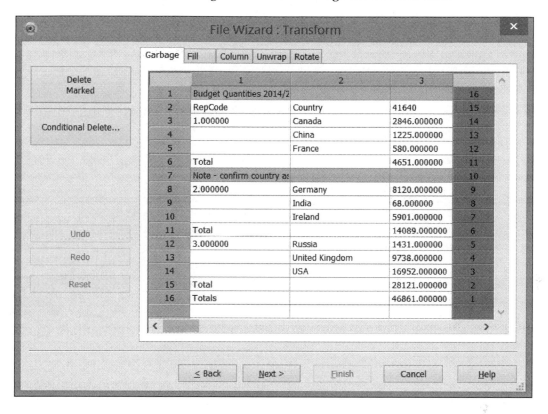

Garbage

The **Garbage** tab allows us to clean out records that are not useful to us. In the preceding screenshot, there are a couple of rows that we can select and click on the **Delete Marked** button to remove. We can also click on the **Conditional Delete...** button and set up a rule to delete particular rows, for example, if they begin with the word **Total**:

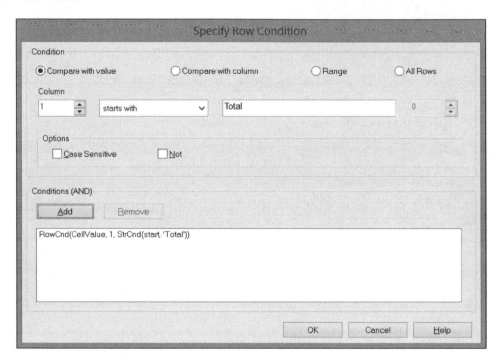

Fill

The **Fill** tab allows us to fill in missing values, or overwrite other values, based on a condition. We can fill data from any direction:

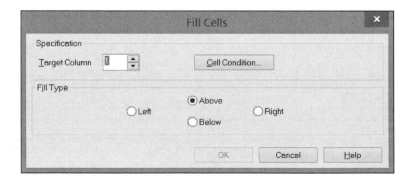

Column

The **Column** feature allows us to create new columns or replace columns, by copying the content of another column:

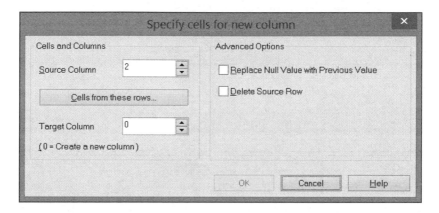

This is quite often used with the **Context** tab because it allows us have two columns: one with the original value and one with the value extracted from the context.

Context

The **Context** tab is only available when working with HTML data. It allows us to extract information from tags in the data. For example, if we go to www.xe.com, we can get a table that lists currencies. In one column, we will have the currency name but this is also a hyperlink. The Context function allows us to interpret the value as HTML and extract the hyperlink href value:

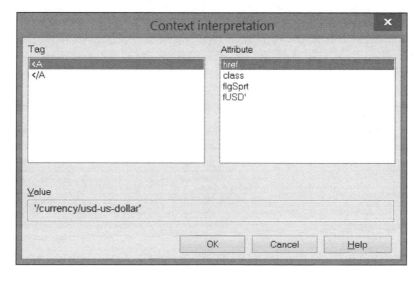

Unwrap

The Unwrap function allows us to take data that might be wrapped across multiple columns and unwrap it. For example, if we have the **Year** and **Value** columns followed by another pair of **Year** and **Value** columns, the Unwrap function will allow us to wrap the second pair of columns back under the first pair where the data should be.

Rotate

The Rotate function allows us to either rotate data to the left-hand side or right-hand side, or transpose the data; that is, columns become rows and rows become columns.

Using the Crosstable wizard

The last couple of pages of Table Files Wizard contain further manipulation options. Probably the most frequently used of these is the **Crosstable** option. This is used, often with Excel files but can also be from any data source, to correct the data where you have what appear to be field names in a two-dimensional matrix and you want to transform them into the field values that they should be. For example, in a budget file, we might have the budget month running across the top of the page:

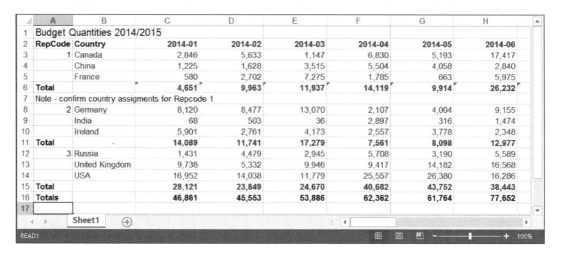

However, the budget month is actually not a field in itself; it should be a field value. This is where the **Crosstable** wizard comes in:

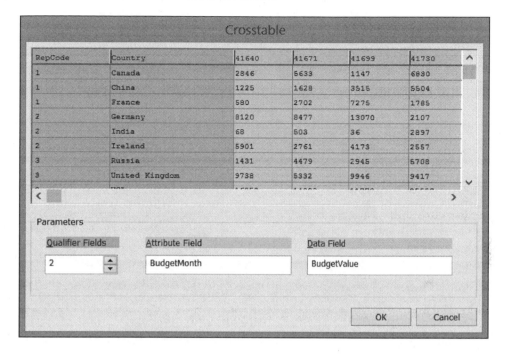

In the wizard, we need to tell it how many fields are **Qualifier Fields**. This means fields that are already correct as field values and don't need to be unraveled. Next, we specify a name that we want to call the new field, for example, BudgetMonth. Finally, we specify a name for the new field that will hold the values that are currently in the matrix, for example, BudgetValue. Luckily, these days, QlikView provides a color coding to show you where each value applies.

When we click on **OK** in the **Crosstable** wizard, we will see a preview of the how the data will look:

When we now click on **OK**, the script to load the table, along with the **Crosstable** prefix, will be inserted into the script editor:

```
CrossTable(BudgetMonth, BudgetValue, 2)
LOAD RepCode,
     Country,
     [41640],
     [41671],
     [41699],
     [41730],
     [41760],
     ...
     [42309],
     [42339]
FROM
[..\Sources\Budget.xls]
(biff, embedded labels, table is Sheet1$, filters(
Remove(Row, Pos(Top, 1)),
Remove(Row, RowCnd(CellValue, 1, StrCnd(start, 'Total'))),
Remove(Row, Pos(Top, 5)),
Replace(1, top, StrCnd(null))
));
```

We can see that the values that we passed in from the wizard have gone in as parameters. Actually, once we understand what the parameters of the CrossTable statement are, we might never use the wizard again!

It is interesting to note that we don't need to actually list all the fields in the file. We can, instead, have a piece of script like this:

```
CrossTable(BudgetMonth, BudgetValue, 2)
LOAD *
FROM
[..\Sources\Budget.xls]
(biff, embedded labels, table is Sheet1$);
```

This will allow different months to be added or removed from the file as time goes on. However, we will need to ensure that the structure of the file doesn't change and no additional columns are added that are not month values (for example, totals)

Another thing to note is that if the column names are numeric (as in this example), they will actually be loaded as text. This is correct because QlikView will otherwise just load the column name into all the values! In that case, we might need to add an additional step:

```
Budget_Temp:
CrossTable(BudgetMonth, BudgetValue, 2)
LOAD *
FROM
[..\Sources\Budget.xls]
(biff, embedded labels, table is Sheet1$);
Budget:
NoConcatenate
Load
  RepCode,
  Country,
  Date(Num#(BudgetMonth,'#####')) As BudgetMonth,
  BudgetValue
Resident
  Budget_Temp;

Drop Table Budget_Temp;
```

Looking at data from different directions

Sometimes, we need to consider data from different directions. In this section, we will examine some advanced techniques for data manipulation that will make our lives easier.

Putting things first

We will often come across situations where we need to consider the earliest values in a dataset, either just the first number of rows or the first value in an ordered set. QlikView has functions for this.

First

The `First` statement will precede a load and states the number of records that should be loaded:

```
First 10
Load *
From Data.qvd (qvd);
```

Sometimes, if we want to just get a fixed set of rows from a file, we can use the **Header** option in Table Files Wizard to remove any rows preceding the rows we want and then use the `First` statement to grab the lines that we do want. This can be an effective strategy where there are several datasets in one worksheet in Excel.

FirstSortedValue

`FirstSortedValue` is a very advanced function that can be used both in the script and in charts. We use it to obtain the top value in a sorted list of values.

As an example, say that we want to retrieve `ProductID` with the highest sales value for each order, the following code can be used:

```
TopProd:
Load
    OrderID,
    FirstSortedValue(ProductID, -LineValue) As TopProduct
Resident
    Fact
Group by OrderID;
```

We retrieve the top product based on the order of the `LineValue` field. The minus sign preceding the field name indicates that this is a descending sort, so the first product should correspond to the highest value.

 Note that this is an aggregation function, so in the script, there must be a `Group by` clause.

We can pass some other parameters. For example, if more than one product had the same value, then the default option is to return `null`. If we specify `Distinct` before `ProductID`, then the duplicate situation will be ignored.

We can also pass a third parameter after the sort weight to, say, get the second or third or n^{th} sorted value instead of the first.

Looking backwards

When loading data, it can be a very neat trick to look at data that we have loaded before. There are two great functions that we can use to do this.

Previous

The `Previous` function can look at a value in the previous input row. This can be really useful. In fact, we can nest multiple previous statements together to look even further back!

Mostly, the function will be combined with an `Order By` clause. This means that we can have some kind of expectation of what the previous record held, and therefore, test for that.

As an example, let's look at this simple dataset:

```
Emps:
Load * Inline [
Employee, Grade, StartDate
Brian, 1, 2010-01-04
Jill, 1, 2011-07-19
Graham, 3, 2010-02-02
Miley, 2, 2011-08-20
Brian, 2, 2012-04-03
Jill, 3, 2013-11-01
Miley, 3, 2014-01-30
];
```

We can see that we have a list of employees with the grade that they are at and the date that they started at that grade. What would be good to be able to calculate is the end date for each of the grades (which would be today for the latest grades) so that we can match these employees to events that happened on particular dates (using `IntervalMatch`).

If we sort the data by employee and then the start date in the descending order, we can compare on each row if we are dealing with the same employee as on the previous row. If we are, we can calculate the end date from the previous date. If not, we just use today's date. Here is the code:

```
Employee:
Load
  Employee,
  Grade,
```

```
    StartDate,
    If(Previous(Employee)=Employee,
      Previous(StartDate)-1,
      Today()
    ) As EndDate
Resident
  Emps
Order By Employee, StartDateDesc;

Drop Table Emps;
```

Peek

Peek is the opposite of the Previous function in that Peek will look at data that has been loaded into memory rather than data that is being loaded from a source. From that point of view, it is always available because the data is just there, whereas the Previous function can only operate during a load. This makes Peek very versatile for accessing data from the in-memory tables.

Peek takes up to three parameters:

Parameter	Description
Field name	The name of the field that you want to retrieve the value from. It is passed as text literal, that is, in single quotes.
Row index	The row of the table from which you want to retrieve the field value. This index starts at 0 for row 1 (just to confuse us) and you can also pass a value of -1, which is the default, to retrieve the value from the last row loaded.
Table name	The name of the data table from which you want to retrieve the value. It is passed as a text literal.

If Peek is used with just the field name, then the most recently loaded value into that field, into whatever table, will be returned. If the row index is passed, then you must also pass the table name, as it doesn't make sense without it.

As an example, let's use a loop to cycle through all the records in a table, extract the field values, and display them using a trace:

```
For i=0 to NoOfRows('Employee')-1

  Let vEmp=Peek('Employee', $(i), 'Employee');
  Let vGrade=Peek('Grade', $(i), 'Employee');
  Let vDate=Date(Peek('StartDate', $(i), 'Employee'), 'M/D/YYYY');
```

```
    Trace Employee, $(vEmp), started Grade $(vGrade) on $(vDate);

    Next
```

As a more advanced example of using `Peek`, let's imagine that we had a sale file output from an ERP system that contained both header and line information in the one file. Here is an example:

```
201A0000120140801
202PR0001000005000366
202PR0002000011001954
202PR0003000017000323
202PR0004000001009999
202PR0005000008003287
201A0000220140802
202PR0001000003000360
202PR0002000111000999
```

Lines beginning with `201` are the order header row. They contain the customer number and the order date. Lines beginning with `202` are order lines and they contain a product code, quantity, and price per unit.

Obviously, we might imagine that we could deal with this using Table Files Wizard as it is a fixed width record. However, the problem here is that there are different width values on different lines. This is a perfect place to use `Peek`! Let's have a look at how we build the code for this.

It can be useful to use the wizard to help us get started, especially if there are many fields. In fact, we can run it twice to help build up the script that we need:

```
LOAD @1:3 as LineType,
     @4:9 as CustomerCode,
     @10:n as OrderDate
     ...
```

The following script has to be run as well:

```
LOAD @1:3 AsLineType,
     @4:9 AsProductCode,
     @10:15 As Quantity,
     @16:n/100 As UnitPrice
     ...
```

Now, we can combine these. We will use Peek to move the CustomerCode and OrderDate values onto the order line rows:

```
SalesFile_Temp:
LOAD
   @1:3 AsLineType,
  If(@1:3=201,
     @4:9,
     Peek('CustomerCode')
     ) As CustomerCode,
  If(@1:3=201,
     Date#(@10:n,'YYYYMMDD'),
     Peek('OrderDate')
     ) As OrderDate,
If(@1:3=202,@4:9,Null()) As ProductCode,
If(@1:3=202,@10:15,Null()) As Quantity,
If(@1:3=202,@16:n/100,Null()) As UnitPrice
FROM
[..\Sources\SalesFile.txt]
(fix, codepage is 1252);
```

Now, the table will contain a mix of row types, but we only need the ones that are type 202, because they have all the good data now:

```
SalesFile:
Load
  CustomerCode,
  OrderDate,
  ProductCode,
  Quantity,
  UnitPrice,
  Quantity*UnitPrice as LineValue
Resident
  SalesFile_Temp
Where LineType=202;

Drop Table SalesFile_Temp;
```

Reusing code

In various areas of this chapter so far, we've suggested that it can be useful to maintain script elements in separate text files that can be included within the QlikView script using an Include or Must_Include construct.

Many organizations, when building their own best practices among their QlikView team, will create a library of such scripts.

One such library that any QlikView developer who is interested in increasing their skill levels should look at is the QlikView Components library created by Rob Wunderlich. Refer to `https://github.com/RobWunderlich/Qlikview-Components` for more information.

This library contains a whole host of functions that, even if a developer wasn't to use them, would be worth reviewing to see how things are done.

As a quick example, something that we do in almost every QlikView application is to generate a `Calendar` table:

```
Call Qvc.Calendar(vStartDate, vEndDate, 'Calendar', 'Cal', 1);
```

That is it!

It is also a good idea to check out Rob's *QlikView Cookbook* (unrelated to the *QlikView for Developers Cookbook, Packt Publishing, Stephen Redmond*) website: `http://qlikviewcookbook.com/`.

Summary

This chapter has given us a lot of good information on functions that we can use when writing scripts.

After reviewing the basics on loading data, we then went into how to count records and the useful functions that we have for that purpose. We had a discussion on the best way to optimize data loading. We then explored variables and the Dollar-sign Expansion in the script. We talked about fundamental control structures and had a good look at Table Files Wizard, followed by a discussion on using different functions to grab data from different directions.

Finally, we had a very brief discussion on reusing code and the use of libraries such as Rob Wunderlich's QlikView components.

In the next and final chapter, we will have a look at the area of data visualization.

7
Visualizing Data

"The greatest value of a picture is when it forces us to notice what we never expected to see."

- John Wilder Tukey, statistician and developer of the box plot

"The purpose of visualization is insight, not pictures."

- Ben Shneiderman, developer of the treemap

These two quotes are interesting in their juxtaposition. One tells us to draw pictures that reveal the unexpected. The other tells us that the purpose of visualization is not pictures but insight. If they were part of the same conversation, one might believe that the two famous contributors to the area of data visualization were in a disagreement.

Of course, this is not true, and these statements were made at different times and in different contexts. However, they could be part of the same conversation. One that extols us to, yes, create pictures, but not just pretty pictures; pictures that deliver insight, pictures that reveal the unexpected.

In this chapter, we are going to explore where data visualization has come from. We will also look at the important things to understand about how humans work with data, and this will lead us to some rules about how to present data most effectively.

These are the topics we'll cover in this chapter:

- Reviewing the history of data visualization
- Understanding the audience
- Designing effective visualizations

Reviewing the history of data visualization

Before we can discuss how best to visualize data, it is useful to understand a little about your audience: humans. The first thing to understand is that humans have been visualizing things for a long, long time. Some people seem to think that data visualization started some time in 1800, but things were happening a long time before that.

Beginning the story

At some unknown stage in human evolution, it suddenly became important to tell stories. In many cultures, the easiest way to tell these stories was to create pictures that would enable the storyteller to show the listeners what was being related:

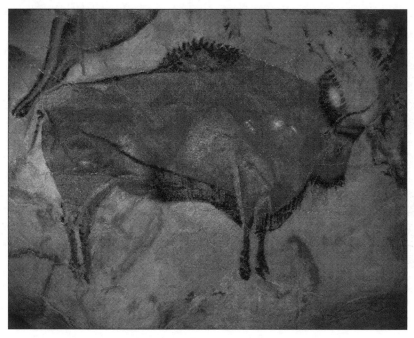

Bisonte Rupestre en Altamira by Baperukamo—own work

This photograph is licensed under Creative Commons Attribution-Share Alike 3.0 via Wikimedia Commons and is available at http://commons.wikimedia.org/ wiki/File:Bisonte_Rupestre_en_Altamira.jpg#mediaviewer/File:Bisonte_ Rupestre_en_Altamira.jpg.

As civilizations grew, the aural transfer of information became more important. Later, the written word became the most important method of transmitting messages. However, art was always the most important way of telling stories and sharing ideas.

As numeracy increased and mathematics developed, methods to use images to understand the numbers started to appear.

Analyzing geometry

The first cases of uses of visualizations to represent numbers come in the area of analytical geometry—using some kind of coordinate system to either resolve or create equations.

Grecian influences

The earliest uses can be traced back to before 300 BC in ancient Greece, during the great era of philosophers, at a time when scholastic pursuits were encouraged.

Menaechmus (around 380 BC to 320 BC) was a Greek mathematician and friend of Plato, who is credited with discovering the conic sections: the realization that shapes like the ellipse and parabola were actually cross-sections of a cone. His methods of proving his theorems had a strong resemblance to the use of coordinates.

Apollonius of Perga (around 262 BC to 190 BC) developed a method that is very similar to those developed by more modern mathematicians. He can't be fully attributed with the development of analytical geometry, because he was also working on conics and his equations related to curves. He was able to come up with equations of the motions of planets, and his work influenced other important mathematicians such as Ptolemy.

Claudius Ptolemy (around 90 AD to 168 AD) created one of the first, widely replicated data visualizations when he created his Geographia. He collected as much data as he could, transformed it using rules that he established himself, and created his famous world maps.

French discord

One of the most interesting debates in Mathematics is that of who really created analytical geometry. The debate centers on two famous French mathematicians and history appears to have come down in the favor of the publishing date.

René Descartes (1596 to 1650) is the historical winner:

René Descartes

This photograph is licensed under Public Domain via Wikimedia Commons and is available at http://commons.wikimedia.org/wiki/File:Ren%C3%A9_Descartes. jpg#mediaviewer/File:Ren%C3%A9_Descartes.jpg.

Descartes is famous as being both a mathematician and philosopher. He coined the often used phrase, "I think, therefore I am". He has also had the honor of having his name applied to the coordinate system used in analytical geometry: Cartesian coordinates.

Descartes published his essay, *La Geometrie*, in 1637. Interestingly, although he reduced geometry down to arithmetic and algebra and he introduced the concepts of the coordinate system that now bears his name, there are no equations actually graphed in this work.

Pierre de Fermat (1601 to 1665) appears to be the loser:

Pierre de Fermat

This photograph is licensed under Public Domain via Wikimedia Commons and is available at `http://commons.wikimedia.org/wiki/File:Pierre_de_Fermat.png#mediaviewer/File:Pierre_de_Fermat.png`.

Pierre de Fermat had also written a work on analytical geometry that was apparently circulating in Paris in the manuscript form in 1637, prior to Descartes publication of *La Geometrie*. It is unlikely that Descartes was aware of this as he was living in the Dutch Republic at the time. So, it appears that both came up with their ideas independently. Descartes was actually published in 1637 (with a Latin translation published in 1649), whereas de Fermat's manuscript was not published until 1679.

The main difference between the two works was a matter of perspective. Descartes' techniques started with a curve and produced the equation of the curve. Pierre de Fermat's techniques started with an equation and then described the curve. Because of this, Descartes had to deal with more complex equations but this meant that he developed methods to deal with higher degree polynomial equations.

Telling stories with diagrams

Mathematicians developed the use of charts to help them work out complex calculations. Over a hundred years after Descartes' *La Geometrie*, scientists and mathematicians emerged who would use charts to educate and persuade. They used them to tell stories.

Educating with charts

One of the earliest recorded uses of using charts to educate was by the polymath, Joseph Priestley (1733 to 1804) who used charts that look very like what we today know as Gantt charts, to help deliver history lectures at Warrington Academy:

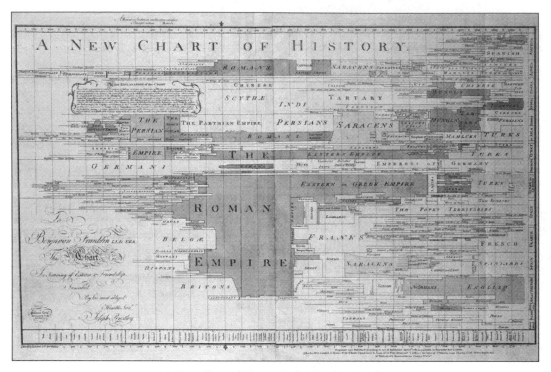

A New Chart of History (color) by Alan Jacobs

The preceding photograph is licensed under Public Domain via Wikimedia Commons and is available at `http://commons.wikimedia.org/wiki/File:` `A_New_Chart_of_History_color.jpg#mediaviewer/File:A_New_Chart_of_` `History_color.jpg`.

His *A New Chart of History* and *Chart of Biography* might have been influenced by an earlier chart created by Jacques Barbeu-Dubourg (1709 to 1779) in 1753 in Paris. However, Priestly's charts were much simplified (Barbeu-Duborg's chart was 54-feet long!) and easier to understand.

His charts were much admired, and along with his influential work in the area of Chemistry, this led him to be nominated by his peers to become a member of the Royal Society.

Inventing new charts

Now entering into this account, we meet one of the most famous individuals in the history of data visualization: William Playfair (1759 to 1823). Playfair, after a long line of interesting employments, became an economic journalist. He was almost certainly influenced by Priestly's time series charts and developed them as a method of representing the change of a value over time—what we would recognize today as a line chart:

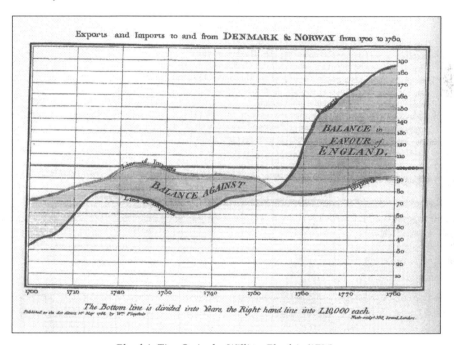

Playfair TimeSeries by William Playfair (1786)

This photograph is licensed under Public Domain via Wikimedia Commons and is available at `http://commons.wikimedia.org/wiki/File:Playfair_ TimeSeries.png#mediaviewer/File:Playfair_TimeSeries.png`.

When creating his work, *Commercial and Political Atlas*, 1786, Playfair had 43 plates that showed these line charts of import and export from various countries over the years. However, he had a problem. He also wanted to include the data for Scotland but did not have all the data. So, he came up with a different solution; he just showed one year's data for Scotland's 17 trading partners with two lines for each that represented the imports and exports:

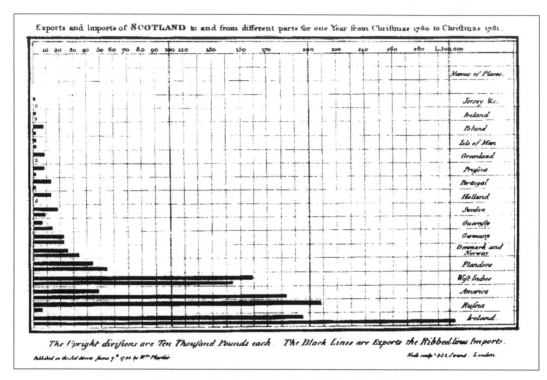

Playfair Barchart by William Playfair, London, 1786

This photograph is licensed under Public Domain via Wikimedia Commons and is available at `http://commons.wikimedia.org/wiki/File:Playfair_Barchart.gif#mediaviewer/File:Playfair_Barchart.gif`.

Of course, this is what we know today as a bar chart.

In his work, *Statistical Breviary*, 1801, Playfair introduced another new chart; the pie chart:

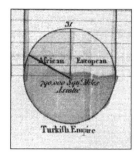

Playfair-piechart by William Playfair

This piechart is taken from *The Commercial and Political Atlas and Statistical Breviary, Cambridge University Press*.

This photograph is licensed under Public Domain via Wikimedia Commons and is available at `http://commons.wikimedia.org/wiki/File:Playfair-piechart.jpg#mediaviewer/File:Playfair-piechart.jpg`.

What Playfair achieved was not just the creation of a new chart type, but it was the use of charts to bring numbers to the public. From that time, the use of charts in financial and statistical publications has become the norm.

Creating infographics

A retired French engineer, Charles Joseph Minard (1781 to 1870), created a visualization that had a big impact on infographics.

Minard retired in 1851 and spent his retirement doing private research. In his career as a civil engineer, he worked on road and bridge projects and used maps extensively. After his retirement, he started to produce some data visualizations that made use of maps to position the data geographically. For example, in 1858, he created a visualization of the cattle being sold in Paris. The chart showed a pie chart on each region, where the cattle were coming from with the segments breaking down the breed of the animals.

The size of each pie chart represented the total sales:

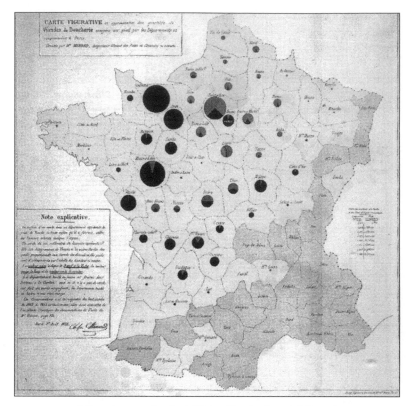

Minard-carte-viande, 1858, by Charles Joseph Minard

This map is taken from *Des chiffres et des cartes: la cartographie quantitative au XIXè siècle, Gilles Palsky, Paris: Comité des travaux historiques et scientifiques.*

This photograph is licensed under Public Domain via Wikimedia Commons—
`http://commons.wikimedia.org/wiki/File:Minard-carte-viande-1858.png#mediaviewer/File:Minard-carte-viande-1858.png`.

His most famous work was published in 1869. Minard combined his ideas around mapping and engineering flow diagrams to show the results of Napoleon Bonaparte's disastrous Russian campaign of 1812/1813. The beauty of this visualization was that the entire campaign was described in one image and the reader required very little effort to understand it:

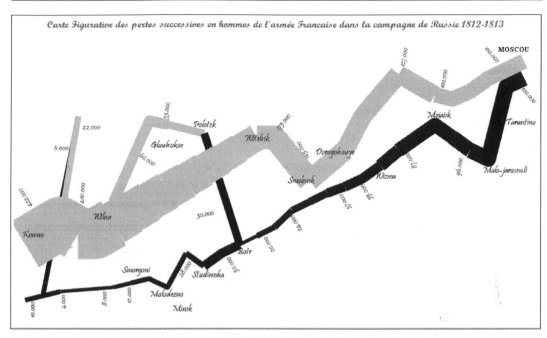

Stephen Redmond's recreation in QlikView of Minard's famous visualization

You can refer to `http://www.qliktips.com/2012/06/homage-to-minard.html` to find out more on how this was created.

Using data visualization to persuade

Florence Nightingale (1820 to 1910) is famous to many people as one of the founders of modern nursing techniques. Her caring work during the Crimean War helped establish her reputation, and she later established a nursing school in St. Thomas's Hospital in London.

What is less well known about her is that she was a brilliant mathematician and became the first female member of the Royal Statistical Society. She wrote extensively on the subject of public health and used her mathematical knowledge to help make her points, quite often including pie charts in her publications to help make her points.

Nightingale's most famous visualization was an early use of a polar chart:

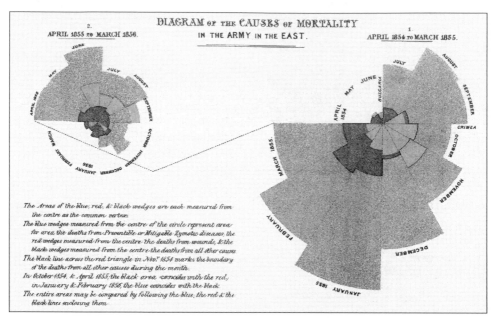

Nightingale-mortality by Florence Nightingale

This photograph is licensed under Public Domain via Wikimedia Commons and is available at `http://commons.wikimedia.org/wiki/File:Nightingale-mortality.jpg#mediaviewer/File:Nightingale-mortality.jpg`.

The segments in this chart show the total deaths of servicemen in the British Army. The red segments in the middle are deaths from wounds. The black segments are "others". The larger blue segments are preventable deaths caused by infections. She used this chart to make the case for better sanitation in hospitals.

Bringing the story up to date

The story didn't end at the beginning of the twentieth century. Mathematicians, statisticians, engineers, economists, and other scientists have continued to use and develop data visualizations.

However, until quite recently, relatively little has been written and broadly published on the subject. One of the best books on data visualization in the modern era is *The Visual Display of Quantitative Data* by Edward Tufte. This book was published back in 1983.

The digital revolution brought data visualization to the masses. Anyone with a PC and Microsoft Excel could now quickly create charts and share them with colleagues. While everyone was doing what they wanted with these tools, the academic study of the subject has been slow to catch up. However, we now have a rich amount of information and research available and there are several leading thinkers in the area.

Following the leaders

There are a number of thought leaders that I follow online and believe that it is worthwhile for others to pay attention to. Of course, following online does not mean blindly following each and every suggestion made by these luminaries. We should always apply our own thoughts and logic to come up with the right solutions for us.

Edward Tufte

Edward Tufte is alive and well and still talking to the world about data visualization. His 1983 book is still in print and widely available. You can follow Edward on Twitter at `@EdwardTufte`.

Few

Stephen Few published his first book on data visualization, *Show Me The Numbers*, back in 2004. This was at a time when there was a real lack of thought-leadership on the subject. He has since published two additional works: *Information Dashboard Design* and *Now You See It*. Both *Show Me the Numbers* and *Information Dashboard Design* have had second editions published in recent years. Stephen regularly publishes blogs and comments to his own website, `www.perceptualedge.com`.

Robert Kosara

Robert Kosara was a professor at the University of Maryland before taking a sabbatical year and joining Tableau Software, where he still works.

His blog, `www.eagereyes.com`, has been very popular for many years, and he also appears at data visualization conferences and is a regular contributor to various media. Robert can be followed on Twitter at `@eagereyes`.

Alberto Cairo

Alberto Cairo is a professor teaching visualization at the University of Miami. His book, *The Visual Art*, is a bestseller in the topic. He has also taught the subject on a **Massive Open Online Course** (**MOOC**). Alberto can be following on Twitter at `@albertocairo`.

Andy Kirk

Andy Kirk is a freelance data visualization specialist, designer, speaker, and researcher. He is the author of *Data Visualization: A Successful Design Process*. He delivers public training on the subject worldwide. His data visualization website is `www.visualisingdata.com` and Andy tweets on Twitter at `@visualisingdata`.

Enrico Bertini and Stefaner Moritz

Enrico Bertini lectures on visualization at NYU. Stefaner is an independent design consultant. Together, they present a biweekly podcast called *Data Stories*. Each episode will involve a guest from one of many subjects within the area of data visualization.

The podcast can be subscribed to on iTunes or via their website, `www.datastori.es`. Enrico tweets at `@FILWD` and Stefaner at `@moritz_stefaner`.

Mike Bostock

Mike Bostock has had a huge influence on the area of data visualization because he is the founder of and chief contributor to the d3.js JavaScript library. This library allows developers to create engaging web content from their data with very little coding. The library can also be relatively easily used within Qlik extension objects.

Mike's day job is working for the *New York Times* as part of their award-winning visualization team where they regularly push the boundaries of how we view data. He has his own blog at `bost.ocks.org` and he tweets at `@mbostock`.

Understanding the audience

To deliver effective data visualizations, we need to understand our audience: human beings.

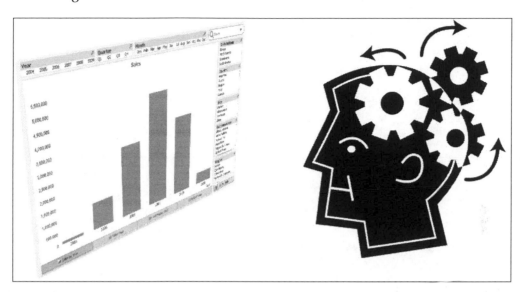

There are some rules that we need to know when dealing with humans. These are based on sound psychological studies, and therefore, aren't always true! They are good guidelines that apply to the majority of the population, but we really need to know that you can't please all of the people all of the time.

Matching patterns

One of the things that humans really excel at is recognizing things that they have seen before or look similar to things that they have seen before and associating those things with other similar things that they have experienced before. As we tend to share a lot of cultural experiences, many of us will share the same generalizations. For example, you might have seen this in your Facebook or e-mail in the recent past:

"Olny srmat poelpe can raed tihs.

I cdnuolt blveiee taht I cluod aulaclty uesdnatnrd waht I was rdanieg. The phaonmneal pweor of the hmuan mnid, aoccdrnig to a rscheearch at Cmabrigde Uinervtisy, it deosn't mttaer in waht oredr the ltteers in a wrod are, t he olny iprmoatnt tihng is taht the frist and lsat ltteer be in the rgh it pclae. The rset can be a taotl mses and you can sitll raed it wouthit a porbelm. Tihs is bcuseae the huamn mnid deos not raed ervey lteter by istlef, but the wrod as a wlohe. Amzanig huh? yaeh and I awlyas tghuhot slpeling was ipmorantt!"

Of course, this isn't true! Consider this sentence:

```
udinsnantderg lugagane sdolem egurecaons ciosonfun
```

In the first paragraph, the letters aren't really completely scrambled. They are close enough to the originals for us to easily read the paragraph as we scan across them and match the patterns to the words. In the second sentence, the letters are truly scrambled, and we need to try and employ our anagram-solving skills to try and understand the sentence: understanding language seldom encourages confusion.

The process of seeing patterns in things that might otherwise be considered random is called apophenia. It is something that we do a lot because we are very good at it. Imagine driving down the freeway and seeing a cloud ahead of you.

What do you see? Is it merely a collection of water droplets, floating on air currents? Or is it a dragon, flying through the sky? It could be anything. To each of us, it is whatever our brains make of it, whatever pattern we match.

We are fantastic at seeing these pictures. We have a large proportion of our brain devoted to the whole area of visuals and matching patterns against our memory, far bigger than for any other sense.

Counting numbers

We, as humans, don't have a very long history with numbers. This is because for very long stretches of our evolution, we just didn't need number systems. As hunter-gatherers, it was not necessary for us to count accurately. All we needed to do was make estimations.

We can still see this today in surviving hunter-gatherer tribes such as the Warlpiri in Australia and the Munduruku in the Amazon. Both tribes have words in their languages for small numbers such as one, two, or three, but after that they either have no words at all or have some words but are inconsistent in their use.

About 10,000 years ago, things started to change. Although there is evidence of limited agriculture in surrounding areas, the real changes happened in and around an area known as Fertile Crescent (`http://en.wikipedia.org/wiki/Fertile_Crescent`), an area sitting between the Nile Delta in the southwest, the Caspian Sea in the northeast, the Black Sea in the northwest, and the Persian Gulf in the southeast. The main rivers of this area, Tigris, Euphrates, and Nile, created a large area of fertile land and agriculture and husbandry of animals exploded. Man started changing from hunter-gatherer to farmer and shepherd.

As we settled down, we started trading with each other. Suddenly, we came up with a reason to count things! When we went to bed with one hundred sheep in the field, it was important to know that there were one hundred sheep still there in the morning.

Given that we have had up to a million years of evolution, it might not be too far a stretch to say that most humans are not as comfortable with numbers as they think.

Estimating numbers

Consider this figure:

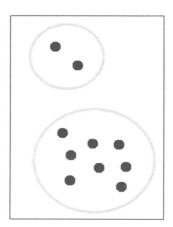

How many dots are in the upper circle?

How many dots are in the lower circle?

Now, consider how you answered both those questions. I would suggest that most people will look at the upper circle and immediately see two dots. However, when most people look at the second circle, they will not immediately see eight dots. Instead, they will often switch to breaking the number down, perhaps see three + two + three (vertically), three + three + two (horizontally), or some other breakdown, and then add those back up to get the number eight. Even for such a relatively small number such as eight, we still tend to break it down into smaller groups. So, how can we count this number of dots?

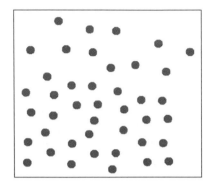

Of course, we can't count these in one go. We could spend a minute counting them one by one, although we still might not get the correct answer as the random arrangement could lead to mistakes. Alternatively, we could just have a guess and estimate the correct answer. Wouldn't that be good enough for most situations? It would be especially good enough if our goal is just to answer the question of which side has more dots:

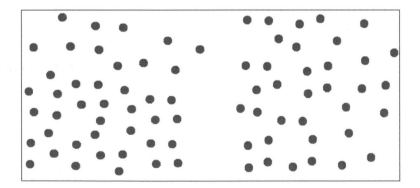

If we have to answer the question with any sort of immediacy, we need to quickly estimate and decide. Quite often though, we will get the right answer! Our brains are actually very good at this estimation, and it comes from a time a long way before numbers existed.

When deciding where to spend valuable energy to chase down or gather food, early man would have had to make the calculations on return on investment. All of these would have been done by estimations: how many wildebeests are there in the herd, how far it was to get to them, or how many people are needed to hunt them down. We still do this today! If we walk into a fast-food restaurant at lunchtime, and you see eight long queues of people waiting to be served, we immediately start making evaluations and estimations about which queue should be the one for us to spend our valuable time in to get the reward; otherwise, we estimate that it is not worth spending time for that reward and we leave.

So, knowing that we are naturally good at estimation, how does this help when we are working with numbers—something that we have, relatively, spent a lot less time with?

It would appear that when it comes to numbers, we still perform estimations. When we see two numbers beside each other, especially large numbers, our brains will make estimates of the size of the numbers and create a ratio, though not always accurately. Let's consider this famous set of numbers:

Row	1 x	1 y	2 x	2 y	3 x	3 y	4 x	4 y
1	10	8.04	10	9.14	10	7.46	8	6.58
2	8	6.95	8	8.14	8	6.77	8	5.76
3	13	7.58	13	8.74	13	12.74	8	7.71
4	9	8.81	9	8.77	9	7.11	8	8.84
5	11	8.33	11	9.26	11	7.81	8	8.47
6	14	9.96	14	8.1	14	8.84	8	7.04
7	6	7.24	6	6.13	6	6.08	8	5.25
8	4	4.26	4	3.1	4	5.39	19	12.5
9	12	10.84	12	9.13	12	8.15	8	5.56
10	7	4.82	7	7.26	7	6.42	8	7.91
11	5	5.68	5	4.74	5	5.73	8	6.89

Anscombe's Quartet, created in 1973 by the statistician, Francis Anscombe

Just spend a minute perusing the numbers and see whether you can see anything interesting in them.

They look reasonably similar. We might think about doing some analysis of the data to see whether there is a major difference. Perhaps, we should average them:

1 avg(x)	1 avg(y)	2 avg(x)	2 avg(y)	3 avg(x)	3 avg(y)	4 avg(x)	4 avg(y)
9.00	7.50	9.00	7.50	9.00	7.50	9.00	7.50

Quite interestingly, it appears that each set of columns has the same average for the **X** and **Y** values. Perhaps, we should look at the standard deviation:

1		2		3		4	
stdev...	stdev...	stdev...	stdev...	stdev...	stdev...	stdev...	stdev...
3.32	2.03	3.32	2.03	3.32	2.03	3.32	2.03

Again, it appears that we have a very similar dataset indeed. Perhaps, we should calculate the slope of the regression line for these numbers:

1	2	3	4
3.00	3.00	3.00	3.00

Statistically speaking, this is a remarkably similar dataset. I wonder how this dataset would look if we actually graphed it:

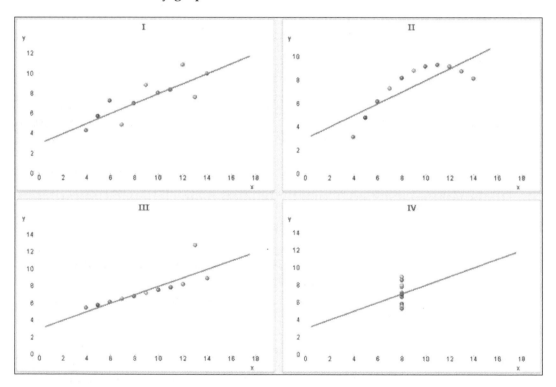

Incredible! We have a dataset that looks quite similar on casual inspection, and even more so when we apply common statistical functions, but when we graph it we can see that it is completely different!

Understanding picture superiority

There have been many studies into the picture superiority effect, where it is shown that we understand and learn far better using pictures than words. For example, a study by Georg Stenberg of Kristianstad University, Sweden, in 2006, entitled, *Conceptual and perceptual factors in the picture superiority effect*, looked at memory superiority of pictures over words.

Every study will show that we remember pictures better and that we can associate pictures with other memory items better; we just process visual images faster than spoken words or sentences written on a page.

A larger portion of our brain's cortex is devoted to visuals as opposed to every other sense. This shouldn't be a surprise as we are a relatively slow and weak animal with an inferior sense of smell and hearing compared with other animals. Our vision and our ability to process visuals is one of the things that has made us the dominant species on this planet.

Drawing conclusions

So, we know that humans are excellent pattern matchers. We can see patterns in shapes and create stories from those patterns that match our experiences. However, we are not really that great with numbers. We like to think that we are, but we often fail to see patterns in sets of numbers.

We are quite comfortable with very small numbers, but even with slightly bigger numbers, we will adopt a strategy of breaking them down to smaller parts to help us understand.

We don't really get exact numbers unless we can directly experience them. For example, for many of us, the phrase, "20 minutes", has no real meaning whereas the phrase, "about 20 minutes", is immediately understood! This is because we have no natural reference point for exactly how long a second or a minute is, let alone 20 minutes, but we can reference our experience and understand exactly how long *about* 20 minutes is.

So, if humans are not very good at dealing with exact numbers, what is the most effective way of communicating with numbers? We cannot rely on people gaining insight from a column of numbers in a spreadsheet. The only way to help us understand numbers is to present them graphically and in context.

We really need to *show* people the numbers.

Designing effective visualizations

It is useful for designers of user interfaces to understand some general design principles. It can only make them better UI designers and deliver a better user experience.

It might seem that the positioning of elements on the screen shouldn't be that important. Surely, it depends on the style of the Qlik developer. However, is it important? It is important because we need to consider the person who is clicking the mouse. The user should always be considered in any design of layout, and we should strive for a clean design, consistency, and ease of use.

Understanding affordances

Donald Norman is a famous person in the area of design. Not in the area of data visualization at all, but just the design of everyday things. In fact, one of his best works is called *The Design of Everyday Things*.

Norman adopted a term that is now central in design: the idea of affordance. Originally, an affordance means all of the things that an item affords you to do with it. For example, a table affords us with many options: we can place things, sit, write or even dance on it! Some other items have very few affordances. For example, a button on a screen has pretty much only one: you can click on it. However, Norman had a closer definition of this term: not all the things that are physically possible, but the possibilities of different actions that will be immediately apparent to the person using the item (we don't all immediately think of dancing on tables!) I like to call these "unwritten rules": you look at something and will just know what to do with it.

A classic example of this is the known as a Donald Door because so many people reference Donald Norman when discussing it. When we see a door that has a flat panel on it, we don't even need to look for the word, "PUSH," above the panel, because we know how to open that door. Similarly, when we see a door that has a long vertical bar, our natural instinct is to grasp the bar and pull—this is the unwritten rule. However, we are often stymied in our attempts to open such a door until we realize that actually we need to push it. Here is an example:

Image courtesy of Colman Walsh, Owner, UXTraining

This image was taken from the UX article, *The Usability of Garda Doors* which can be found at `http://iqcontent.com/blog/2007/01/`.

Here, we see a door that users want to grab and pull, but they should grab and push. It is clear, from the wear on the word, **PUSH**, on the panel, that regular users of this door completely bypass the use of the handle and push against the panel instead. They choose to do the natural thing and reject the unnatural.

As user interface designers, we should always think about how the user will actually use our layouts. We might do things that cause minor irritations to users that become major irritations over extended use. If we have difficulty getting into the mind of a user, it is useful to engage with users and talk to them about how they like or dislike using an interface.

Grading your screen's real estate

Not all areas of the screen are equal. Depending on the user and their connection with the data, how they look at it will also be different, but with some similarities.

Nielsen's F

Jakob Nielsen is the cofounder, along with the aforementioned Donald Norman, of the Nielsen Norman Group, a major design consultancy. He has done a large amount of work in the area of user experience and has created several usability methods.

One of his experiments was to use eye-tracking equipment to track how users viewed websites. You can refer to `http://www.nngroup.com/articles/f-shaped-pattern-reading-web-content/` for more information.

The interesting thing for us to take note of is that when users first look at a page on the screen, their gaze is directed immediately to the top-left area of the screen. They will spend some time here and across the top and then move down and to the left again, but spend less time on the lower areas. The gaze pattern often looks like the shape of the capital letter, F.

There might be a difference in other cultures; however, a learned response by web users in those cultures might also cause them to look to the upper-left area first.

The important conclusion for us is that the upper-left area of the screen is the most important real estate and should contain the most important information.

The Gutenberg diagram

The theory of the Gutenberg diagram, created by Edmund Arnold (1913 to 2007), a newspaper layout designer, is that a page can be divided into four main areas like this:

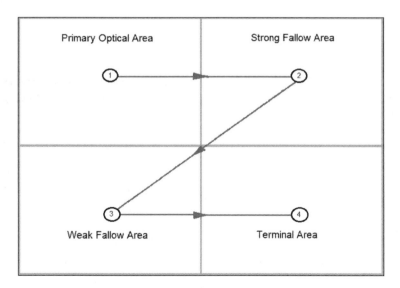

Similar to Nielsen's F pattern, the upper-left area (**1**) is the primary area in which information is inserted. Unlike the F pattern, the fallow areas are taken in, but only if the user has a level of interest in the content. In this model, the lower-right area (**4**) is actually an important area because it is the area where the gaze pattern will terminate.

This technique has been used by newspaper and magazines and latterly for web designs, and it has been shown that the terminal area is the correct area to place items where the user might take action. In this model, the lower-left area (**3**) is the least important.

Preference for the right

Studies by marketing experts have shown that people are more likely to click on action items on the right-hand side of the screen. These studies are backed up by research by Daniel Casasanto of the Psychology Department of the University of Chicago. Casasanto found that people who are right-handed (90 percent of us) have a natural tendency to prefer things that are positioned to the right.

Positioning screen elements

Based on the scientific evidence, we can now derive some rules about where various screen elements should be positioned.

Charts on the left

We know that the most important real estate on the screen is the upper-left. Therefore, this is the area that we should place our most important information: the charts that show the information that users need to see.

Listboxes on the right

People who are right-handed (most of us) are more comfortable clicking on things on the right-hand side of the screen. Therefore, we should place our listboxes, the things that users will click on, on the right-hand side of the screen.

The scientific reasons are not the only reasons why we should consider placing listboxes on the right-hand side. Another reason to consider is the use of Qlik products on mobile devices. Right-handed people tend to hold their devices in their left hand and use their right hand to tap the screen. So, what happens when the listboxes are on the left:

Every time the user has to make a new selection, their hand covers most of the screen, so they have to then move their hand out of the way to see the effect of the change. Now, what if the listboxes are on the right-hand side?

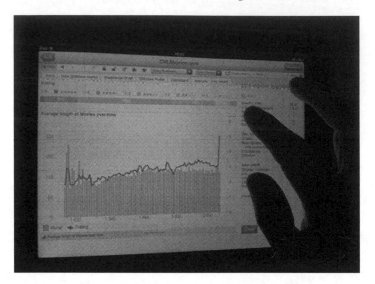

Now, the user can make selections and see the changes as they happen without having to move their hand. This is a preferable situation.

Dates on top

Because of their nature, field values, such as year and month, lend themselves to being rendered as horizontal listboxes. These are quite often rendered across the top of the screen in QlikView applications.

It appears that this is acceptable because users will accept a certain amount of header and navigation elements across the top of the screen and the date filters, as they are horizontal across the top, become a part of this.

Using the layout grid

In the QlikView **View** menu, there is an option to turn on a design grid that assists us with our layout (this is the default behavior in Qlik Sense). We can define the size of the grid and the snap steps in **User Preferences**:

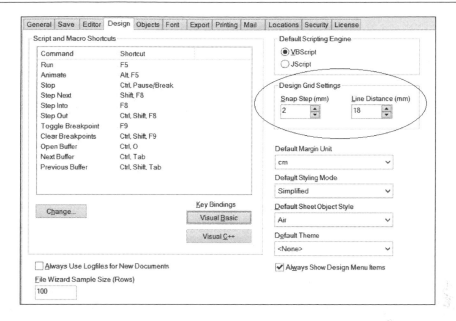

We can use this design grid to help implement a grid baseline design such as those recommended by many web designers. By setting the **Line Distance** and **Snap Step** values appropriately and then following the rule of always keeping objects one snap step from the edge of the grid, we can achieve a clean and consistent layout with regular spacing between objects:

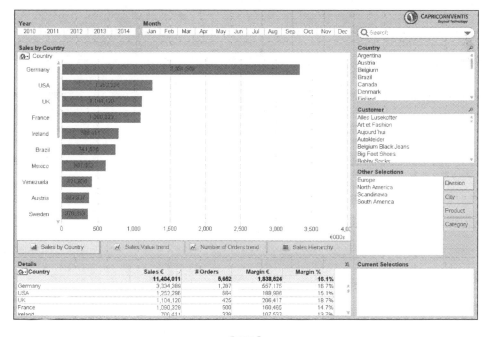

Thinking quantitatively

There is an excellent show on BBC Radio 4 called *More Or Less* (http://www.bbc.co.uk/radio4/moreorless) that takes statistics that have been presented in the media and explains or debunks them. For a show about numbers, it is quite amusing and worth listening to. Their podcasts can be downloaded worldwide.

They have a concept on the show of "big numbers". A big number is a number that sounds quite big, is usually quite round, but is usually presented without any additional context. It is the kind of number that headline writers love to use and that the *More Or Less* team love to debunk. There are examples of them everywhere.

The important thing to do with big numbers or any number is to put it in context. Otherwise, we face the prospect of the dreaded SFW question.

Understanding the SFW question

SFW stands for **So What**. A client once explained to me the SFW question in relation to a dashboard that was being built. If you look at a number on a dashboard, no matter how big that number, it is completely meaningless if there is no context around it.

One morning, TV3 News led with the story that the public prosecution service had not pursued 2,000 cases in the previous year:

Of course, 2,000 is a big number. The news article gave zero context to the number. We don't know what types of cases they were. We don't know how many cases were pursued and what the total was. Is the number 2,000 more or less than that of other years, versus the crime rate of other years?

This was the lead story and presented as a major scandal. The reality is that we should say: 2,000 cases? So what?

Every number that is presented in a Qlik application should have some context. Whether that is a breakdown by category in a bar chart, a ratio versus a target or previous period, or a trend over several periods, it is vital to give the users information about where that number sits. Otherwise, the users will just be asking, so what?

Designing dashboards

For me, the ultimate design of a dashboard is the one sitting in front of me when I drive my car. It gives me all of the information that I need to know to be able to manage my progress along the road.

It contains indicators vital to the current situation of the car: my speed, the engine oil temperature, and the engine RPMs. It doesn't have any information about the speed I was driving at the same time last week; this isn't important for me to drive the car along the motorway right now. I don't have an indicator for the amount of oil that I have in my engine, but this is something that I can find out by opening the hood and checking the dipstick; something that I should do on a semiregular basis, but not something that I need to know when I am behind the wheel.

For a business, the dashboard should be designed along the same lines. It should only show the information needed for the users to understand what is happening right now in their business: their key performance indicators. There should be very limited selectability, if any, on a dashboard and there should be no date selectors. The dashboard shouldn't show us the KPI value last week; it should show it right now. We can provide analysis sheets for users to investigate values at different time periods if that is important to them.

Choosing charts

When picking the chart to display numbers, there is often a balance to achieve between effective visualization and attractive visualization. Users will appreciate an attractive display and will get the most information out of an effective chart. Luckily, with QlikView and Qlik Sense, we often can usually achieve both.

Categorical comparison

For a normal day-to-day comparison between different values in a category, it is hard to beat a bar chart for simplicity and accuracy. Humans appear to have a very good ability to discern differences in length, even if this is just a very small difference. Bar charts beautifully encode their values by their lengths, so we can quickly see the differences between the different categories:

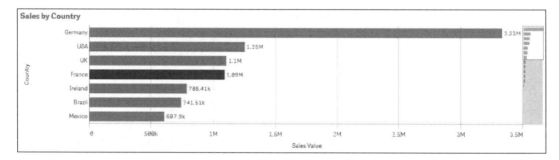

Bar charts are also very effective when comparing two measures across category values. It is important that the magnitude of the measures being compared be similar, or they are at least expected to be similar; for example, budget versus actual, so that they can share a common axis, and therefore, be comparable by length. We should also be careful that if we put two bar charts side by side, the different axis lengths could cause confusion for users and lead them to take up the wrong idea. For example, does black tea have as much caffeine as brewed coffee?

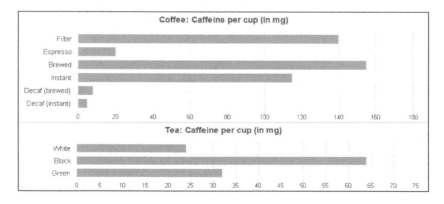

One of the things that we need to be aware of is that bar charts, as they encode their values in their length, must always begin their axis at zero. If we are tempted to change this, perhaps because the data doesn't look good, we are actually not telling the truth about our data!

Back in 2007, the Quaker Oats company was making some quite interesting claims about oatmeal and its effect on cholesterol in the body. They marketed this with a graph showing the effect of consumption of oatmeal on cholesterol over a four-week period:

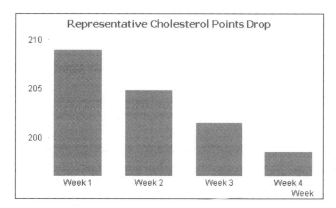

At first glance, it appears that we should rush out and buy oatmeal! But wait! We should notice that the axis here starts at about 195, not zero. How would it look if we redraw with a zero axis:

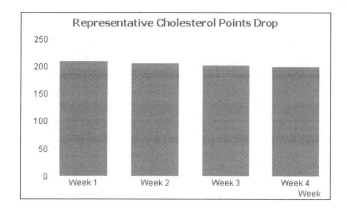

Now we see that the change is not quite so drastic! The company was later forced to remove the graph, along with some of the other more exaggerated claims.

Trend analysis

When looking at patterns of change over time, there is no better chart than the simple line graph. While a bar chart allows us to focus on the difference between individual bars, a line graph is all about the shape of the line: peaks and troughs:

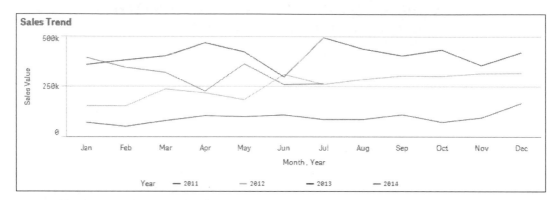

By adding additional expressions, usually an average along with control lines based on standard deviations, we can create a statistical control chart to look out for times where peaks and troughs are not just normal variation:

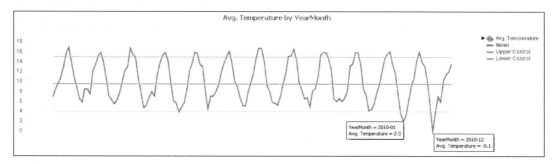

The rules about zero on the axis that we have for bar charts do not have to be applied to line charts. This is because the important thing about line charts is the shape of the line, and we might need to change the axis bounds to properly see that.

Comparing measures

When we are comparing measures, we can, of course, use a bar chart to juxtapose one measure against another. However, this does not reveal whether there is any correlation between the two measures, to see whether one measure appears to be a driver for another. For this purpose, a scatter chart is the best choice:

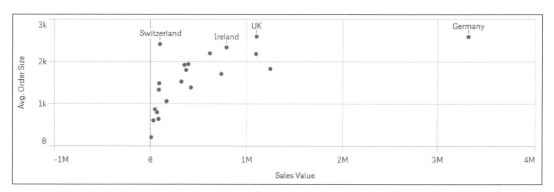

As well as being able to see correlations, we can also spot outliers. We can also interact with the chart and zoom in on areas of interest.

It can also be useful to be able to set the size of each of the bubbles based on a different measure. We can also define the color of each bubble based on yet another measure.

Low cardinality, part-to-whole comparison

Many people quite like pie charts. There is something about them that is familiar and comfortable about them. This is possibly because we learn things based on circles, such as fractions and time, from a young age.

However, there are many people in the data visualization world who will tell you that pie charts should be avoided at all costs! The respected expert, Stephen Few, has written an interesting article that explains why pie charts should never be used, and it can be found at `http://www.perceptualedge.com/articles/08-21-07.pdf`.

The equally well-respected expert, Robert Kosara, has written an equally interesting article, *In Defense of Pie Charts*, which can be found at `http://eagereyes.org/criticism/in-defense-of-pie-charts`.

There is merit in both arguments and both are not actually wrong. What we should consider is not whether we should use pie charts, but what we are going to use the pie chart for.

Pie charts are all about ratio comparison. We are trying to compare a segment with the whole of the circle. We should not be using a pie chart to compare one segment with another; that task is much better served by a bar chart. Consider this example:

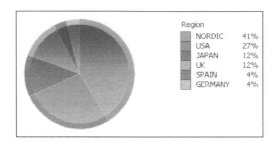

In this example, it becomes hard to separate the different segments from each other. It can be argued that the legend on the right-hand side delivers more information than the pie. We might also consider whether all regions are represented on the chart; if not, then this is not a valid part-to-whole comparison.

A pie chart should really have a low number of segments (low cardinality) so that a user can focus on the part-to-whole comparison. Ideally, this should be just one segment versus the whole. We should also be sure that the whole does represent the whole and not just a selected part.

Of course, QlikView and Qlik Sense are interactive, so they do give interesting information when we hover over the segments, and we can add additional information to that pop up using a pop-up text expression. We can also click to make a selection that gives additional information.

It can also be interesting to do a true part-to-whole comparison by having one segment representing the currently selected values and the whole showing all values:

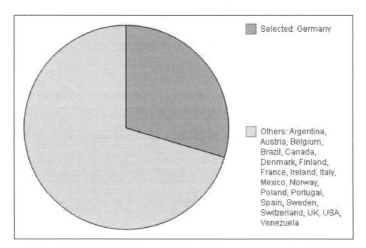

You can refer to `http://www.qliktips.com/2011/04/defending-pie-charts.html` for more information.

Recently, I wrote a blog post on key performance indicator approaches that included a proposed new KPI visualization called **Pie-Gauge**, which can be found at `http://www.qliktips.com/2013/12/key-performance-indicator-approaches.html`.

Pie-Gauge is an interesting use of pie charts. It is a part-to-whole but the whole depends on whether we have exceeded the target or not. If not, the whole is the target value and we have a segment representing the shortfall. If we have exceeded the target, then the whole is the actual value and we have a segment representing the amount by which we have exceeded the target:

Europe	North America	Scandinavia	South America

Tabular information

The straight table is a very powerful tool to represent actual numbers. In general, it will be used to show several calculations versus one-dimension category. However, we know that raw numbers are not always processed well by humans, so we can add additional graphical elements to aid understanding:

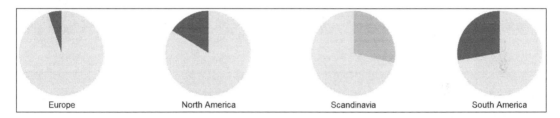

Regional Scorecard									
Region	Sales EUR 2009	Ranking 2009	Sales EUR 2008	%	Sales Trends 2008 - 2009	Budget EUR 2009	Budget EUR 2009	%	Sales vs Budget 2009
Total	21,421,961		58,279,041	37%			66,043,534	32%	
NORDIC	10,237,751		22,633,998	45%			25,394,817	40%	
USA	5,211,325		16,394,030	32%			18,905,175	28%	
JAPAN	2,390,335		7,386,439	32%			8,900,320	27%	
UK	1,925,049		7,404,419	26%			6,630,265	29%	
GERMANY	934,179		2,100,962	44%			2,759,447	34%	
SPAIN	723,323		2,359,194	31%			3,453,510	21%	

We can see two uses of horizontal gauge here: one with an indicator and one using the **Fill to Value** setting to represent a bar chart. We also have a sparkline, which is an example of a mini line chart that shows just the trend of a value over a period without showing magnitudes. We also see a whisker chart here that shows values above or below a value, in this case, budget and over time.

Another visual that we can add in straight tables is setting the color of the text to indicate positive or negative results.

Using color

It is good to use color in charts, but it is important to consider how we are going to use it and what we are going to do with it.

Color should have meaning

We have an option in QlikView to turn on **Multicolor** as an option in some charts. This will give us a pleasant result:

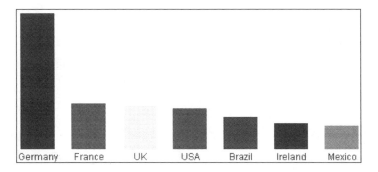

However, we should consider whether there is any additional information given to the user by adding this option. If the chart has only one color, it looks like this:

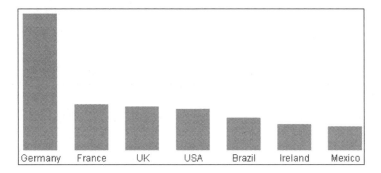

The chart with only one color gives the same information as the chart with multicolors. In fact, it can be argued that the chart with all the colors might actually add some confusion to what should be a simple chart.

We should, perhaps, learn a lesson from nature. Things that stand out from the background can be seen. Things that stand out more than other objects will be noticed even more. However, if everything is standing out, then nothing will come to the forefront of our attention.

If we use softer colors for most of our bars, with a plain white background, then we can see those bars very well. If we need one of the bars to stand out, because it needs some action, then we can have just that bar can have a stronger color to attract attention:

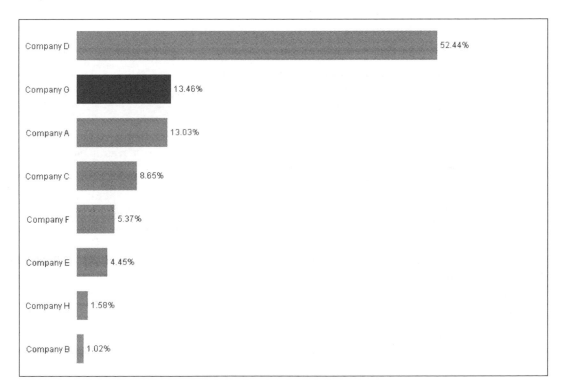

In a QlikView chart, we can specify a calculation for the background color of an expression by clicking the + button beside the expression and entering a color expression for the background.

What does RAG mean?

Many businesses will implement a RAG system for dashboards, where they use red for bad, amber for slightly bad, and green for okay. We should challenge this and ask what the action is, that is, what behavior do we want to drive?

Anything that is okay should probably have no coloring at all. This means that other areas are easier to find. Anything that is bad can remain red and should be a call to action to have users click and discover.

But what about amber? We really need to think about this. Do we want users to click and discover? If so, then perhaps it should be red. If not, perhaps it should have no color at all.

So, instead of RAG, perhaps we should be implementing R.

The ink-to-data ratio

The ink-to-data ratio is a term coined by Edward Tufte in his 1983 book, *The Visual Display of Quantitative Data*. Of course, back in 1983, Tufte was not talking about displaying something on the computer screen but on printed reports. Therefore, he was talking about ink and not pixels. Perhaps, we can restyle it as the pixel-to-data ratio.

What this ratio means is that any pixel that is not representing data needs to justify its existence. If it is not useful, then it should be removed. Consider this table:

Country	Sales $	COGS $	Margin $	Margin %
	3,191,394	2,682,628	508,767	15.9%
Argentina	38,746	30,517	8,230	21.2%
Austria	180,990	148,951	32,039	17.7%
Belgium	47,618	41,679	5,939	12.5%
Brazil	358,390	297,030	61,360	17.1%
Canada	113,129	96,800	16,329	14.4%
Denmark	152,299	123,508	28,792	18.9%
Finland	21,865	18,783	3,082	14.1%
France	504,712	421,150	83,562	16.6%
Germany	1,487,317	1,256,424	230,894	15.5%
Ireland	286,327	247,786	38,540	13.5%

We have some common elements here: background color, striped rows, and grid lines. By making a few tweaks to the **Style** tab of this chart, we can clean up superfluous pixels:

Country	Sales $	COGS $	Margin $	Margin %
Argentina	38,746	30,517	8,230	21.2%
Austria	180,990	148,951	32,039	17.7%
Belgium	47,618	41,679	5,939	12.5%
Brazil	358,390	297,030	61,360	17.1%
Canada	113,129	96,800	16,329	14.4%
Denmark	152,299	123,508	28,792	18.9%
Finland	21,865	18,783	3,082	14.1%
France	504,712	421,150	83,562	16.6%
Germany	1,487,317	1,256,424	230,894	15.5%
Ireland	286,327	247,786	38,540	13.5%
	3,191,394	2,682,628	508,767	15.9%

We can see that the background color has been removed completely. The vertical grid lines have also been removed as the white areas in between the columns act as very effective separators. The horizontal grid lines have been left but are now almost transparent; they serve as effective guidelines, but are not impactful in the cleaner display.

It is not just in tables that we should keep things clean. In bar charts, there are options to have backgrounds on the display area and lines around the bars:

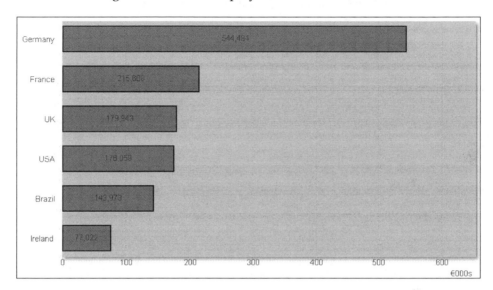

These are really superfluous and unnecessary in a clean chart:

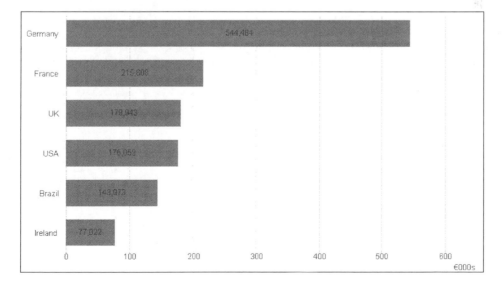

Color blindness

Color blindness is something that affects up to eight or nine percent of the male population. It is almost exclusively a male issue, as female color blindness is extremely rare, and the colors affected are, in the majority, between red and green.

Of course, when we consider things such as RAG beacons on dashboards, we can see that there might be problems for quite a large number of people in even seeing data. We should really be aware of this and consider the colors that we choose for different purposes.

> A great resource for color selection is the Color Brewer website: http://www.colorbrewer2.org.

This website suggests color ranges that we can use, including color-blind-safe selections.

In general, we should avoid juxtaposing green and red. If we are using diverging hues, we should not use green and red and instead use blue along with either green or red. This gives most people the greatest chance of seeing the data.

Using maps

A lot of data that we deal with might have a spatial component. This could be a post code or address that can be geocoded, or we might already have latitude and longitude information. Just because we have this, it doesn't mean that we need to plot the information on a map!

While the data might have a spatial component, it usually doesn't have a special dependency; it doesn't really matter to our analysis exactly where the data occurred. In these cases, a map is just a pretty display, while a bar chart is a better option.

Quite often, people use colored areas on a map to indicate information. This is known as a choropleth, the classic example being used with US election polls and results:

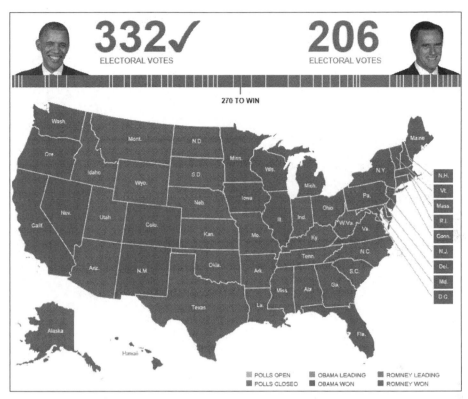

US election results

The image is taken from `http://elections.huffingtonpost.com/2012/results`.

If we look at this map, with large swathes of red, we might be surprised that Obama won the election! The problem is that quite a lot of the land area of the US, especially in the mid-west, has a low population, so contributes less votes to the overall result. The *New York Times* came up with a novel approach to solving this—resizing the states based on electoral vote size:

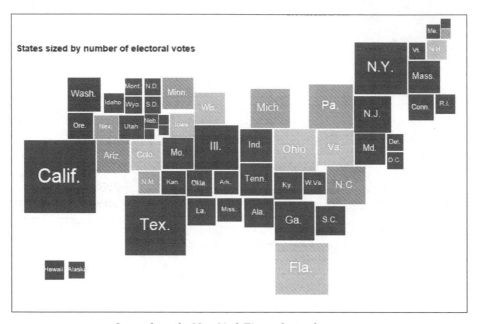

Image from the New York Times electoral coverage

This image is taken from `http://elections.nytimes.com/2012/ratings/electoral-map/`.

One other issue that we must consider with the use of maps is the general level of education. Several studies have shown that a percentage of the population is unable to correctly identify states and countries on a map. Consider whether a simple bar chart would be more appropriate.

Summary

This has been quite an interesting chapter because a lot of the content wasn't true!

We can have some confidence about the historical information. We found out that the beginnings of data visualization started with mathematics and analytical geometry. Once the use of charts was established—largely by Joseph Priestly and then followed by William Playfair—their use became more and more commonplace as useful ways of telling stories with data.

We should have a better understanding of our audience. Of course, this can only apply to most of our audience because there are always outliers.

Design guidelines are never set in stone. What is correct in design today will have changed tomorrow—just look at the iPhone. However, fundamentals will not change and we should be aware of them.

We have reached the end of the road for this book. By now, hopefully, your Qlik education will have advanced towards mastery. Of course, you will not become a master until you start to implement these practices and even create your own best practice. Let's hope that this book is a good foundation.

Index

Sort 183
Unique 183

V

variables
about 245
applying, in script 308-310
parameters, passing to 315, 316
parameters, using with 262
SET versus LET 245-247
use cases 310-312
used, for calculations 251, 252
used, for holding common
    expressions 247, 248
used, in expressions 262
used, with Dollar-sign
    Expansion 248, 249
values, examining during
    reloads 313, 314
vertical calculation
advanced aggregations, creating
    with Aggr 275, 276
inter-record function, using 271, 272
range function, using 271, 272
Total qualifier, applying 273, 274

W

Web Files button 284
When statement 320
wildcard search
about 236
advanced search 239
associative search 237, 238
characters 236
example searches 236
fuzzy search 237
normal search 236

workspace
about 161
creating 161, 162
repository workspace 161
standalone workspace 161
Write Custom operator 181
Write Excel operator 181
Write File operator 181
Write Lookup Table operator 181
Write Parameters operator 181
Write QlikView operator 181
Write Table operator 181
Write Teradata PT operator 181

X

XML files 289, 290

Thank you for buying
Mastering QlikView

About Packt Publishing

Packt, pronounced 'packed', published its first book "Mastering phpMyAdmin for Effective MySQL Management" in April 2004 and subsequently continued to specialize in publishing highly focused books on specific technologies and solutions.

Our books and publications share the experiences of your fellow IT professionals in adapting and customizing today's systems, applications, and frameworks. Our solution based books give you the knowledge and power to customize the software and technologies you're using to get the job done. Packt books are more specific and less general than the IT books you have seen in the past. Our unique business model allows us to bring you more focused information, giving you more of what you need to know, and less of what you don't.

Packt is a modern, yet unique publishing company, which focuses on producing quality, cutting-edge books for communities of developers, administrators, and newbies alike. For more information, please visit our website: www.packtpub.com.

About Packt Enterprise

In 2010, Packt launched two new brands, Packt Enterprise and Packt Open Source, in order to continue its focus on specialization. This book is part of the Packt Enterprise brand, home to books published on enterprise software – software created by major vendors, including (but not limited to) IBM, Microsoft and Oracle, often for use in other corporations. Its titles will offer information relevant to a range of users of this software, including administrators, developers, architects, and end users.

Writing for Packt

We welcome all inquiries from people who are interested in authoring. Book proposals should be sent to author@packtpub.com. If your book idea is still at an early stage and you would like to discuss it first before writing a formal book proposal, contact us; one of our commissioning editors will get in touch with you.

We're not just looking for published authors; if you have strong technical skills but no writing experience, our experienced editors can help you develop a writing career, or simply get some additional reward for your expertise.

QlikView for Developers Cookbook

ISBN: 978-1-78217-973-3   Paperback: 290 pages

Discover the strategies needed to tackle the most challenging tasks facing the QlikView developer

1. Learn beyond QlikView training.

2. Discover QlikView Advanced GUI development, advanced scripting, complex data modeling issues, and much more.

3. Accelerate the growth of your QlikView developer ability.

4. Based on over 7 years' experience of QlikView development.

QlikView Scripting

ISBN: 978-1-78217-166-9   Paperback: 138 pages

Your comprehensive guide to scripting powerful QlikView applications

1. Understand everything about QlikView, from structuring a script to fixing it to charting object problems.

2. Packed full of information and code examples to help you to understand the key concepts and features of QlikView.

3. Informative screenshots help you navigate QlikView's scripting menus and dialogs.

Please check **www.PacktPub.com** for information on our titles

Made in the USA
Middletown, DE
13 September 2017